GENERAL EDITORS

Jeffrey R. Dickson, PhD

JEFFREY R. DICKSON is the Senior Pastor of Salem Baptist Church in Goochland, VA and the Program Director of the PhD in Applied Apologetics at Liberty Theological Seminary. He lives outside of Richmond, VA with his wife and family.

Daniel R. Sloan, PhD

DANIEL SLOAN is the Associate Pastor of Safe Harbor Community Church in Bedford, VA, and the Program Director of the MA in Biblical Studies and MA in Biblical Exposition at Liberty Theological Seminary. He lives in Lynchburg, VA with his wife and family.

CONSULTING EDITOR

David Mappes, PhD

DAVID MAPPES is an Associate Professor and Subject Matter Specialist in several courses at Liberty Theological Seminary along with directing Nobility and Knowability Truth Ministries (https://www.davidmappes.com/) and serves as the senior Content Editor for Lampion House Publishing. David and his wife reside in Tennessee.

CONTRIBUTORS

JEFFREY R. DICKSON (PhD) is the Senior Pastor of Salem Baptist Church in Goochland, VA and the Program Director of the PhD in Applied Apologetics at Liberty Theological Seminary. He lives outside of Richmond, VA with his wife and family.

MARK HITCHCOCK (PhD, Dallas Theological Seminary) serves as the Senior Pastor of Faith Bible Church in Edmond, OK and as Research Professor of Bible Exposition at Dallas Theological Seminary. Dr. Hitchcock has authored over 20 books, primarily on end-time prophecy, and speaks throughout the country and internationally at churches and conferences.

H. WAYNE HOUSE (ThD, Concordia Seminary; JD, Regent University) serves as a Distinguished Professor of Theology, Law, and Culture at Faith International University and Seminary and an adjunct Professor at the Liberty Theological Seminary. He is also a conference speaker, international lecturer, has authored or co-authored nearly 40 books, and is the owner of Lampion House Publishing.

TOMMY ICE (PhD, Tyndale Theological Seminary) serves as the Executive Director of The Pre-Trib Research Center. He co-founded the Center in 1994 with Dr. Tim LaHaye to research, teach, and defend the pretribulational rapture and related Bible prophecy doctrines. Dr. Ice has authored and co-authored over 30 books, written hundreds of articles, and is a frequent conference speaker.

WALTER KAISER (PhD, Trinity International University) is retired from serving as president of Gordon-Conwell and is the President Emeritus and Distinguished Professor of Old Testament and Ethics at Gordon-Conwell Theological Seminary. He has authored or contributed to over 50 books.

DAVID MAPPES (PhD, Dallas Theological Seminary) teaches courses in New Testament, Old Testament, hermeneutics, theological method, and theology at numerous schools including Liberty Theological Seminary, Columbia International University (CIU), Calvary University (CU), College of Biblical Studies (CBS). He is also the director of Nobility and Knowability Truth Ministries and serves as the senior Content Editor for Lampion House Publishing. See publications and various conference papers at https://www.davidmappes.com/.

RANDALL PRICE (PhD, University of Texas) serves as the President of World of the Bible Ministries, Inc., conducts international tours, and has authored or contributed to over 25 books. He formerly served as a Distinguished Research Professor of Biblical and Judaic Studies at the Liberty University John Rawlings School of Divinity.

RON RHODES (ThD, Dallas Theological Seminary) serves as the President of Reasoning from the Scriptures Ministries (a nonprofit ministry), lectures on cult apologetics, addresses current issues in the national media, serves as a keynote speaker at conferences across the United States, and has authored over 80 books including three Silver Medallion winners.

TIM SIGLER (PhD, Trinity International University) is the CEO2 at Ariel Ministries and previously served as Provost and Dean at Shepherds Theological Seminary and Professor of Hebrew and Biblical Studies at the Moody Bible Institute. He has been studying and teaching about the land and people of Israel for 35 years.

DANIEL SLOAN (PhD) is the Associate Pastor of Safe Harbor Community Church in Bedford, VA, and is the Program Director of the MA in Biblical Studies and MA in Biblical Exposition at Liberty Theological Seminary. He lives in Lynchburg, VA with his wife and family.

THE KING IS COMING

Dispensational Essays
Commemorating the Life and Ministry
of Dr. Ed Hindson

Jeffrey R. Dickson & Daniel Sloan

GENERAL EDITORS

LAMPION HOUSE PUBLISHING LLC
Navasota, Texas 77868

2024

The King is Coming: Dispensational Essays
Commemorating the Life and Ministry of Dr. Ed Hindson

Copyright © 2024 Lampion House Publishing LLC

All rights reserved. No part of this publication may be reproduced, distributed or transmitted in any form or by any means, without prior written permission.

Biblical citations are from various translations of the Scripture including the author's own translation.

Lampion House Publishing LLC
P.O. Box 1295
Navasota, TX 77868
Website: http://lampionhousepublishing.com/

Printed in the United States of America

ISBN: 979-8-9878598-9-6 (softcover)

First Edition, October 2024

Cover and interior design/formatting by Vickie Swisher, Studio 20|20

FOREWORD

It is an honor and privilege to dedicate this volume to the life and ministry of Dr. Ed Hindson. He has set an example for all of us to follow. His life and ministry touched many thousands of Christians through his television program, many books, and public ministry. As well, his ministry and influence at Liberty University was profound as an academic-minded professor and godly person, who taught his subject matter in such a winsome manner, in addition to his work as a dean at Liberty.

I knew Dr. Hindson for many years in our association at the Pretribulation Conference that has met each year in Dallas for decades, and through the years we became good friends. Dr. Hindson's influence on prophetic teaching, the dispensational pre-tribulational view of the rapture, and his robust defense of the Scripture and inerrancy, is well known.

This volume to honor Dr. Ed Hindson focuses on the return of Christ. His love for the coming Savior and King Jesus was obvious to all who knew him. It is my hope that this book will encourage new scholarship and even further Dr. Hindson's love for the Lord and his passion for the return and exaltation of Christ.

H. WAYNE HOUSE
(ThD, Concordia Seminary; JD, Regent University)

PREFACE

One constant in higher education is change—change can be intentionally positive or negative or change can occur simply through drift. The oft-quoted phrase, *being missional changes everything*, is fundamentally flawed. Being missional does entail some change but being missional also entails preserving the non-changing truth of Jesus and the Scriptures. The author of Hebrews exhorts his readers that "Jesus Christ is the same yesterday and today and forever" and to "not be carried away by varies and strange teaching" (Heb 13:9–10).

Any Christian institution of higher education needs a consistent, clear mission, godly policies and practices, and most importantly competent, well-trained, academic, godly leaders and staff who have an a priori commitment to the knowability of truth as revealed in the Scriptures and living out that truth.

The biblical authors provide a deposit of truth referred to as *the faith, apostolic traditions,* and sound doctrine to denote a fixed body of doctrine that includes both doctrinal orthodoxy (correct belief) and orthopraxy (upright and godly biblical conduct). Paul reminds Timothy to guard the *sound words* (2 Tim 1:13, 14) and *sound doctrine* (2 Tim 4:3), which he also refers to as *the truth* in 2 Timothy 4:4. Jude reminds his readers to contend for this truth which he calls *the Faith*.

This book celebrates and honors the life and ministry of Dr. Ed Hindson. He accepted God's free gift of salvation as a young boy when he was six years old and entered the presence of his Lord and Savior on Saturday, July 2, 2022. He was known as a faithful follower of Jesus, a prominent biblical scholar who authored over

40 books, edited five major study Bibles, and provided 48 years of service to Liberty University in His ministry to Christ.

He was a speaker on "The King is Coming" telecast and was a visiting lecturer at Oxford University and Harvard Divinity School, as well as numerous evangelical seminaries including Dallas, Denver, Trinity, Grace, and Westminster.

He also served as Dean at the John W. Rawlings School of Divinity—he was an academic cornerstone for Liberty University. He was both a friend and godly mentor to those who knew him. He apprehended Jesus' teaching that, "A disciple is not above his teacher, but everyone when he is fully trained will be like his teacher" (Luke 6:40). He personified Paul's imitation motif that teaching must entail modeling personal godliness (1 Tim 6:3 and Titus 1:1). Christian leaders are called to consistently display a life of godliness so others can imitate them. Paul encouraged the Corinthian believers, "Be imitators of me, just as I also am of Christ" (1 Cor 11:1) and Paul commends the Thessalonian believers in writing, "You also became imitators of us and of the Lord...so that you became an example to all the believers in Macedonia and in Achaia" (1 Thess 1:6-7). Peter emphasizes that Elders are to be "examples to the flock" (1 Peter 5:3).

We are indebted to our dear brother for his life, academic prowess, ministry, and above all his imitation of Christ. Thank you, Dr. Hindson for fighting the good fight, finishing the course, and keeping the faith (2 Tim 4:7).

– David Mappes, PhD

TABLE OF CONTENTS

Preface vii

CHAPTER ONE
The Coming Lamb: John's Apocalyptic Introduction
of the Hero of Revelation *by Jeffrey R. Dickson, PhD*. 1

CHAPTER TWO
Evidence for the Pre-Tribulation Rapture in
1 Thessalonians *by Dr. Mark Hitchcock* 25

CHAPTER THREE
A Theological Discussion Nuancing Dispensational
Views of the Kingdom-Age *by Dr. H. Wayne House*. 47

CHAPTER FOUR
God's Purpose Within His Overall Plan for a
Pretribulational Rapture *by Dr. Thomas Ice*. 69

CHAPTER FIVE
The New Heavens and The New Earth in The Eternal
State: Isaiah 65:17–25; 66:18–24 *by Walter C. Kaiser, Jr.*. 109

CHAPTER SIX
Where is The Kingdom of God in The Social Gospel?
by David Mappes, PhD 123

CHAPTER SEVEN
Premillennialism and The Dead Sea Scrolls
by J. Randall Price, PhD 147

CHAPTER EIGHT
The Timing of the Ezekiel Invasion *by Dr. Ron Rhodes* 191

CHAPTER NINE
The Capital of The Coming King in Psalm 2:6
by Tim M. Sigler, PhD. 219

CHAPTER TEN
The Kingdom of God and The Kingdom of Man
in the Book of Daniel *by Dr. Daniel Sloan*. 245

Epilogue 271

CHAPTER ONE

THE COMING LAMB: JOHN'S APOCALYPTIC INTRODUCTION OF THE HERO OF REVELATION

by Jeffrey R. Dickson, PhD

In epic literary and/or cinematic works, heroes are typically easy to spot. Complete with larger-than-life personas and even grander abilities, these over-the-top characters arrive on the scene with corresponding puffs of smoke, bolts of lightning, pithy lines, and bright colors that accentuate their obvious power. Such phenomena establish these protagonists as formidable forces against the influences of evil that they will inevitably confront, and audiences wait with bated breath for the fight to ensue. Given that many hero archetypes in storytelling find their genesis in ancient writings, it is little wonder that the Bible has many such characters in its pages. However, in perhaps the most visually stimulating and apocalyptic contributing volume of the canon—the Book of Revelation—the hero that is described and referred to most often takes a surprisingly unexpected shape. Amid the cosmic conflict, spectacular images, glorious battles, and colorful cast of characters, a lamb emerges that takes center stage and serves as the hero of this prophetic drama. Why so?

The word "lamb" (ἀρνίον) occurs 30 times in the NT—once in John 21:15 and twenty-nine times throughout the book of Revelation.[1] In fact, the "Lamb" (ἀρνίον) is by far the most prolific title given for Christ in John's latest work, appearing more than twice as often as any other Christological label. Also, although John uses ἀρνίον liberally in Revelation, he is the only biblical writer who uses this particular term for Jesus.[2] While it would seem this peculiar and yet heavily endorsed title for Revelation's principal character is deserving of special attention, only recently has any rigorous study been leveraged toward understanding what John is accomplishing with this term. Even then, conclusions that have been reached are unnaturally univocal and do not reflect the sophistication of the Apocalypse of John in general and the apostle's use of this title in particular. Therefore, after perusing several incomplete interpretive options for ἀρνίον, this chapter will demonstrate a responsible biblical interpretation of John's humble and glorious Lamb as witnessed in his apocalyptic introduction using a contextual-grammatical-canonical-historical hermeneutic that is focused on the authorial intent of a Holy Spirit-inspired apostle and what is reflected in what the church refers to as the Book of

---

1 Peter Whale, "The Lamb of John: Some Myths about the Vocabulary of the Johannine Literature." *Journal of Biblical Literature* 106 No. 2 (1987): 289-95. Whale is quick to correct the assumption that John reserves ἀρνίον exclusively for Revelation and points out that John does, in fact, use it once in his Gospel. However, this is a moot point as John uses the term consistently for lamb in Revelation while he endorses multiple words for the same in his Gospel. This suggests that John is trying to say something deliberate and distinct about Christ in his apocalypse.

2 For more discussion on John's unique use of ἀρνίον in Revelation see Loren Johns, *The Lamb Christology of the Apocalypse of John: An Investigation into its Origin and Rhetorical Force* (Eugene, OR: Wipf and Stock, 2014), 22-25. See also Jeffrey Dickson, *The Humility and Glory of the Lamb: Toward a Robust Apocalyptic Christology* (Eugene, OR: Wipf and Stock, 2019).

Revelation. This modest task will no doubt provide a richer and more resplendent understanding of exactly WHO is expected to return in the future and what he will accomplish (which is the principal preoccupation of the apocalypse in the first place).[3]

Interpretive Options and Considerations

First, ἀρνίον is a peculiar choice for Lamb, especially as a reference for Christ, given what is used elsewhere of Jesus in the New Testament. For instance, John could have adopted what Paul employs in 1 Corinthians 5:7 when he calls Jesus the πάσχα (Paschal/Passover Lamb).[4] Such a choice would have immediately transfixed the literal image of a lamb to a familiar salvific, historically rooted, and figurative antitype. An even more obvious choice would have been ἀμνὸς which is what John the Baptist endorses when he introduces Jesus as "the Lamb of God who takes away the sin of the world" (quoting the LXX).[5] Ἀμνὸς is also used for Jesus in Acts 8:32 when Philip quotes Isaiah 53:7-8 (again from the LXX) saying, "a sheep [πρόβατον] is brought to the slaughterhouse, and as a lamb [ἀμνὸς] before its shearer is silent, thus he did not open his mouth." First Peter 1:18-19 makes use of the same word when it says, "by means of the valuable blood of Christ, like that of a lamb (ἀμνὸς) without defect or blemish." A third choice for lamb was also available to John in the word ἀρήν, a term used in Luke 10:3.[6]

---

3 See Rev 1:1's provided title of the work—"the revelation of Jesus Christ." Whether "of Jesus Christ" (Ἰησοῦ Χριστοῦ) is intended to function as an objective genitive ("revealing Jesus' Christ"), a possessive Genitive (as in "Jesus Christ's revelation"), a genitive of content ("revelation containing Jesus Christ"), or even genitive of apposition (as in "revelation that is Jesus Christ"), the preoccupation of the "unveiling" to be presented in the rest of the work is focused on the protagonist, not the timing, secondary characters, or other phenomena in the book. See Daniel Wallace, *Greek Grammar Beyond the Basics: An Exegetical Syntax of the New Testament* (Grand Rapids, MI: Zondervan, 1996), 72ff for discussion on genitive case functions.

4 "Clean out the old leaven so that you may be a new lump, just as you are in fact unleavened. For Christ our Passover [πάσχα] also has been sacrificed."

5 John 1:29. John, the apostle, even repeats this title himself in John 1:36.

6 See Luke 10:3, "Go; behold, I send you out as lambs [ἀρνά, plural of ἀρήν] in the midst of wolves." Although technically, ἀρήν is the noun of which ἀρνίον is the diminutive, these forms had lost their diminutive force by the time the NT was written. Johns, *Lamb Christology*, 26.

Any of these choices (πάσχα, ἀμνὸς, or even ἀρήν) would have been more literally consistent with the existing biblical literature that was already being circulated by the end of the first century. One might also argue that these choices would have been better suited to connect the person of Jesus in the eschaton to a specific and previously developed Christological motif.[7]

So from where does John derive ἀρνίον and what must he mean? Examination of biblical and extra-biblical literature has unfortunately yielded a multiplicity of potential meanings assigned to this word. Though Louw and Nida claim that ἀρνίον can refer to either a sheep of any age, a lamb, or a ram,[8] Loren Johns points out that "all occurrences of the word ἀρνίον in biblical and classical Greek refer to a young sheep or lamb."[9] Robert M. Mounce believes that John's use of Lamb in Revelation is derived from the literature of Jewish apocalyptic, holding that John is merging the two ideas of the Lamb as victim and the Lamb as leader.[10] Evidence for this interpretation of John's Lamb can be found in 1 Enoch 90 in which the Maccabees are described as "horned lambs" (similar to what is envisioned in Rev 5). Also, in the Testament of Joseph, a lamb destroys the enemies of Israel.[11] David Macleod believes that, in part, John uses the "unusual Lamb" in Revelation to suggest that like these other apocalyptic works, Jesus is the "warrior Lamb."[12] Beale reaches a similar conclusion

---

[7] For instance, πάσχα would have immediately connected Jesus to his Christological function of appeasing God's wrath, ἀμνὸς would have highlighted his Christological ministry of atoning sacrifice, and ἀρήν would have identified him with his people and as one who suffers alongside his fellow lambs.

[8] Louw and Nida, *Greek-English Lexicon*, s. v. ἀρνίον.

[9] Johns, *Lamb Christology*, 22.

[10] Mounce, "The Christology of the Apocalypse." *Foundations* 11 No. 1 (Spring 1968): 42–45. R. H. Also see, Charles, *A Critical and Exegetical Commentary on the Revelation of St. John*. Vol. 1 (Edinburgh: T&T Clark, 1920) for discussion.

[11] Testament of Joseph 19:3, "And I saw that from Judah a virgin was born, wearing a linen garment; and from her a lamb without spot came forth, and on its left side it was as a lion; and all the beasts rushed against it, and the lamb overcame them and destroyed them to be trodden."

[12] Donald Macleod, "The Christology of Chalcedon," in *The Only Hope Jesus: Yesterday, Today, Forever*, ed. Mark Elliot and John McPake (Fearn: Christian Focus, 2001), 337.

when, based on the same grouping of texts, he states, "The slain lamb thus represents the image of a conqueror who was mortally wounded while defeating an enemy...the messianic Lamb, becomes interpreted as a sacrifice that not only redeems but also conquers."[13] However, though John may have had this in mind, he would have served this interpretation better if he had used ἀμνὸς instead of ἀρνίον as these other apocalyptic sources have.

Perhaps what is meant by ἀρνίον in Revelation might be ascertained by looking at the potential predicates and/or Old Testament types John may have had in mind. Allusions to the Hebrew Scriptures abound in John's work, and the Septuagint even uses ἀρνίον on occasion.[14] With this in mind, the apocalyptic Lamb could be a reference to the sacrificial system (after all, the Lamb is depicted as slain, his death has some expiatory force, and the phrases "in the blood" and "redeem" elicit this association). However, the apocalyptic vocabulary is not sacrificial, and the OT primarily uses ἀμνὸς for these atoning lambs. Second, Revelation's Lamb could be understood as the Paschal Lamb of the Exodus (since Passover Christology existed in the early first century, there is widespread critical support for this interpretation, and literary similarities between Revelation and the Exodus abound). However, πάσχα, not ἀρνίον, would have made for a more distinct connection between Revelation and Exodus, and the Passover victim was not always a lamb. Third, the Lamb of the Apocalypse may serve as the antitype for Isaiah 53:7 (as both contexts include the image of the slaughter). However, ἀμνὸς, not ἀρνίον, is used in Isaiah and the suffering servant motif at work in Isaiah is absent in Revelation. Fourth, Daniel's vision of a ram and a goat in Daniel 8 might provide a potential background for the apostle's Christology (as this passage is one of the only OT passages in which humans are symbolized as animals, both have apocalyptic undertones, and

---

13 G. K. Beale, *The Book of Revelation*, NIGTC (Grand Rapids, MI: Eerdmans, 1999), 351.
14 It is used on rare occasions to speak of lambs in the LXX (Jer 11:19; 50:45; Ps 114:4, 6; Isa 40:11)

both contexts cry out for justice). However, Daniel reveals that the two horns of the ram and the male goat are not Christ.[15] Fifth, the Lamb could be understood in comparison with the Aqedah of Genesis 22 (the tradition of the story believed that the ram had been prepared before the foundations of the world and, according to John's *The Lamb Christology*, both contexts involve vulnerability. However, no explicit appeal is made to the Abraham episode in the Apocalypse and the traditions surrounding the Abrahamic story could have been later than the writing of Revelation. Finally, the vulnerable Lamb might be ascertained by a cursory look at ἀρνίον's usage in the LXX, however, delimiting the victorious Christ to such proves precarious and unnaturally univocal.[16] Ultimately, each of these choices for their own set of reasons is found wanting. Therefore, an alternative must be pursued that can provide a more robust and altogether more fitting interpretation of Revelation's protagonist—an alternative that allows the text of the Apocalypse to supervene on the meaning of its important terms.

---

15 Dan 8:21 states "The shaggy goat represents the kingdom of Greece, and the large horn that is between his eyes is the first king."

16 Upon closer inspection, the verses upon which Loren Johns leans so heavily (Jer 11:19; 50:45; Ps 114:4, 6; Isa 40:11) to reach such a conclusion do not necessarily nor explicitly convey a vulnerable subject nor do they even apply to God's people. Despite this, Johns assumes that vulnerability is nearly always associated with ἀρνίον and even endorses this meaning in the very few places it is found in extra-biblical literature. In so doing, Johns proves guilty of what D. A. Carson calls a "false assumption of technical meaning" in which an interpreter falsely assumes that a word nearly always has a certain technical meaning usually derived from either a subset of the evidence or from the interpreter's personal systematic theology. Not only is Johns guilty of this fallacy, but one might also argue that Johns is guilty of "semantic obsolescence." This infraction is defined as follows: "Here the interpreter assigns to a word in his text a meaning that the word in question used to have in earlier times, but that is no longer found within the live, semantic range of the word. That meaning, in other words, is semantically obsolete." Johns commits this when he assumes that the vulnerability associated with ἀρνίον remains consistent in the ever-fluid and evolving literary world (especially as one considers the time difference between the completion of the LXX and the writing of Revelation). Could not the connotation of ἀρνίον have changed between the writing of the LXX and the writing of the Apocalypse of John? A third hermeneutical strike against Johns' program is his endorsement of "an appeal to unknown or unlikely meanings." Johns commits this when he assumes that in Revelation—in which Jesus is clearly depicted as a conquering, victorious, powerful warrior king—ἀρνίον must continue to convey something about vulnerability. However, vulnerability as a theme in Revelation does not seem tenable, especially as it pertains to how Christ is delineated. This list of potentialities articulated in this paragraph is elucidated by Johns in *Lamb Christology*, 128ff. For discussion on hermeneutical fallacies see D. A. Carson, *Exegetical Fallacies*. 2nd ed (Grand Rapids, MI: Baker, 1996), 35, 37, 45.

The Humble and Glorious Lamb of Revelation

What follows is a contextual-grammatical-canonical-historical approach to interpreting the Lamb of Revelation, particularly as he emerges in Revelation 5:6-10. Few passages are more contextually significant, literarily meaningful, and vividly presented in the book of Revelation than this group of verses.[17] Even Caird refers to these verses as some of the most important in the Book of Revelation[18] because it is in this passage that the main protagonist is introduced (that is, in the prophetic section of Revelation) and sets in motion the judgment that envelopes the better part of the Book of Revelation. It is also in this passage that ἀρνίον is used for the first time and the only time this term is employed without the definite article. Though every other use of ἀρνίον is arthrous (containing the definite article), in Revelation 5:6 the term is anarthrous (absent a definite article), thereby indicating that at least potentially, every subsequent use refers in some way to the first occurrence connotatively and/or hermeneutically.[19]

---

17 Donald Guthrie, "The Lamb in the Structure of the Book of Revelation," *Vox Evangelica* 12 (1981): 64-71. "Indeed it is part of the intention of the whole scene in chapters 4 and 5 to set the stage for the dramatic introduction of the Lamb to the readers" (64). Here, Guthrie also points out that Rev 4-5 is the first worship passage of the Apocalypse.

18 G. B. Caird, *The Revelation of St. John the Divine* (New York: Harper & Row, 1966), 73. On these verses William Hendrickson writes "They relate Jewish Messianic hopes to the distinctively Christian good news of the advent of the Messiah in the person of Jesus of Nazareth, but a Messiah of a character so wholly unexpected by the Jews that they rejected him." *More than Conquerors* (Grand Rapids, MI: Baker, 1967), 109.

19 Possible functions of the definite articles attached to the "lamb" as it is found elsewhere in the book of Revelation include the following: anaphoric (denoting previous reference—a reference that is typically anarthrous because in its original or first occurrence it is being introduced), par excellence (pointing out that the Apocalyptic Lamb is in a class by itself as introduced in Rev 5:6-10), monadic (indicating that, as in Rev 5, the Lamb is one-of-a-kind). Though a case might be made for each of these in the various contexts in which ἀρνίον is found, these possibilities in general and the anaphoric function in particular indicate that the first anarthrous use of Lamb is of special interpretative significance, especially as it pertains to the arthrous examples that follow. For discussion on these possible functions see Wallace, *Beyond the Basics*, 217ff.

Contextual Analysis

In the verses leading up to 5:6-10, there is a great deal of potential literary energy that when released successfully instigates the judgments that are unleashed upon the earth through the seals, trumpets, and bowls thereafter. "After these things" (Μετὰ ταῦτα) in 4:1 successfully divides chapters 1-3 and the next major unit (chapters 4-22). Not only does the temporal change marked in 4:1 suggest a degree of literary separation, but phrases like "in the Spirit" and pervasive use of "like" followed by vivid descriptions of places (4:2), people (4:4), phenomena (4:5), and creatures (4:8) successfully imbue the text with a worshipful and otherworldly connotation that is absent from the previous chapters. This worship reaches a climax in 4:8 when a doxology rings out over the halls of a heavenly scene—"Holy, Holy, Holy, is the Lord God, the Almighty, who was and who is and who is to come." This worshipful verse is then, in many ways, mirrored by three stanzas of praise that are offered in the remainder of chapter 4 and into chapter 5.[20] However, the worship that is expressed by the heavenly inhabitants of these two chapters is temporarily interrupted by a scene that breaks out in the beginning of chapter 5.

The interruption is introduced by a phrase indicating a new observation—"I saw in the right hand..." (5:1).[21] Here, John witnesses a seven-sealed book and hears "a strong angel proclaiming with a loud voice...'Who is worthy to open the book and to break its seals?'" (5:2). Though the reader might assume that the one who was holding the book (the one who "sat on the throne") could break this volume open, John learns that no one yet pres-

---

20 4:11, "Worthy are You, our Lord and our God, to receive glory and honor and power; for You created all things, and because of Your will they existed, and were created." 5:9-10, "Worthy are You to take the book and to break its seals; for You were slain, and purchased for God with Your blood men from every tribe and tongue and people and nation. You have made them to be a kingdom and priests to our God; and they will reign upon the earth." 5:12, "Worthy is the Lamb that was slain to receive power and riches and wisdom and might and honor and glory."

21 See the major division suggested in 4:1 by "After these things I looked and behold...".

ent in the scene can, by all appearances, expose the contents of this mysterious scroll. Fearing that no one can open the book, break its seals, and thereby implement the things that are revealed therein, John weeps.[22] John's weeping ceases when he is told that "the Lion that is from the tribe of Judah, the Root of David, has overcome to open the book and its seven seals" (5:5). In other words, a hero exists that has provided salvation and as a direct result is qualified to provide salvation for John's present distress (opening the seven-sealed scroll and paving the way for the eschatological judgment and salvation to be disclosed in the remainder of the Apocalypse).[23] The description attributed to this hero is two-fold. First he is described as the "Lion of the tribe of Judah," indicating a "kingly might and boldness" that is similar to what is portrayed in Genesis 49:9 and Proverbs 28:1.[24] Second, he is depicted as the "root of David," a title that John will eventually use again in 22:16. In Isaiah 11:1, 10, this label identifies the Lion as the head of the Davidic kingdom that was prophesied in the OT. Taken together, these messianic labels indicate that it is by this hero's unique membership in David's family that he is called the greatest of the tribe of Judah and a branch from the root of this regal line.[25]

---

22 John had been promised in 4:1 that he would be shown "what must take place after these things." Therefore, this closed book, for John, represents a barrier keeping him from seeing/experiencing what God is going to do. John is therefore weeping over the apparent indefinite postponement of God's final and decisive action. See Robert L. Thomas, *Revelation, An Exegetical Commentary*, 2 vols. (Chicago: Moody, 1992), I.386.

23 David MacLeod, "The Lion Who is a Lamb: An Exposition of Revelation 5:1-7." *Bibliotheca Sacra* 164 No. 655 (Summer 2007): 328-29. "The breaking of the seals is preparatory to God's people entering the promised inheritance...".

24 Thomas, *Revelation*, I.387. Gen. 49:9, "Judah is a lion's whelp; from the prey, my son, you have gone up. He couches, he lies down as a lion, and as a lion, who dares rouse him up?" Prov. 28:1, "The wicked flee when no one is pursuing, but the righteous are bold as a lion."

25 A. T. Robertson, *Word Pictures in the New Testament*, 6 vols. (Nashville: B&H, 1933), 6:333-34.

However, the figure that appears after this introduction does not match the title and description he is given in verse 5. When John turns to look at the regal hero, not a lion, but a "Lamb" (ἀρνίον) emerges onto the scene, "standing as if slain, having seven horns and seven eyes, which are the seven Spirits of God, sent out into all the earth" (5:6). This Lamb takes the scroll from the hand of the one who sits on the throne, thereby eliciting the worship and praise of those present in verses 9-10. While praise was limited to the one who occupied the throne in chapter 4, worship is extended to this Lamb in verses 9-10 and then again in verse 12 in response to his ability to take the scroll and set into motion what John and the world have been waiting for—the eschaton complete with its judgment and final victory.

Grammatical Analysis of Revelation 5:6–10

Before a complete interpretation of this passage can be achieved, special attention needs to be given to what the diagrammatical analysis demonstrates. Much of what this passage has to say is contingent on the understanding of ἀρνίον.[26] Again, 5:6 contains the first time that John employs this term. Additionally, and as mentioned earlier, ἀρνίον is by far the most frequent designation for Christ in Revelation (appearing more than twice as frequently as any other label for Jesus in the Apocalypse). For John this is

---

26 Grammatical analysis reveals that in 5:6 the interpretation of the direct object of the main independent clause (ἀρνίον) is dependent on the two complex dependent participial phrases that are used by John to describe him ("standing as if slain, having seven horns and seven eyes..."). Also, as mentioned earlier, it is worth reiterating that ἀρνίον in verse 6 is anarthrous, indicating that it is without previous reference in the Apocalypse and thereby requiring special interpretative care. The relative temporal phrase in verse 8–"when he had taken the book," - betrays why the Lamb was worshipped. This "worthiness" is further evidenced in verses 9-10 by means of the explanatory ὅτι clauses that are attached to the phrase "worthy are you." The horned and slain Lamb is described as worthy not only because of what he is presently doing (taking the book), but because of what he has already accomplished–"...purchased for God with Your blood men from every tribe and tongue and people and nation. You have made them to be a kingdom and priests to our God..." (5:9-10).

especially telling, for, as witnessed in his Gospel, John often uses different synonyms for the same concept.[27] Therefore, the consistent use of ἀρνίον for Christ in Revelation might indicate that John is deliberately conveying something of theological significance. However, understanding what this significance is requires that the reader pay close attention to how John juxtaposes the "Lamb" in verse 6 with the "Lion" in verse 5.

Toward an Interpretation of the Lamb

John appears to be intentionally highlighting the antithetical nature of these two images—Lion and Lamb—and their connection to one figure who embodies the connotations of both. As has already been determined, "Lion" is a direct reference to the powerful and royal line of Judah and David. Its use appears to present Christ as the prophesied Davidic King.[28] This particular title refers back centuries to the days of Jacob who, while on his deathbed, blessed his sons and prophesied over them saying "Judah is a lion's whelp from the prey, my son, you have gone up. He crouches, he lies down as a lion, and as a lion, who dares rouse him up?"[29] As Judah is perpetually connected to Christ (as Jesus emerges from his family line), this eschatological connection helps demonstrate Christ's place as the long-awaited champion of the Jews. Employing this figure of the lion, 2 Esdras 12:31 says, "This is the Messiah"[30] and appreciates him for his glory, strength, and

---

27 See John's use of ἀγαπάω and φιλέω in John 21 as an example.
28 Andreas L. Kostenberger, Scott Kellum, and Charles L. Quarels, *The Lion and the Lamb: New Testament Essentials from the Cradle, the Cross, and the Crown* (Nashville: B&H, 2012), 387.
29 Gen 49:9. See also Macleod, "Lion who is a Lamb," 332.
30 The full quote of 2 Esdras 12:31–33 reads "And as for the lion whom you saw rousing up out of the forest and roaring and speaking to the eagle and reproving him for his unrighteousness, and as for all his words that you have heard, this is the Messiah whom the Most High has kept until the end of days, who will arise from the offspring of David, and will come and speak with them. He will denounce them for their ungodliness and for their wickedness and will display before them their contemptuous dealings. For first he will bring them alive before his judgment seat, and when he has reproved them, then he will destroy them."

worthiness to judge the wicked. The description of this Lion does not cease with this reference to Judah. Instead, John also calls the Lion the "Root of David."[31] Alluding to Isaiah 11:10, this title describes the Lion as that descendent of David who will restore the long-awaited Davidic kingdom.[32] These references imbue the figure in question with connotations of victory, power, and prestige.

However, when John turns to view this "Lion," he beholds something unexpected—a "Lamb." "Lamb" hardly denotes the same prestigious connotations as "Lion of the tribe of Judah" (and "Root of David"). The former is one of the humblest creatures while the latter is regal, powerful, and glorious. The theme of humility in connection with ἀρνίον (distinct from other words for lamb in the remainder of Scripture) is consistent with how this word is used in the LXX. Jeremiah 11:19 employs ἀρνίον alongside the qualifier "gentle" and "led to the slaughter," demonstrating the humble ways in which a lamb was both viewed and used in connection with sacrifice for sin. Not only that, but Isaiah 40:11 states "like a shepherd He will tend His flock, in His arm He will gather the lambs and carry them in His bosom; He will gently lead the nursing ewes." This demonstrates that the humility of a lamb is so severe that its survival depends on the care and protection of a shepherd. Therefore, while πάσχα and ἀμνὸς are employed elsewhere in the NT for lamb (to draw more specifically from the Passover tradition and the pervasive sacrifices of the OT respectively), John chooses a more connotatively neutral and altogether unique term in an effort to highlight something different—humility (especially when juxtaposed alongside the use of "Lion" in verse 5)—and applies this to Revelation's most important character.

---

31 Rev 5:5.

32 Caird, *Revelation of St. John*, 74, Robert H. Mounce, *The Book of Revelation*, New International Commentary on the New Testament. Grand Rapids: Eerdmans, 1997, 131; David Aune, *Revelation 1-5*, Word Biblical Commentary (Dallas: Word, 1997), 350-51. Grant Osborne, *Revelation*, Baker Exegetical Commentary on the New Testament (Grand Rapids, MI: Baker, 2008), 254.

This interpretation is supported by the participial phrases attached to this term in verse 6 beginning with "standing, as if slain...." The only way for a lamb to be more humiliated than it already is entails having it slain. Here, the obvious reference is to the death of Christ, who, even though slain, is erect and alive in this heavenly scene.[33] In other words, while the marks of death are visible, they are not debilitating.[34] This provocative image, along with the descriptions that follow of the Lamb, helps demonstrate that while John may be capitalizing on the humility of the Lamb, there is more at work in this term and the connotations it is capable of eliciting.

This becomes clearer as the next participial phrase is uttered "having seven horns and seven eyes, which are the seven spirits of God" (5:6). In one breath, John depicts the Lamb as slain, and in the next, he assigns images of dominion and rule to this humble figure. Since the OT uses the horn as a symbol of strength and power,[35] seven of them together in this context indicate the fullness of power that rests on this all-powerful warrior-like Lamb.[36] Something similar may be said about the seven eyes which indicate the inescapable view by which the Lamb discerns the world and all that happens within it. Some have connected this set of eyes to Zechariah 3:9 and 4:10, believing that they indicate the

---

33 Thomas, *Revelation*, I.391.
34 Henry Alford, *The Greek Testament*, 4 vols. (London: Longmans, Green, 1903), 4:607. H. B. Swete, *The Apocalypse of St. John* (London: Macmillan, 1906), 78. Isbon T. Beckwith, *Apocalypse of John* (New York: Macmillan, 1919), 510.
35 See Num 23:22; Deut 33:17. See also 1 Sam 2:1; 2 Sam 22:3; 1 Kgs 22:11; Pss 75:4; 132:17; Dan 7:20-21; 8:5. Thomas also points out that later books in the OT "symbolizes dynastic force or kingly dignity and is thus used in Apocalypse several times (Rev. 12:3; 13:1; 17:3, 12)." *Revelation*, 392.
36 Beale, *Revelation*, 351, "That the Lamb has seven horn signifies the fullness of his strength, since 'seven' is figurative for fullness elsewhere in the Apocalypse and in biblical literature." William Kelly, *The Revelation* (London, Thomas Weston, 1904), 90. George Ladd, *A Commentary on the Revelation of John* (Grand Rapids, MI: Eerdmans, 1972), 87. "Here, we must guard against the temptation to visualize the Lamb...the symbols of Revelation are intended to communicate truth, not to serve as photographic reproductions...". Mounce, "Christology of Apocalypse," 44. See also Swete, *Apocalypse*, 78-79.

Lord's ability to remove iniquity from the land of Israel.[37] However, the explanatory relative clause that closes verse 6 ("which are the seven spirits of God sent into all the earth"), seems to support what Thomas and others have concluded concerning the Lamb's eyes—that "not only is he omnipotent, as indicated by his seven horns, he is also omniscient."[38]

The greatness of the Lamb is further illustrated in his being "worthy...to take the book and break its seals" (5:9-10). This is why the Lamb is worshipped in the same manner as the occupier of the throne in 4:8. "Worthy" (ἄξιος) was applied to the enthroned figure first in 4:11. This same worthiness is applied to the Lamb in 5:9-10 and then again in 5:12. John connects the worship of the Lamb to the worship of the Father to demonstrate their shared divinity (as only God is an appropriate recipient of worship in John's writings). As Macleod rightly concludes, "His worthiness to open the scroll and inherit the kingdom is based on the victory he won as the Lamb on the cross"[39] —Jesus' greatest and most humble act.

A tentative interpretation of this passage and its most central term, especially given the context in which it is found, involves Jesus' unique ability to set in motion the eschaton and thereby the ultimate salvation (glorification) of his people. This ability is afforded him because he (the Lion of the Tribe of Judah) humiliated himself to the point of death (a Lamb standing as if slain)[40]

---

37   Zech 3:9, "For behold, the stone that I have set before Joshua; on one stone are seven eyes. Behold, I will engrave an inscription on it,' declares the Lord of hosts, 'and I will remove the iniquity of that land in one day." Zech 4:10, "For who has despised the day of small things? But these seven will be glad when they see the plumb line in the hand of Zerubbabel—these are the eyes of the Lord which range to and fro throughout the earth."

38   Thomas, *Revelation*, I.392. Thomas believes that those who believe the "eyes" are connected to Zech 3:9 and 4:10 are pressing the meaning of the OT source of the words too far. See also Mounce, "Christology of Apocalypse," 44, Swete, *Apocalypse*, 78-79, Charles, *Revelation*, 141, Robertson, *Word Pictures*, 6:334-35, Caird, *Revelation*, 75.

39   Macleod, "Lion who is a Lamb," 335.

40   Macleod, "Lion who is a Lamb," 334, "John was assured that the Lion 'has overcome,' which, as noted earlier, refers to His defeat of Satan, sin, and death at the cross." Osborne calls this "a great Christian paradox—Jesus has 'conquered' primarily not through military might, though that is to come, but through his sacrificial death (5:6, 9, 12)... As the Royal Messiah, Jesus wages

and as such has been given all power (seven horns) and perception (seven eyes), to continue to perform God's will. Because of this, he is worthy of worship. The Christological statement made here (accentuated by the image of the ἀρνίον) successfully portrays Jesus in his humblest and therefore most glorious light (His passion).[41] This symbol affords Christ equal status with God, the praise of all present in this heavenly spectacle, and the kind of literary capacity necessary to house many other Christological themes within its domain.[42] It is this image in which John decides to cast Jesus throughout the remainder of Revelation.

Canonical and Historical Analysis

Beginning with what is more contextually significant (Johannine literature, the NT, and the OT) and continuing to what is more contextually remote (extra-biblical literature), the remainder of this study will investigate whether the interpretation already given requires any alteration or nuance. First, the tentative interpretation above is analogous to what is found in Johannine literature. For example, Paul Rainbow acknowledges that in the beginning of John's Gospel, Jesus is described as the "Word made flesh" (λόγος made σάρξ).[43] According to his view, "the evangelist wants us to read the entire book as the story of the Logos-become-flesh who laid down his life as God's lamb."[44] Immediately after this

---

a messianic war against evil, and the major weapon that defeats the enemies of God is the cross. This cosmic victory enables him 'to open' the scroll." Osborne, *Revelation*, 254.

41 "The crucified Christ is central to the Book of Revelation." Macleod, "Lion Who as a Lamb," 331.

42 The conclusion reached thus far desires to extend what others like Beale have already argued. Beale says, "there are two different proposals for the background of the 'slain Lamb.' Some prefer to see it as a reference to the OT Passover lamb, while other favor Isa. 53:7...However, neither should be excluded..." Beale, *Revelation*, 351. A robust understanding of ἀρνίον demonstrates that it is inclusive of potentially many Christological motifs between the paradoxical domain of utter humility and superior glory.

43 John 1:14.

44 Paul A. Rainbow, *Johannine Theology: The Gospel, the Epistles, and the Apocalypse* (Downers Grove, IL: InterVarsity, 2014), 183.

claim, Rainbow draws parallels between "Word made flesh" and "Lamb as if slain." John uses the former ("Word made flesh") in his Gospel to highlight the divinity of the Son by emphasizing his incarnation while John uses the latter ("Lamb as if slain") in his apocalypse to demonstrate the glory of the Son by accentuating his humility.[45]

That Jesus is depicted as gloriously humble in Johannine literature is evident in passages like John 4:34 in which Jesus says, "My food is to do the will of Him who sent me and to accomplish His work." Such a statement renders Christ a uniquely modest deity. This sentiment is repeated just one chapter later when Jesus says "I can do nothing on My own initiative. As I hear, I judge; and My judgment is just because I do not seek My own will, but the will of Him who sent Me."[46] However, perhaps one of the most humble descriptions of Jesus is made in John 10:11ff when in another pastoral passage Jesus speaks about his unique authority alongside his utter humiliation saying—"I am the good shepherd; the good shepherd lays down his life for the sheep." Here, goodness/greatness is juxtaposed alongside a willingness to humble oneself—particularly, as it pertains to Jesus' humblest act on the cross.

However, the theme of humble greatness is not limited to Christ's passion. While in the upper room, John describes how Jesus "began to wash the disciples' feet and to wipe them with the towel with which He was girded."[47] Though a foreshadowing of an even greater act of service that he would soon accomplish,[48] the lesson is explained by Jesus as follows—"If I then, the Lord and the Teacher, washed your feet, you also ought to wash one another's feet. For I gave you an example that you also should do as I did to

---

45 Rainbow, *Johannine Theology*, 183. Here, Rainbow draws special attention to the Lamb's humility as witnessed in Christ's atoning sacrifice.
46 John 5:30.
47 John 13:5.
48 D. A. Carson, *John*, Pillar Commentary Series (Grand Rapids, MI: Eerdmans, 2016), 463. "Peter and the others will understand later...[that] this does not refer to the footwashing, but to the passion to which the footwashing points."

you."[49] The acuity of Jesus' humiliation in this act is highlighted by Peter's revulsion at the idea that Jesus, his teacher and Lord, would stoop to wash his feet—an act reserved for the humblest of servants.[50] However, this is exactly Jesus' point: the greatest is not the one who would never wash feet, but the one who will choose to humble himself even to the point of performing such an activity.

These findings prove consistent with what is found elsewhere in the NT. In Matthew 23:11-12 Jesus says "but the greatest among you shall be your servant. Whoever exalts himself shall be humbled; and whoever humbles himself shall be exalted."[51] Applied to the interpretation already given of Revelation 5:6-10, the one who humbled himself the most as the slain Lamb is the same one who is exalted high enough to be able to break open the seven-sealed book.

The dispute concerning greatness among the disciples in Luke 22:23ff echoes these principles. In response to their quarrel Jesus states,

> The kings of the Gentiles lord it over them; and those who have authority over them are called 'Benefactor.' But it is not this way with you, but the one who is the greatest among you must become like the youngest, and the leader like the servant. For who is greater, the one who reclines at the table or the one who serves? Is it the one who reclines at the table? But I am among you as the one who serves.[52]

To silence the argument the disciples were endorsing, Jesus turns greatness on its head and introduces his followers to the paradox of humility affording that which is praiseworthy, pointing to himself as the example *par excellence* of this phenomenon.

---

49 John 13:14-15.
50 Andreas Kostenberger, *John*, Baker Exegetical Commentary on the New Testament (Grand Rapids, MI: Baker, 2004), 405.
51 See also Lk 14:11; 18:14.
52 Lk 22:25-27.

These concepts are also found in the OT. Therein, God makes a habit of choosing the humblest people to do the most extraordinary things. Throughout the OT, the barren,[53] youngest,[54] fearful,[55] hesitant,[56] sorrowful,[57] and cowardly[58] were used by a mighty God to do what was praiseworthy and glorious. Not only that, but the people of God were in a perpetual state of humility (i.e., slavery or exile) and yet remained the Lord's promised ones. In many ways, the OT is full of ἀρνίovs—the humblest of creatures—who are used for glorious purposes.

That ἀρνίον conveys humility and subsequent glory is supported not only by the few OT passages in which this word is used[59] but also by the extra-biblical usage of this term. Though Louw and Nida's lexicon claims that this term can refer to either a sheep of any age, a lamb, or a ram,[60] as was mentioned earlier, Loren Johns reveals that all examples of the word in biblical and classical Greek refer to a young sheep or lamb.[61] Nowhere does it refer to an adult ram in literature that predates the Apocalypse."[62] This is confirmed later by passages in the Mishnah which state, "Lambs must be no more than one year old..." in the context of types of sacrifices offered.[63] These humble creatures, made even more humble by their youth, were especially qualified for sacrificial use. Therefore, the semantic range of ἀρνίον as witnessed in extra-bibli-

---

53   See Sarah in Gen 11:27ff, Rachel in Gen 29:29ff, and Hannah in 1 Sam 1:1-2.
54   See David in 1 Sam 17:14.
55   See Moses in Exod 3-4 and Elijah in 1 Kgs 19.
56   See Jonah in Jonah 1-2.
57   See Ruth and Naomi in Ruth 1-4.
58   See Gideon in Judges 6.
59   Jer 11:19; Jer 50:45; Ps 114:4, 6; Isa 40:11; Song 8:23.
60   Louw and Nida, *Greek-English Lexicon*, s. v. ἀρνίον
61   Johns, *Lamb Christology*, 22.
62   Johns, *Lamb Christology*, 22.
63   Mishnah Para 1:3. This passage defines "lamb" (ἀρνίον) more precisely as not more than one year old. Though this occurrence is two centuries removed from the writing of John's Apocalypse, it demonstrates that at least on a historical level, there are uses of the term that appear to imbue ἀρνίον with some level of meaning that renders the humility of the creature in question especially humble.

cal literature suggests that humility of a very special kind is at least potentially integral to the connotation of this term.

The image of humble sheep also emerges in 1 Enoch 89. Although God's people were described as bulls early in the chapter, Isaac's son Jacob is depicted as a sheep as is Jacob's twelve sons and Moses after him. One might say that bulls become sheep upon the emergence of Israel (Jacob). These sheep spawn other sheep who are then led by a series of "seventy shepherds" (alluding perhaps to Jeremiah's prediction that Israel's exile will last for seventy years).[64] Once strong bulls, these apocalyptic sheep demonstrate the humble place that God's people occupied on the world's stage, especially in times of tribulation and exile. At times this apocalyptic tribulation is self-induced, as witnessed in Zechariah 11:4-17. Here, the shepherd/sheep imagery takes on a new flavor when the prophet is depicted as a "shepherd of the flock doomed to slaughter."[65] Having disobeyed their natural shepherd, Yahweh, the sheep are handed over by God to other shepherds to be disciplined[66] for a time.

The word ἀρνίον itself along with the preexistent themes of humility and greatness seem to work together on both a linguistic, historical, and thematic level outside of and within the Canon to support the interpretation given for Revelation 5:6-10—namely that Jesus' unique status, as witnessed in his ability to take the scroll and set in motion the end times, is confirmed in his matchless glory which is wondrously encased in the humblest of forms—"the Lamb standing as if slain." Because none could humble themselves greater than Jesus did, no one is as gloriously capa-

---

64 F. J. Murphy, *Apocalypticism in the Bible and its World* (Grand Rapids, MI: Baker, 2012), 90. See also 1 Enoch 89:59. Others hold that the number seventy corresponds to Daniel's seventy weeks of years and the common division of history into seventy generations. See Jer 25. J. Collins, *The Apocalyptic Imagination: An Introduction to the Jewish Matrix of Christianity* (New York: Crossroad, 1984), 68ff.

65 Zech 11:4.

66 Greg Carey, *An Introduction to Jewish and Christian Apocalyptic Literature* (St. Louis, MO: Chalice Press, 2005), 59. David L. Petersen, *Zechariah 9-14 and Malachi* (Louisville: Westminster John Knox Press, 1995), 90. "Yahweh cedes power to malevolent human rulers."

ble of doing what he will accomplish in the *eschaton*. This renders Jesus a uniquely fitting/capable and yet altogether peculiar hero/protagonist in the apostle's Apocalypse.

Conclusion

In Revelation 5:6–10, Jesus is cast as a brilliant paradox that accentuates not only his matchless glory but also his uncompromising humility. Augustine reached a similar conclusion regarding this term as connected to this passage when he said,

> Who is this, both Lamb and lion? He endured death as a lamb; he devoured it as a lion. Who is this, both lamb and lion? Gentle and strong, lovable and terrifying, innocent and mighty silent when he was being judged, roaring when he comes to judge.[67]

The words used (particularly ἀρνίον), descriptions offered (seven horns and seven eyes), worship witnessed, precedent given (in both the Old and NTs), and even the extra-biblical usage of the same term support these claims. By employing a peculiar term amid his opening description of Christ, John allows himself the literary freedom to accomplish his goal of describing a humble and therefore glorious God-Man that he calls to mind no less than 28 additional times throughout the remainder of this letter in a variety of contexts (always, following Revelation 5:6, with the definite article of previous reference). Because John endorses a relatively unique term (ἀρνίον) bereft of formal historical connotations, it is malleable enough to be imbued with more general themes like humility and glory. Because of its unique semantic range bookended by the related poles of utter humility and supreme glory, ἀρνίον is not as limited as other more developed terms and

---

[67] Augustine, "Sermon 275A: On the Sacraments" in *Sermons (341-400) on Various Subjects* (New York: New City Press, 1995), 330.

can therefore encompass a variety of multivalent Christological considerations (including but not limited to the more univocal interpretive options of the Passover Lamb, superior sacrifice, victorious one, etc.). For these reasons—the fitting introduction of Revelation's protagonist and the carefully selected verbiage that is employed—the Lamb is not only a fitting hero for the last chapter of God's canon, but the greatest ever hero.

BIBLIOGRAPHY

Alford, Henry. *The Greek Testament*, 4 vols. London: Longmans, Green, 1903.

Augustine, "Sermon 275A: On the Sacraments" in *Sermons (341-400) on Various Subjects*. New York: New City Press, 1995.

Aune, David. *Revelation 1–5*, Word Biblical Commentary. Dallas: Word, 1997.

Beale, G. K. *The Book of Revelation*, New International Greek Testament Commentary. Grand Rapids, MI: Eerdmans, 1999.

Beckwith, Isbon T. *Apocalypse of John*. New York: Macmillan, 1919.

Caird, G. B. *The Revelation of St. John the Divine*. New York: Harper & Row, 1966.

Carey, Greg. *An Introduction to Jewish and Christian Apocalyptic Literature*. St. Louis, MO: Chalice Press, 2005.

Carson, D. A. *John*, Pillar Commentary Series. Grand Rapids: Eerdmans, 2016.

Charles, R. H. *A Critical and Exegetical Commentary on the Revelation of St. John*. Vol. 1. Edinburgh: T&T Clark, 1920.

Collins, J. *The Apocalyptic Imagination: An Introduction to the Jewish Matrix of Christianity*. New York: Crossroad, 1984.

Dickson, Jeffrey. *The Humility and Glory of the Lamb: Toward a Robust Apocalyptic Christology*. Eugene, OR: Wipf and Stock, 2019.

Guthrie, Donald. "The Lamb in the Structure of the Book of Revelation." *Vox Evangelica* 12 (1981): 64–71.

Hendrickson, William. *More than Conquerors*. Grand Rapids, MI: Baker, 1967.

Johns, Loren. *The Lamb Christology of the Apocalypse of John: An Investigation into its Origin and Rhetorical Force*. Eugene, OR: Wipf and Stock, 2014.

Köstenberger, Andreas. *John*, Baker Exegetical Commentary on the New Testament. Grand Rapids, MI: Baker, 2004.

———. L. Scott Kellum, and Charles L. Quarels. *The Lion and the Lamb: New Testament Essentials from the Cradle, the Cross, and the Crown*. Nashville: B&H, 2012.

Ladd, George. *A Commentary on the Revelation of John*. Grand Rapids, MI: Eerdmans, 1972.

MacLeod, Donald "The Christology of Chalcedon." *The Only Hope Jesus: Yesterday, Today, Forever*, ed. Mark Elliot and John McPake. Fearn: Christian Focus, 2001.

———. "The Lion Who is a Lamb: An Exposition of Revelation 5:1-7." *Bibliotheca Sacra* 164 No. 655 (Summer 2007): 323-40.

Mounce, Robert H. *The Book of Revelation*, New International Commentary on the New Testament. Grand Rapids: Eerdmans, 1997.

———. "The Christology of the Apocalypse." *Foundations* 11 No. 1 (Spring 1968): 42-45.

Murphy, F. J. *Apocalypticism in the Bible and its World*. Grand Rapids, MI: Baker, 2012.

Osborne, Grant. *Revelation*, Baker Exegetical Commentary on the New Testament. Grand Rapids, MI: Baker, 2008.

Petersen, David L. *Zechariah 9-14 and Malachi*. Louisville: Westminster John Knox Press, 1995.

Rainbow, Paul A. *Johannine Theology: The Gospel, the Epistles, and the Apocalypse*. Downers Grove, IL: InterVarsity, 2014.

Robertson, A. T. *Word Pictures in the New Testament*, 6 vols. Nashville: B&H, 1933.

Swete, H. B. *The Apocalypse of St. John*. London: Macmillan, 1906.

Thomas, Robert L. *Revelation*, An Exegetical Commentary, 2 vols. Chicago: Moody, 1992.

Wallace, Daniel. *Greek Grammar: Beyond the Basics*. Grand Rapids, MI: Zondervan, 1996.

Whale, Peter. "The Lamb of John: Some Myths about the Vocabulary of the Johannine Literature." *Journal of Biblical Literature* 106 No. 2 (1987): 289-95.

Kelly, William. *The Revelation*. London: Thomas Weston, 1904.

CHAPTER TWO

EVIDENCE FOR THE PRE-TRIBULATION RAPTURE IN 1 THESSALONIANS

by Dr. Mark Hitchcock

Before we get into the topic at hand, I want to share a brief word about my relationship with Ed Hindson. I met Ed at the Pre-Trib Research Center annual meeting in 1994, which was my first year to attend. The meeting was held at the headquarters of Precept Ministries in Chattanooga, TN. It was the only time it had been held outside the Dallas area. Ed and I were assigned to the same cabin. We slept in a rustic bunk bed—Ed on top, me on bottom. Although initially I had no idea who Ed was, and he certainly had no idea who I was, we quickly became friends. I sensed that our meeting was providential. After those three days together, including some late-night conversations, our relationship deepened as our paths crossed many times over the next almost thirty years. I highly valued and appreciated my friendship with Ed.

I had the privilege to co-author two books with Ed, serve with him on the board of the Pre-Trib Research Center, and speak at numerous churches and prophecy conferences together. He was a respected friend, mentor, colleague, and inspiration.

I'm grateful for the opportunity to write a chapter in this *festschrift* for my dear friend. I decided to write a chapter focused on the rapture—a topic Ed loved and spoke about often. I pray the Lord will continue to honor the life and ministry of His faithful servant and spur all who read these pages to live and look for the blessed hope.

The Eschatological Epistles

My simple purpose in this article is to examine some of the relevant evidence in 1 Thessalonians for the pretribulation rapture of the church. It goes without saying that in one brief chapter, I will not be able to plumb the depths of every issue and text, but I hope to give a helpful sketch or overview of the timing of the rapture presented in 1 Thessalonians.

The Thessalonian letters were written by the Apostle Paul on his second missionary journey. Acts 17 records that during his initial visit to Thessalonica Paul ministered in Jewish synagogues for three weeks reasoning each Sabbath from the Scriptures. Paul was probably in the northern Greek city of Thessalonica for six to eight weeks.[68]

After Paul and his associates were run out of town, they headed south to Berea, then to Athens, and eventually to Corinth where Paul settled and set up his headquarters for eighteen months (Acts

---

[68] Three factors indicate that Paul was in Thessalonica for more than three weeks during his initial visit in Acts 17. 1) During Paul's stay in Thessalonica, the believers in Philippi sent at least two financial gifts to Paul. Since Thessalonica is about 100 miles away this points to a considerable lapse of time (Phil 4:16). 2) Paul was in Thessalonica long enough to pursue his secular trade (1 Thess 2:9). 3) The fact that most of the members of the Thessalonian church were Gentiles indicates that after reasoning with the Jew for three weeks in the synagogue, Paul had some time of ministry among the Gentiles in Thessalonica.

18:11). While in Corinth, Paul authored his two letters to the Thessalonians in which he focused on issues related to the end of time. For that reason, the Thessalonians letters are often referred to as Paul's "eschatological epistles." There are twenty different references to the coming of Christ, and the Lord's coming is mentioned in every chapter. Eighteen percent of 1 Thessalonians (16 of 89 verses) are prophetic in nature and content.[69] Second Thessalonians is forty percent prophecy (19 of 47 verses).[70] Neither book contains any direct Old Testament quotations.

The epistles refer to a variety of end-time events and persons: the rapture, the day of the Lord, the man of lawlessness or the son of destruction, the apostasy, the removal of the restrainer, Satanic deception, and the strong delusion sent by God in the end times. One of the key issues in the Thessalonian letters centers on the timing of the rapture. Is it a separate event from the return of Christ at the culmination of the tribulation? How is the rapture related to the day of the Lord?

There are at least five compelling points in 1 Thessalonians that indicate the church will be exempt from the coming wrath of the tribulation by being transported to heaven before the day of the Lord arrives.

Delivered from Wrath

In 1 Thessalonians 1:9–10 Paul reminds the believers at Thessalonica how they readily turned to God from dead idols to serve the living God and wait for the coming of Jesus from heaven.

> For they themselves report about us as to the kind of reception we had with you, and how you turned to God from idols to serve a living and true God, and to wait for His Son from heaven, whom He raised from the dead, that is, Jesus who rescues us from

---

[69] *Tim LaHaye Prophecy Bible* (Chattanooga, TN: AMG Publishers, 2001), 1406.
[70] *Tim LaHaye Prophecy Bible*, 1411.

the wrath to come.

Exemption from wrath is explicitly promised. "Jesus, who *delivers us from the wrath to come*" (italics added). The preposition *ek* ("from"/"out of") appears three times in 1:10. Without some clear signal in the text, one assumes that all three uses have the same meaning. The believers were waiting for Jesus to come from (*ek*) heaven, the One who was raised "from (*ek*) the dead." This same person would deliver the believers "from (*ek*) the wrath to come." The first two uses of *ek* clearly mean "from" or "out of." Jesus came *out of* heaven and was raised *out from* the dead, so it makes sense that the final use of *ek* in reference to God's wrath must have the same connotation. The preposition *ek* "emphasizes the completeness of our rescue by Christ—we are rescued out of the time of distress itself."[71]

The word "delivers" (*rhuomai*) is an action word that refers to rescue from something by a forcible act.[72] The word "places the emphasis on the greatness of the peril from which deliverance is given by a mighty act of power."[73] This word is used of the extraction or rescue of Lot from the wicked city of Sodom in 2 Peter 2:7. The word "delivers" is a present tense participle which stresses that the church's "deliverance or separation from the future wrath was already a present reality when Paul wrote 1 Thessalonians 1:10."[74] Since our deliverance or separation from wrath is already a present reality, we can rest assured that we will be separated from the wrath in the future.

---

71 Paul N. Benware, *Understanding End Times Prophecy* (Chicago: Moody Press, 1995), 174.
72 C. F. Hogg and W. E. Vine, *The Epistles of the Thessalonians* (Fincastle, VA: Scripture Truth, 1959), 48.
73 D. Edmond Hiebert, *1 & 2 Thessalonians*, rev. ed. (Chicago: Moody, 1992), 211.
74 Renald Showers, *Maranatha Our Lord, Come!* (Bellmawr, NJ: Friends of Israel Gospel Ministry, 1995), 194.

Eschatological Wrath or Eternal Wrath?

Once exemption from divine wrath for the church is established, the key question is—what specific aspect of God's wrath is in view? The word "wrath" (*orge*) has the definite article, so it is not just any wrath, but *the* wrath to come. Many commentators view this as eternal wrath in hell since in the preceding context in 1 Thessalonians Paul has been discussing the doctrine of election and salvation, not eschatology.[75] Richard Mayhue, who holds to a pretribulation rapture, appeals to the immediate context to support his view that eternal wrath is in view. "The whole of this chapter has been devoted to remembering the salvation of the Thessalonians... in context, it is best seen as God's eternal wrath. Thus, the deliverance is not in the sense of evacuation but rather of exemption."[76] John MacArthur, who also supports a pretribulation timing for the rapture, agrees with Mayhue. MacArthur states: "Some believe the wrath to come refers to the Great Tribulation, viewing this rescue as the promise of the pretribulation Rapture, expounded upon later in this epistle. But the immediate context of Paul's discussion of election and salvation rather than eschatology rules out the temporal wrath and points to eternal wrath."[77]

Of course, there is unanimous agreement that believers are protected from God's eternal wrath in hell; however, in the overall context of 1 Thessalonians, which contains frequent reference to the Lord's coming, the wrath in 1:10 seems to point to eschatological wrath. Believers will be delivered from wrath by the Lord's coming. His coming is not what delivers believers from the wrath of hell, but his coming will deliver us from the wrath of the Day of

---

75 I. Howard Marshall, *1 & 2 Thessalonians*, The New Century Bible Commentary, ed. Matthew Black (Reprint, Grand Rapids, MI: Eerdmans, 1990), 59; G. K. Beale, *1-2 Thessalonians*, The IVP New Testament Commentary Series, ed. Grant R. Osborne (Downers Grove, IL: InterVarsity Press, 2002), 62.

76 Richard Mayhue, *First and Second Thessalonians*, Focus on the Bible (Great Britain: Christian Focus, 1999), 62-3.

77 John MacArthur, Jr., *1 & 2 Thessalonians*, The MacArthur New Testament Commentary (Chicago: Moody, 2002), 2.9

the Lord. Paul Feinberg agrees that eschatological wrath is in view.

There are, I think, three reasons for thinking that the wrath spoken of is that of the Tribulation. First, the general context of the Thessalonian epistles is the day of the Lord. While this includes the final judgment, the focus of these epistles is the judgment of God that precedes and is associated with Christ's coming. Second, the text itself states that is a "coming wrath" and implies that rescue is related to Christ's return. Third, the wrath of 1 Thessalonians 1:10 seems related to that of 5:9 where the advent of eschatological woes is in view.[78]

Based on the language of 1 Thess 1:10 and the overall eschatological thrust of the entire epistle, the wrath believers are exempt from by means of Christ's coming is the wrath of the day of the Lord or tribulation period.

When Does the Day of the Lord Wrath Begin?

Once it is agreed that church-age believers are exempt from divine wrath and that the wrath under question is the wrath of the day of the Lord, the final key question is—when does that wrath begin? This is a critical question in determining the timing of the rapture.

All the main views of the timing of the rapture, except the partial rapture view, agree that church-age believers are exempt from God's wrath during the Great Tribulation or day of the Lord.[79] All the views also concur that the protection from the divine wrath of the day of the Lord does not mean the church is exempt from all suffering, trial, persecution, and trouble. Jesus was clear with His followers, "In the world you have tribulation" (John 16:33b). The apostle Paul was clear about the struggles of the church during

---

78 Paul D. Feinberg, "The Case for the Pretribulation Rapture Position," in *The Rapture: Pre-, Mid-, or Post-Tribulational?* ed. Ben Chapman (Grand Rapids, MI: Academie Books, 1984), 53.

79 The partial rapture view holds that only believers who are prepared, ready, and faithful will be raptured before the tribulation while those left behind on earth will endure all or part of the wrath of the tribulation. Many who hold to this view believe there will be various raptures throughout the tribulation as believers achieve a sufficient state of readiness.

this age: "Through many tribulations we must enter the kingdom of God" (Acts 14:22b). Many other passages underscore this truth (John 15:18–20; 1 Thess 3:3; 2 Tim 3:12; 1 Pet 4:12–16). All believers encounter trials, trouble, and tribulations in daily life, but believers are specifically promised deliverance from the divine wrath of the day of the Lord.

The issue at hand, then, is determining the time when the wrath of God begins, and the means God uses to protect the church from that time. Paul Feinberg notes, "It should be clear that the question of divine wrath is a fundamental one for the Rapture positions. The difference of opinion centers on the *commencement* of divine wrath and the *nature* or *means* of divine protection from that wrath."[80] Or to put it another way, how long will the wrath last and how will God keep the church from experiencing it?[81]

Here is a very succinct summary of how the four main views of the timing of the rapture address these issues.

Pretribulationism maintains that the entire seven-year tribulation "is a time of divine wrath" and "the means of protection for the church is removal from this period by the Rapture."[82]

Midtribulationists believe the first half of the final seven years the world experiences the wrath of man and the wrath of Satan, and the wrath of God is relegated to the final three and one-half years. The church will be caught up to heaven at the mid-point of the tribulation before the wrath of God is poured out.

Pre-Wrath Rapturism contends that all the judgments preceding the sixth trumpet in Rev 6 are human and satanic in nature; thus, the day of the Lord (God's wrath) commences with the seventh trumpet. The pre-wrath view places the rapture about three-fourths of the way through the tribulation between the sixth and seventh trumpets.

---

80 Feinberg, "The Case for the Pretribulation Rapture Position," 223.
81 Paul N. Benware, *Understanding End Times Prophecy* (Chicago: Moody Press, 1995), 171.
82 Feinberg, "The Case for the Pretribulation Rapture Position," 58.

Posttribulationism believes the church will be present on earth during the entire seven years of the tribulation but will be protected by God. The church will not be removed from the tribulation, but God will preserve the church in and through it.[83] The church will be raptured at the time of the Second Advent when Jesus returns to earth (Rev 19). Another form of this view holds that God's wrath is concentrated and compressed to the closing days of the tribulation, and the church will be raptured right before Armageddon at the consummation.[84] In either form, posttribulationists believe the church is present on earth for the entire span of the tribulation.

The following chart shows how the different approaches to the timing of the rapture deal with the onset of God's wrath and the means of deliverance from it.

	When Wrath Commences	Means of Divine Protection
Pretribulation	Beginning of the Tribulation	Removal to Heaven
Midtribulation	Mid-point of the tribulation	Removal to Heaven
Posttribulation	The wrath of God is concentrated at the end of the tribulation	Protected on Earth
		Removal at the Second Advent
Pre-Wrath	After the 6th trumpet	Removal to Heaven

---

83   George Eldon Ladd, *The Blessed Hope* (Grand Rapids, MI: Eerdmans, 1956), 129.
84   Robert H. Gundry, *The Church and the Tribulation* (Grand Rapids, MI: Zondervan, 1973), 63.

The mid-tribulation, pre-wrath, and post-tribulation positions all believe the wrath of God begins at some point in the tribulation after its apparent commencement in Rev 6:1 with the opening of the seals. They all view some portion of the tribulation as the wrath of man and the wrath of Satan but not the wrath of God. They contend, to differing degrees, that war, famine, and disease are not the direct wrath of God.

The difficulties these views face is that human activity and divine wrath cannot be separated so precisely. Distinctions between human and divine wrath dissolve when we recognize that human action is one means by which divine wrath is accomplished.[85] Paul Feinberg notes:

> To identify the wrath of God simply with His direct intervention is to overlook the fact that primary and secondary agency both belong to God. Would anyone deny that the Northern Kingdom had been judged by God because Assyria conquered her? Did the Southern Kingdom escape the wrath of God for her sin because the instrument of judgment was Nebuchadnezzar and Babylon? Surely the answer is no. Then why should anyone think that because the early seals and trumpets relate to famine and war as well as natural phenomena that they cannot and are not expressions of the wrath of God?... The incident in David's life where he numbered Israel shows that God used Satan in bringing judgment (2 Sam 24:1; cf. 1 Chron. 21:10). The activity of the whole period proceeds from the activity of the worth Lamb; it is He who breaks the seals.[86]

---

85 Craig Blaising, "A Case for the Pretribulation Rapture," *Three Views on the Rapture: Pretribulation, Prewrath, or Posttribulation*, ed. Alan Hultberg, 2nd ed. (Grand Rapids, MI: Zondervan, 2010), 247.

86 Feinberg, "The Case for the Pretribulation Rapture," 62.

Famine, war, and plagues are often tied to God's wrath in other places in Scripture (Jer 14:12; 15:2; 24:10; 29:17; Ezek 5:12, 17; 14:21). The character of the entire tribulation period points toward Christ's bride's exemption from all of it, not just some lesser segment.

All three waves of judgment in Revelation 6–18 (seals, trumpets, and bowls) are God's wrath. The seal judgments, which commence the tribulation, are opened by the Lamb (Rev 6:1). Jesus opens the seals. They are being unleashed by Him from the outset. To suggest that the wrath of God is somehow limited to the last half, last one-fourth, or very end of the tribulation ignores the source of the seven seal judgments that commence the seven-year tribulation. Feinberg states,

> Christ alone has the authority to take the scroll and break its seals. Every judgment from the first seal to the last judgment comes as the retributive wrath of God.... It is the Lamb, Christ, who breaks the seals before the wrath proceeds (Rev 6:1, 3, 5, 7, 9, 12).... The entire Tribulation period is a time of God's wrath, from the first seal to the last bowl. The judgments of God fall universally upon all the earth.[87]

The judgments indeed increase in intensity and frequency as the Tribulation progresses, but this has no bearing on their source.

Craig Blaising points to the integrated structure of the tribulation as an indication that all the judgments are God's wrath. "Pretribulationists believe, however, that the church is promised exemption from a unique future time of tribulation. This tribulation is a unique, integrated, complex, structured event that can be considered as a unified whole.... The deliverance promised to the church is from this particular complex event considered as a whole."[88] I agree. To attempt to break up the day of the Lord into

---

[87] Feinberg, "The Case for the Pretribulation Rapture," 62, 223.
[88] Blaising, "A Case for the Pretribulation Rapture," 244.

separate segments is not consistent with the integrated nature of the day of the Lord presented in the Book of Revelation.

Revelation 3:10 provides further support for the evacuation of the church from the entire time of the tribulation. "Because you have kept My word of perseverance, I also will keep you from the hour of the testing, that hour which is about to come upon the whole world, to test those who live on the earth." Notice, believers are not just promised exemption from the wrath, but exemption from the *time* of the wrath, that is, the tribulation period. The very next verse, Rev 3:11a, provides the means God will use to keep His people from the time of the tribulation. "I am coming quickly." If the wrath of God is falling everywhere on earth during the tribulation, the only way for God to keep His people from it is by the rapture—removal from the earth.

Getting Things in Order

Paul's extended discussion of the day of the Lord in 1 Thessalonians 5:1-8 comes right on the heels of the classic rapture passage in 1 Thessalonians 4:13-18. The sequence or chronology of these two passages is instructive. First Thessalonians 4:13-18 deals with the resurrection of dead believers and the rapture of living saints to meet the Lord in the air at His coming.

This text is followed in 1 Thessalonians 5:1 by the introduction of a new topic. The transition is marked by the words, "Now as to" (*peri de*) which signals a change of subjects in Paul's writings (1 Cor 7:1, 25; 8:1; 12:1; 16:1, 12; 1 Thess 4:9; 5:1).

Now as to the times and the epochs, brethren, you have no need of anything to be written to you. For you yourselves know full well that the day of the Lord will come just like a thief in the night (1 Thess 5:1-2).

The introduction of a fresh, but related, eschatological topic is significant because of the order of the events. The rapture is presented in 1 Thessalonians 4:13–18, and then the day of the Lord or tribulation is discussed in 1 Thessalonians 5:1–8. This clear sequence indicates the rapture is followed by the day of the Lord. As different, but related topics, they are presented as *sequential*, not *simultaneous*. The rapture must transpire before the day of the Lord, not consummate it. Mark Howell highlights the distinction between the two events.

Paul does not combine the two discussions. Had he done so, we might conclude that the rapture is somehow to be included in the events surrounding the Day of the Lord. However, rather than tying these events together, he appears to separate them purposely into two distinct events.... Paul chooses to address the rapture and the Day of the Lord separately. It is not coincidental that the rapture discussion precedes the Day of the Lord discussion. The natural reading of the text implies the Day of the Lord would follow the rapture of the church."[89]

In short, the tribulation is pictured as a *separate* and *subsequent* event from the rapture. The order is clear.

1 Thessalonians 4:13-18 portrays The Rapture
　　1 Thessalonians 5:1-9 portrays The Day of the Lord/Tribulation

The rapture and the day of the Lord can hardly be parts of the same event as posttribulationists maintain.[90] The rapture precedes the day of the Lord in 1 Thessalonians 4–5.

Two Topics

Another distinction between 1 Thessalonians 4:13–18 and 1 Thessalonians 5:1–8 that strengthens their separation from one another is that the believers were "uninformed" concerning the truth of the rapture in 4:13, while in 5:1 they are well aware of the

---

89　Mark Howell, *Exalting Jesus in 1 & 2 Thessalonians*, Christ-Centered Exposition, ed. David Platt, Daniel L. Akin, and Tony Merida (Nashville, TN: Holman Reference, 2015), 128.

90　Gleason L. Archer, Jr., "The Case for the Mid-Seventieth Week Rapture Position," in *The Rapture: Pre-, Mid-, or Post-Tribulational?* (Grand Rapids, MI: Zondervan, 1984), 117-18.

truth of the day of the Lord. The rapture and the day of the Lord are two distinct but connected topics, with the rapture preceding the day of the Lord.

A Common Argument against the Pretribulation Rapture
There's one main argument from 1 Thessalonians that is often raised by posttribulationists against the pretribulation rapture. I struggled with where to place a discussion of this argument, so I guess this is as good a place as any. Posttribulationists hold that the word "meet" (*apanteesis*) in 1 Thessalonians 4:17 is a technical term that refers to the citizens of a community who would pay tribute to a visiting dignitary by going out of the city to meet him and then ceremonially "accompany him back to the city he was planning to enter."[91] The conclusion from the use of this word is that when believers are raptured they return immediately back to earth escorting Jesus, which is consistent with the post-tribulation view and inconsistent with the pretribulation rapture which holds that raptured believers are transported immediately to heaven.

Shogren supports the technical meaning of *apanteesis* and its implications for the post-tribulation view. "Based on this conventional usage of 'meeting'...it may be concluded with a relatively high degree of certainty that Paul envisions Jesus coming in the air; resurrected believers and then living ones will ascend to honor him, and *they will accompany him back to the earth.*"[92]

John Piper cites the meaning of *apanteesis* as one of his key reasons for rejecting the pretribulation view. He leans on the other two uses of *apanteesis* in the New Testament in Matthew 25:6 and Acts 28:15-16.

The word translated "to meet" in the ESV occurs only two other places in the New Testament, and in both of them, the word

---

91 Gary S. Shogren, *1 & 2 Thessalonians*, Zondervan Exegetical Commentary on the New Testament, ed. Clinton E. Arnold (Grand Rapids, MI: Zondervan, 2012), 189.
92 Shogren, *1 & 2 Thessalonians*, 190.

refers to a meeting in which people go out to meet a dignitary and then accompany him to the place from which they came out.... This suggests strongly that the picture before us in 1 Thessalonians 4:17 is one of Christian believers rising to meet the Lord in the air and accompany him back to his rightful kingdom on earth. The word does not suggest any departure with Christ from the earth."[93]

While that interpretation, based on lexical evidence, is certainly possible, there's insufficient evidence that *apanteesis* always carries this technical meaning, and the context is key to its meaning in a specific text.

No specific indication is given as to where God's people go following this reunion. However, the logical reading of the passage suggests that they go to be with the Lord in heaven (John 14:1-3). There is no reason to believe Paul has in mind a return to earth. Why would he gather His people "in the air" only to bring them back to earth? He will return to earth one day. When He does return, He will not be coming for His church; He will be coming with His church.[94]

Catching-up His people in the air seems pointless unless God's people continue on to heaven with Jesus.

John 14:1-3 indicates that when Jesus comes, He will transport His people to the Father's house, not return right back to earth with them.

Do not let your heart be troubled; believe in God, believe also in Me. In My Father's house are many rooms; if that were not so, I would have told you, because I am going there to prepare a place for you. And if I go and prepare a place for you, I am coming again and will take you to Myself, so that where I am, there you also will be.

---

[93] John Piper, *Come, Lord Jesus: Meditations on the Second Coming of Christ* (Wheaton, IL: Crossway, 2023), 207.

[94] Howell, *Exalting Jesus in 1 & 2 Thessalonians*, 122; cf. Robert L Thomas, "1, 2 Thessalonians," in The Expositor's Bible Commentary, ed. Frank E. Gaebelein, vol. 11 (Grand Rapids, MI: Zondervan, 1978), 279.

The linguistic similarities between John 14:1-3 with 1 Thessalonians 4:13-18 lends support to believers going to heaven after the rapture, not returning immediately back to earth. Jesus' teaching recorded in John 14:1-3 may have been Paul's primary source for 1 Thessalonians 4:13-18.

Parallels Between John 14:1-3 and 1 Thessalonians 4:13-18

John 14:1-3	1 Thess 4:13-18
trouble (1)	sorrow (13)
believe (1)	believe (14)
God, me (1)	Jesus, God (14)
told you (2)	say to you (15)
come again (3)	coming of the Lord (15)
receive you (3)	caught up (17)
to myself (3)	to meet the Lord (17)
be where I am (3)	ever be with the Lord (17)

Based on the similarity between these two texts, Hiebert says, "From John 14:2-3 it is clear that Christ's coming to take His own unto Himself is for the express purpose of taking them to the heavenly mansions now being prepared for them."[95] For this reason, *apanteesis* provides no support for the post-tribulation view, rather the context and parallel passage in John 14:1-3 undergirds the catching away of the bride to the Father's house while the tribulation rages on earth.

---

95 Hiebert, *1 & 2 Thessalonians*, 215.

Pretribulation Pronouns

The alternating pronouns in 1 Thessalonians 5:1–4, shifting between two different audiences, are noteworthy concerning the timing of the rapture. Pay special attention to the italicized pronouns in these verses.

Now as to the times and the epochs, brethren, *you* have no need of anything to be written to *you*. For *you yourselves* know full well that the day of the Lord will come just like a thief in the night. While *they* are saying, 'Peace and safety!' then destruction will come upon *them* suddenly like birth pangs upon a woman with child; and *they* shall not escape. But *you*, brethren, are not in darkness, that they day should overtake *you* like a thief; for *you* are all sons of light and sons of the day. *We* are not of night nor of darkness.

The sudden shift in this text between *you* and *we* (the believers) in the first and second person, and *they* and *them* (the unbelievers) in the third person is a significant signal. The strategic shift in wording indicates that when the tribulation comes there will be two groups of people each exclusive of the other. One group will be exempt from the darkness and destruction, and the other group will enter and experience the darkness and destruction.

Note the striking contrast. The day of the Lord will come upon *them*, and *they* shall not escape (5:3). Unbelievers will find themselves in the crosshairs of God's retribution. Then, in 5:4 there is an abrupt contrast: "But *you* are not in the darkness." *They* (unbelievers), who will not escape, stand in sharp contrast to the believers ("you") in 5:4–11 who will escape. The patent distinction between unbelievers, who will not escape the destruction of the day of the Lord, and believers, who will escape the destruction of the day of the Lord, is a strong signal that believers are exempt from the wrath of the day of the Lord.

The future judgment of those who ignore God is described as "surprise, destruction, darkness, pain, and no escape"; whereas the future destiny of those who honor Him is "light salvation, and alive with Christ."[96] They are complete opposites when it comes to experiencing the wrath of the day of the Lord. Here is a simple chart highlighting the contrasts.

Unbelievers	Believers
darkness (5:4, 5)	light (5:5)
night (5:5, 7)	day (5:5, 8)
sleep (5:6, 7)	watch (5:6)
drunk (5:7)	sober (5:6, 8)

Blaising summarizes the point well. "In 1 Thessalonians 5 this language of 'salvation' for 'you' as opposed to 'destruction' for 'them' refers to the separation that takes place at the onset, the beginning of the day of the Lord, with the 'salvation' taking place by means of the rapture described in 4:13–17."[97]

No Instruction for Preparation

A related point that is germane to the timing of the rapture in 1 Thessalonians 4–5 is an argument from silence. I recognize that arguments from silence are not always the strongest, but in this case, the silence is suggestive and significant. The argument goes like this: If Paul expected the Thessalonian believers to endure the destruction of the day of the Lord, then why is there no instruction or preparation for how to endure and survive its horror? This omission is inexplicable if believers must endure part or all the most horrific era of human history.

There is no doubt that Paul taught them about the Day of the Lord. Yet there is no suggestion that he ever sought to prepare them to be in it. Rather, his intention was to give them sufficient

---

96 Howell, *Exalting Jesus in 1 & 2 Thessalonians*, 134-35.
97 Blaising, "A Case for the Pretribulation Rapture," 57.

truth to clarify the confusion about it. The implication is that Paul knew the church would be gone because Jesus was coming to rapture the church out of the world before this day would come (John 14:1-3). The focus of the passage is encouragement. Just as Paul sought to comfort the Thessalonians about their departed loved ones, so also he attempted to reassure them about their future. If he knew that believers would be alive at the time of the Day of the Lord, he would have most certainly sought to prepare them for such a time.[98]

Mayhue questions:

Let us suppose that postribulationism is true? What would we expect to find in 1 Thessalonians?... We would expect Paul, even in the absence of interest or questions by the Thessalonians, to have provided instruction and exhortation for such a supreme test which would make their present tribulation seem microscopic in comparison. *But* there is not one indication of any impending tribulation.[99]

This argument from significant silence is further evidence of a pretribulation rapture in 1 Thessalonians.

Keeping Your Appointment

The point here is a reinforcement of the exemption from divine wrath presented in 1 Thessalonians 1:10. It supplies another layer of the argument. First Thessalonians 5:9 says, "For God has not destined us for wrath, but for obtaining salvation through our Lord Jesus Christ." Like 1 Thess 1:10, the readers are promised exemption from divine wrath, but again, as in that text, the question is, which aspect of God's wrath is in view?

Many commentators believe the "wrath" in this verse refers to the eternal wrath of God in hell from which believers will be

---

[98] Howell, *Exalting Jesus in 1 & 2 Thessalonians*, 120.
[99] Mayhue, *First and Second Thessalonians*, 218-19.

spared.[100] However, two points support understanding the wrath of God in 1 Thessalonians 5:9 as the wrath of the day of the Lord. First, the Thessalonians already knew they were not destined for God's eternal wrath in hell. Paul had told them this very clearly in 1 Thessalonians 1:4. Second, in the entire context of 1 Thessalonians 5:1–8 Paul been discussing not the wrath of hell but rather the wrath of the tribulation or day of the Lord. Ryrie says, "The wrath is the anguish and tribulation associated from the beginning of the Day of the Lord (v. 3), and it is from this that the believer has been delivered by the One who 'delivers us from the wrath to come.'"[101]

Mark Howell summarizes the issue well:

> The context seems to favor that Paul has in mind the wrath associated with the Day of the Lord (5:1–8). The Thessalonians clearly knew that Christ had pardoned their sin, purchased their redemption, and delivered them from death (1:4-5). Their present struggles do not appear to be related to questions about their eternal destiny. As the letter reveals, their present struggles were related to questions about future events, namely, the destiny of their dead friends and the coming of the Day of the Lord.[102]

Church-age believers are appointed for salvation or deliverance and not appointed to the wrath of the Day of the Lord. Believers are promised "exemption for the entirety of the future horrors of the earthly tribulation period."[103] Dr. John Walvoord

---

100 Leon Morris, *The First and Second Epistles to the Thessalonians*, New International Commentary on the New Testament, ed. F. F. Bruce (reprint, Grand Rapids, MI: Eerdmans, 1959), 160. Pretribulationist Richard Mayhue also supports this view of wrath in 1 Thess 5:9, as he does in 1 Thess 1:10 (Mayhue, *First and Second Thessalonians*, 135).

101 Charles C. Ryrie, *First & Second Thessalonians*, Everyman's Bible Commentary (Chicago: Moody Press, 2001), 72.

102 Howell, *Exalting Jesus in 1 & 2 Thessalonians*, 140-41.

103 Mike Stallard, *The Books of First & Second Thessalonians*, Twenty-first Century Biblical Commentary Series, ed. Mal Couch and Ed Hindson (Chattanooga, TN: AMG Publishers, 2009), 96.

puts it simply: "In this passage he is expressly saying that our appointment is to be caught up to be with Christ; the appointment of the world is for the Day of the Lord, the day of wrath. One cannot keep both of these appointments."[104] We make our appointment for salvation and rescue, both from eternal wrath and eschatological wrath, when we trust Jesus Christ as our personal Savior from sin—the One who bore our wrath and judgment on the cross and rose from the dead.

Conclusion

There are many excellent biblical and theological arguments in favor of the pretribulation rapture, but the most concentrated section of Scripture for convincing evidence is 1 Thessalonians. I pray that the four simple arguments presented in this article will serve to enforce the conviction of those who hold to the pretribulation coming of Jesus and to encourage those who hold a different view to thoughtfully re-examine their position considering these points.

---

[104] John F. Walvoord and Mark Hitchcock, *1 & 2 Thessalonians*, The Walvoord Prophecy Commentaries, ed. Philip E. Rawley (Chicago: Moody Publishers, 2012), 94.

BIBLIOGRAPHY

Archer, Gleason L., Jr., "The Case for the Mid-Seventieth Week Rapture Position," in *The Rapture: Pre-, Mid-, or Post-Tribulational?* Grand Rapids: Zondervan, 1984.

Beale, G. K. *1–2 Thessalonians*. The IVP New Testament Commentary Series, edited by Grant R. Osborne. Downers Grove, IL: InterVarsity Press, 2002.

Benware, Paul N. *Understanding End Times Prophecy*. Chicago: Moody, 1995.

Blaising, Craig. "A Case for the Pretribulation Rapture," *Three Views on the Rapture: Pretribulation, Prewrath, or Posttribulation*, edited by Alan Hultberg, 2nd ed. Grand Rapids: Zondervan, 2010.

Feinberg, Paul D. "The Case for the Pretribulation Rapture Position," in *The Rapture: Pre-, Mid-, or Post-Tribulational?*, edited by Ben Chapman. Grand Rapids: Academie Books, 1984.

Gundry, Robert H. *The Church and the Tribulation*. Grand Rapids: Zondervan, 1973.

Hiebert, D. Edmond. *1 & 2 Thessalonians*, rev. ed. Chicago: Moody, 1992.

Hogg, C. F. and W. E. Vine, *The Epistles of the Thessalonians*. Fincastle, VA: Scripture Truth, 1959.

Howell, Mark. *Exalting Jesus in 1 & 2 Thessalonians*. Christ-Centered Exposition, edited by David Platt, Daniel L. Akin, and Tony Merida. Nashville, TN: Holman Reference, 2015.

Ladd, George Eldon. *The Blessed Hope*. Grand Rapids: Eerdmans, 1956.

LaHaye, Tim. *Prophecy Study Bible*. Chattanooga, TN: AMG Publishers, 2001.

MacArthur, John, Jr. *1 & 2 Thessalonians*. The MacArthur New Testament Commentary. Chicago: Moody, 2002.

Marshall, I. Howard. *1 & 2 Thessalonians*. The New Century Bible Commentary, edited by Matthew Black. Reprint. Grand Rapids: Eerdmans, 1990.

Mayhue, Richard. *First and Second Thessalonians*. Focus on the Bible. Great Britain: Christian Focus, 1999.

Morris, Leon. *The First and Second Epistles to the Thessalonians*. New International Commentary on the New Testament, edited by F. F. Bruce. Reprint. Grand Rapids: Eerdmans, 1959.

Piper, John. *Come, Lord Jesus: Meditations on the Second Coming of Christ*. Wheaton, IL: Crossway, 2023.

Ryrie, Charles C. *First & Second Thessalonians*. Everyman's Bible Commentary. Chicago: Moody, 2001.

Shogren, Gary S. *1 & 2 Thessalonians*. Zondervan Exegetical Commentary on the New Testament, edited by Clinton E. Arnold. Grand Rapids: Zondervan, 2012.

Showers, Renald. *Maranatha Our Lord, Come!* Bellmawr, NJ: Friends of Israel Gospel Ministry, 1995.

Stallard, Mike. *The Books of First & Second Thessalonians*. Twenty-first Century Biblical Commentary Series, edited by Mal Couch and Ed Hindson. Chattanooga, TN: AMG Publishers, 2009.

Thomas, Robert L. "1, 2 Thessalonians," in *The Expositor's Bible Commentary*, edited by Frank E. Gaebelein, vol. 11. Grand Rapids: Zondervan, 1978.

Walvoord, John F. and Mark Hitchcock, *1 & 2 Thessalonians*. The Walvoord Prophecy Commentaries, edited by Philip E. Rawley. Chicago: Moody, 2012.

CHAPTER THREE

A THEOLOGICAL DISCUSSION NUANCING DISPENSATIONAL VIEWS OF THE KINGDOM-AGE

by Dr. H. Wayne House

Introduction

This chapter overviews various dispensational views of the future earthly Kingdom-age while nuancing the traditional dispensational theological method.[105]

---

[105] The following is a modification of "A Biblical and Theological Discussion of Traditional Dispensational Premillennialism," *The Journal of Ministry and Theology* (Spring 2013), 5-56 by Drs. David Mappes and H. Wayne House (©2024 H. Wayne House. All Rights Reserved).

All orthodox Christians agree on the scriptural-prophetic facts of the personal, visible, sudden, and bodily return of Jesus Christ referred to as his second coming. Jesus Christ himself promised his return (Matt 24:27, 30, 37, 39, 42, 44; 25:31), which was announced by angelic beings (Acts 1:9-11) and proclaimed in the early church (Acts 3:19-21). The author of Hebrews guarantees Christ's return when he writes, "so Christ also, having been offered once to bear the sins of many, will appear a second time for salvation without reference to sin, to those who eagerly await him" (Heb 9:28). Christians, however, disagree on the specific details surrounding his return, including the nature of the rapture and the nature of his earthly reign referred to as the millennium.

Theological Summary of Dispensational Views

The word *millennium* is derived from a Latin term meaning one thousand. The term appears six times in Revelation 20:1-7, referring to a one-thousand-year period when Jesus Christ physically, spatially reigns on earth with glorified, resurrected (as well as non-resurrected) believers, while Satan is bound and spatially removed from the earth. Premillennialism entails the view that Jesus will physically return prior to the millennium to establish his earthly reign after which eternity will begin with the establishment of the new heavens and new earth. When Jesus returns to the earth, he establishes his millennial, earthly kingdom.

Classic (or historical) premillennialism and dispensational premillennialism are primarily distinguished by their hermeneutical system with respect to how OT promises to national Israel relate to the millennium. Progressive dispensationalists and traditional/classic dispensationalists are distinguished with respect to the question of whether the church has inaugurated the OT prophesied kingdom age. By way of contrast, amillennialists do not believe in a future, bodily, earthly reign of Christ.

Common features among all premillennialists entail the following: (1) Jesus himself institutes his earthly reign as described in Revelation 19:11-21. This future millennium will not be a gradual extension of Christ's current session in heaven. Rather Christ himself will return in a sudden, dynamic, cataclysmic manner and render Satan completely inactive by spatially removing him and his followers. Jesus Christ will personally end the wars, famines, great apostasy, and the antichrist that are all part of the prophesied Great Tribulation; (2) the two resurrections in Revelation 20:1-6 are chronologically separated by the one-thousand-year reign and are actually two distinct resurrections. The first resurrection in 20:4 indicates that the millennium contains believers in their glorified state inhabiting the millennial reign while the second resurrection refers to the judgment of non-believers; (3) similarities, though also distinct differences, exist between Christ's future millennial reign vs. his reign in the eternal state as described in Revelation 21-22; thus they are separate periods; (4) Christ's current rule in heaven vs. his future earthly reign as described in Revelation 20:1-6 cannot be reduced to a mere apocalyptic metaphorical description of a past or current event(s) nor reduced to an apocalyptic metaphorical description of Christ's current rule in heaven.

Traditional Dispensational Distinctives

Traditional dispensationalism is currently nuanced by its (1) consistent practice of literal hermeneutics and theological method in the Old and New Testament; (2) the nature of the church as a mystery and Christ's current heavenly session as a priestly, non-Davidic reign; and (3) the non-fusing nature and relationship between Israel and the church. Consequently, traditional dispensationalists hold to the *not-yet view* of the messianic kingdom and *deny an already-not-yet view of the Messianic kingdom.* Christ inaugurates the Messianic kingdom age in his second coming, not in his first Advent.

Traditional Dispensationalism and the *Sensus Literal* Hermeneutic

As previously stated, all orthodox Christians hold to the scriptural facts of the bodily return of Christ to judge the living and the dead. This interpretative view has been held throughout the ages because believers apply a common, single, consistent, literal hermeneutic in addressing the repeated assertions in the NT that describe the visible, glorious return of Jesus Christ.

Interestingly, evangelical Christians who were both millenarians and non-millenarians alike continued to hold to these common eschatological truths even when liberal rationalistic theologians sought to apply anti-supernatural views in de-eschatologizing and consequently redefining the kingdom motif, including the return of Christ as being only ethical in nature.

Traditional dispensationalists seek to practice this common, consistent hermeneutical historical-grammatical-literal (*sensus literal*) method of interpretation to *discern the intention of the human author by examining what the author affirms in the historical context of his writing* and then correlate all the material related to a topic in a compressive manner.[106] Rather than re-interpret the OT or practice a complementary hermeneutic proposed by progressive dispensationalists, traditional dispensationalists seek to understand the *literal meaning of a text by its immediate historical-textual parameters* and then understand how this meaning relates to God's over-

---

106 Ryrie writes, "Literal interpretation is not the exclusive property of dispensationalists.... The difference between the dispensationalist's use of this hermeneutical principle and the nondispensationalist's...lies in the dispensationalist's claim to use the normal principle of interpretation *consistently* in *all* his study of the Bible" (Charles C. Ryrie, *Dispensationalism: Revised and Expanded* [Chicago: Moody, 1995], 92-93; emphasis original).

all program.[107] This system of interpretation allows the immediate historical context of a passage to define and limit textual meaning.

Any theological system encounters difficulties with the NT use of the OT and all systems acknowledge it is not possible to exhaustively classify all NT uses of the OT in a simple, single usage. Bateman correctly summarizes that theological arguments to fully nuance and address the future millennial kingdom rest upon the "presuppositional preference on one testament over the other"[108] and those presuppositions then determine one's hermeneutical starting point.

Traditional dispensationalists support a single historical, human/divine authorial meaning for any given text. While some traditional dispensationalists support a controlled form of *sensus plenior* or *reference plenior*, any fuller NT explanation is only an extension and development of the OT authorial verbal meaning and is thus always governed by the initial pattern of human authorial meaning.

Since all dispensationalists insist on a higher degree of consistency in following the *sensus literal* hermeneutic, they then have a larger amount of material to synthesize and collate. So then naturally the dispensationalists have more nuanced specificity in their eschatology as well as more complex problems for resolution.

---

107 Traditional dispensationalists believe that issues of intertexuality and NT use of the OT are too complex and too varied to justify a hermeneutic that allows a re-interpretation or resignification of an OT text based upon the NT usage. The use of the fulfillment formula in the NT is simply too broad to suggest that its mere appearance indicates a historical completion of a prophetic promise. The context and use of each passage must be compared to the antecedent historical promise to validate a fulfilled prophecy. See Charles H. Dyer, "Biblical Meaning of Fulfillment," in *Issues in Dispensationalism*, ed. Welsey R. Willis and John R. Masters (Chicago: Moody, 1994), 51-72. Zuck who allows for a controlled *sensus plenior* describes ten different ways in which a NT author may use an OT text without altering the historical meaning or claiming exhaustive, complete fulfillment: (1) to point up the current accomplishment or realization of a prediction; (2) to confirm that a NT incident is in agreement with an OT principle; (3) to explain a point given in the OT; (4) to support a point being made in the NT; (5) to illustrate a NT truth, (6) to apply the OT to a NT truth; (7) to summarize an OT concept; (8) to use OT terminology;(9) to draw a parallel with an OT incident; (10) to relate an OT situation to Christ. (Roy Zuck, *Basic Bible Interpretation* [Wheaton, IL: Victor, 1991], 260-67).

108 Herbert W. Bateman IV, "Dispensationalism Yesterday and Today," in *Three Central Issues in Contemporary Dispensationalism*, ed. Herbert W. Bateman IV (Grand Rapids: Kregel, 1999), 38.

Nonetheless, dispensationalists would rather allow for both complexity and tension without creating a forced harmony or worse, a progressive reinterpretation of a historically conditioned text that alters the human author's meaning of Scripture.

The general parameters of this theological method include a stratified process that collates and analyzes data first at the exegetical level to form a biblical theology which then serves as the basis for systematic theology. Biblical theology here refers to the "historically conditioned progress of the self-revelation of God as deposited in the Bible."[109] Once the human authorial meaning is determined, then that meaning becomes fixed in time and does not change. The reader then examines how a later author uses that historically conditioned meaning in subsequent writings. Since the OT provides the foundational building block for NT theology, the traditional dispensationalist argues that the OT's literal interpretation must be preserved in light of later progressive revelation.

Traditional Dispensationalism and the Current Session of Christ

The current heavenly reign of Christ is understood as his high priestly Melchizedekian ministry over the church rather than a Davidic rule. His current heavenly priestly reign does not inaugurate nor fulfill the Davidic promise since this Davidic covenant relates to a future, political, earthly, king who rules over the future, earthly, national Israel in their regenerated status. The messianic kingdom age and messianic kingdom and messianic ruling king are inextricably and historically linked together: one cannot have the messianic kingdom or kingdom age without the physical presence of the ruling messianic king.

---

[109] Charles Ryrie, *Biblical Theology of the New Testament* (Chicago: Moody, 1959), 12.

The NT authors clearly identify Jesus Christ as the descendant of David (Luke 1:31–33), and the fulfillment of this promise is found in Jesus Christ. Christ satisfied the provisions of the Davidic covenant, and he is the Davidic king. The question, however, remains as to when fulfillment occurs. Traditional dispensationalists argue that Christ's Davidic reign is inaugurated in the millennial kingdom when Jesus Christ returns (Rev 19:11–16) to reign over Israel and the nations of the earth (Rev 20:4–6). The kingdom age entails the inaugural millennial kingdom and the future eternal state in order to fulfill the eternal dimensions of the covenant-promises. The Davidic reign is presented as territorial, political, national, earthly reign and not as a celestial, heavenly reign.

Traditional dispensationalists certainly agree that some aspects of the Davidic and new covenant have been satisfied. Christ is indeed the seed of the woman who did defeat the Serpent (Gen 3:15). He is the singular seed of Abraham, and he is the Davidic king. Many contemporary traditional dispensationalists agree that the church currently participates in the new covenant blessings through Christ's Melchizedekian priestly ministry as described in Hebrews. Either Christ mediates the actual new covenant of Jeremiah 31 to believers, or he mediates blessings of the new covenant to church believers today. Since Christ is said to be the spiritual seed of Abraham who embodies the covenant promise to Abraham (Gal 3:16), the church as a spiritual offspring of Abraham partakes (not fulfills) in some of these spiritual promises to Abraham by virtue of being in Christ (Gal 3:29).

The aspect of the worldwide blessing promise through Abraham as expanded by the new covenant in Jeremiah 31 and Ezekiel 36 was satisfied by Christ and then provided to the church. This provision entails soteriological and pneumatological aspects (2 Cor 3) rather than the political and land territorial aspects of the new covenant. This provision entails spiritual cleansing (i.e., regeneration) both for Israel in the future (Zech 12:10–13:1, cf. Jer 31:33–34) and for the church of God today (1 Cor 11:23–26; 2

Cor 3:11–18). Applying a provision of Jeremiah 31 and Ezekiel 36 to the church does not imply substitution, abrogation, nor final covenant fulfillment. The actual new covenant of Jeremiah and Ezekiel will not be fulfilled until all the historically stated parameters of the covenant have been satisfied.

God's Mediatorial Peoples/Programs and Traditional Dispensationalists

The church and Israel are considered as two separate mediatorial programs through which God administers his glory. While this distinctive is debated, most traditional dispensationalists agree on this distinctive though nuance it in various ways. There is only one people of God soteriologically in the sense that everyone in any time period is saved by God's grace; thus, any believer of any age shares in the grace-promises of God through faith alone. There are, however, two distinct peoples/programs of God historically and teleologically in accomplishing God's purpose of glorification. This multi-faceted plan is how God chose maximally to glorify himself. This distinction is maintained throughout eternity.

In summary, since OT promises were made to Israel and since the church is portrayed as a mystery in the NT that does not correspond with OT kingdom prophecies, traditional dispensationalists deny that the church is fulfilling OT kingdom promises.

Consequently, the notion of an already-not-yet view of the messianic kingdom age is denied. The NT describes why the anticipated OT prophesied messianic kingdom age was delayed, though they do not deny its future, nor do the New Testament authors redefine the nature of the kingdom age from their OT counterparts. The NT explains the nature of the church as a spiritual-priestly-royal-people representing Jesus Christ to mediate God's current purposes, though not as fulfilling the OT expectation of the messianic age. Other theological systems assert the NT authors either deny or in some fashion redefine the anticipated messianic kingdom age.

Traditional and Progressive Dispensational Differing Theological Views

All dispensationalists form their theological framework around three biblical covenants made in the Scripture—the Abrahamic covenant, the Davidic covenant, and the new covenant. These covenants are viewed as unconditional and irrevocable promises to Israel which progressively build upon one another. As House notes, "Dispensationalists do not see covenants made during subsequent dispensations as replacing the covenants made earlier, unless it is specifically so stated in the Scriptures."[110] Dispensational premillennialists then include OT teaching on the millennial reign of Christ and thus recognize a distinct, future place for national Israel in the millennium as prophesied in the OT.

Primarily, traditional dispensationalists disagree with progressive dispensationalists on their practice of complementary hermeneutics and their understanding of what constitutes fulfillment and/or inauguration of an OT covenant. This complementary hermeneutic led progressive dispensationalists to assert the church is currently an expression of the messianic kingdom, thus advancing the already-not-yet view of the messianic kingdom age.

Traditional dispensationalists believe that each aspect of an unconditional promise-covenant is historically governed by the textual parameters of that initial promise. Therefore, a strict one-to-one correspondence between details of a prophetic prediction and fulfillment of a prophecy must occur. This correspondence includes the details and "essentially the same message expressed

---

110 H. Wayne House, "The Future of National Israel," *BSac* 166, no. 664 (Oct 2009): 472.

in both passages."[111] Fulfillment does not occur until all aspects of the initial promise have been satisfied. Since the promises to Israel in the OT always refer to the physical posterity of Jacob's physical descendants, then these promises to Israel cannot be fulfilled by the NT church. For these covenant promises to be "fulfilled there must be a future [earthly] kingdom"[112] as described by the OT prophets.

Elliott Johnson correctly posits that covenant fulfillment necessarily entails the keeping or satisfying of the commitments and all provisions in the agreement with the specified recipient or partner. Covenant fulfillment is only *inaugurated* when all the provisions are kept in a partial or incomplete or limited manner and *covenant fulfillment only occurs* when all provisions are met in a complete manner per the historical covenant statement. Differences exist then between select provisions of the covenant being fulfilled (or satisfied) vs. inauguration of the entire covenant vs. the actual fulfillment of the covenant.[113]

The original promise should not be reinterpreted apart from the intention of the initial promise-covenant; thus, *prophetic fulfillment* occurs only when all the commitments and provisions in a promise have been realized. Kaiser correctly states, "The theological interpretation or exegesis of a given piece of text must be understood only in light of the antecedent revelations of God to that biblical author and those writers of scripture who historically preceded him...and who shared the same technical terms or analogous concepts in the progress of revelation...[and analogy of faith principle must not be used] until the present text's author

---

111 Elliott E. Johnson, "Premillennialism Introduced: Hermeneutics" in *A Case for Premillennialism: A New Consensus*, ed. Donald K. Campbell and Jeffrey L. Townsend (Chicago: Moody, 1992), 19.

112 Arnold Fruchtenbaum, "The Land Covenant" in *Progressive Dispensationalism: An Analysis of the Movement and Defense of Traditional Dispensationalism*, ed. Ron J. Bigalke Jr. (Lanham, MD: Univ Press of America, 2005), 87. Also see Arnold Fruchtenbaum, *Israelology: The Missing Link in Systematic Theology* (San Antonio: Ariel Ministries, 1993).

113 Elliott E. Johnson, "Covenants in Traditional Dispensationalism," in *Three Central Issues in Contemporary Dispensationalism*, 121-55.

has had a chance to indicate his own distinctive verbal meaning and theological contribution in light of the Bible available to him up to the time of writing."[114]

At times a prophecy may have referred to more than one single future event (what scholars call double fulfillment), but *double fulfillment* does not signify double meaning. The original prophetic promise remains the determiner of what governs its fulfillment. *Prophetic typology* occurs when "points of commonality between Old Testament events and symbols illustrate or foreshadow New Testament truths."[115] However, the original meaning (or pattern of meaning) always controls what constitutes the antitype. *Prophetic significance* refers to events occurring that appear to set the stage for actual prophetic fulfillment. Many current events could be interpreted as having prophetic significance, but this does not mean they are prophetic fulfillment.[116]

Progressive dispensationalists proffer that if one element or provision of a covenant is satisfied, then the entire covenant is inaugurated. Darrell Bock writes, "One does not need every element of the promise to be fulfilled to have the beginning of fulfillment. In contrast to more traditional approaches fulfillment is not an 'all elements present' or 'no fulfillment present affair.'"[117] Blaising explains that "the New Testament does introduce change and advance; it does not merely repeat Old Testament revelation. In making complementary additions, however, it does not jettison old promises. The enhancement is not at the expense of the original promise."[118] This means that the NT authors can make

---

[114] Walter C. Kaiser Jr., "The Fallacy of Equating Meaning with the Reader's Understanding," *TJ* 6 (1977): 192.

[115] H. Wayne House in *Dictionary of Premillennial Theology*, ed. Mal Couch (Grand Rapids: Kregel, 1997), 316.

[116] David Mappes, "Recalculating: Why We're Still Here After Another Round of Failed Rapture Predictions," *Baptist Bulletin* (May/June 2011): 30-34.

[117] Darrell L. Bock, "Covenants in Progressive Dispensationalism," in *Three Central Issues in Contemporary Dispensationalism*, 170.

[118] Craig A. Blaising and Darrell L. Bock, eds., *Dispensationalism, Israel and the Church* (Grand Rapids: Zondervan, 1992), 392-93.

complementary changes to the OT prophecies, though not deny the OT promises.

In this progressive model, OT promises are expanded and re-applied by the NT authors, though not replaced. This complementary hermeneutic leads to prophetic fulfillment/inauguration with less than a one-to-one correspondence to the initial promise. Bock illustrates this less than one-to-one correspondence as he explains, "One of the ways Jews showed fulfillment of an OT passage was to cite the language in alluding to a second passage, thus linking the two texts conceptually. So by his use of the verb 'to sit' (Acts 2:30, 34) Peter links Psalm 132:11 (cited in 2:30) with Psalm 110 (cited in 2:34)."[119] Traditional dispensationalist Mike Stallard evaluates this hermeneutic as he writes, "The promise can have a coinciding or overlapping fulfillment [emphasis original] through NT expansions of the promise...[and] this concept helps form the basis of an 'already, not yet' approach to various texts in the Bible."[120] An example of this hermeneutic is the assertion that the church's participation in the new covenant taught in the NT can add the church to the actual list of recipients of the new covenant promises made in the OT.[121] Thereby claiming the church as an intended recipient of the kingdom age promise is now an inaugural expression of the Messianic kingdom.

Through this complementary hermeneutic, progressives use verbal analogy to link passages by associating words that are common to both passages. Stallard writes,

> In Acts 2:24, the fact that Jesus was "raised up" from the dead is associated with the fact that God promised David in 2 Samuel 7:12 that he would "raise up" from history a descendent to sit on his throne. In spite of the fact that the idea of "raising up" is not

---

119 Darrell L. Bock, "Evidence from Acts," in *A Case for Premillennialism*, 192.

120 Mike Stallard, "Progressive Dispensationalism," <http://faculty.bbc.edu/mstallard/wp-content/uploads/2009/10/PD Challenge.pdf and http://our-hope.org/blog/2012/05/> (accessed 1 September 2012), 4.

121 Stallard.

equivalent in the passages, the similarity of language is used to link the two passages and justify the pouring of the Davidic Covenant into Acts 2. A second example would be the association of the word "to seat" with respect to the throne of David in Acts 2:30 with "sit" in Acts 2:34 (from Ps 110) which refers to the ascension throne of Christ. The text does not explicitly make the equation of the two thrones and traditionalists have understood them as distinct.[122]

The similarity of language is used within complementary hermeneutics to link these passages together in the sense of making them identical.

Psalm 110 portrays both a kingly and priestly emphasis of Messiah and is one of the most quoted and cited Psalms in the NT. The Psalmist, David records a heavenly conversation between the LORD (Yahweh) and his Lord (Adonia the Messiah) (v.1). The Psalm describes a future descendant of David who would not only be David's son but also his Lord. Yahweh shared that the Messiah is seated (enthroned) at his heavenly, celestial right hand until the consummation of the ages when all enemies would be abolished, and Messiah would himself return and territorially rule the earth.

Yahweh specifically links Messiah's celestial heavenly rule with the priestly ministry of Melchizedek as he writes, "You are a priest forever/According to the order of Melchizedek" (110:4). he also portrays the future kingly-warrior aspect of Messiah. This Kingly-warrior aspect most likely refers to Messiah's future Davidic earthly rule during the Kingdom age as portrayed in Daniel 7:14, "And to him was given dominion, glory and a kingdom, that all the peoples, nations, and men of every language might serve him." However, some traditional dispensationalists think this kingly rule is also restricted to his Melchizedekian ministry in heaven preparing the world for Davidic rule.[123]

---

122 Stallard, 6
123 George Gunn and Jerry Neuman, "Psalm 110 and Progressive Dispensationalism," <http://

The NT authors repeatedly appealed to this Psalm to prove that Jesus was the Messiah and not simply a human descendant of David. The determinative issues here in Psalm 110 entail the location of the throne as a heavenly, celestial throne and the authority of the heavenly throne being different than the messianic authoritative rule on earth.

Traditional dispensationalists argue that the Lord Jesus Christ, the Messiah, is now seated in heaven at the right hand of the Father, in satisfying (or partially fulfilling) the high priestly Melchizedekian aspect of Psalm 110 (cf. Mark 16:19; Acts 2:34, 35; Rom 8:34; Eph 1:20; Col 3:1; Heb 1:3; etc.). Messiah's current enthronement is in heaven with a priestly emphasis while his future Davidic seat of rule will take place on earth.

The author of Hebrews argued that Christ is a priest forever according to the Melchizedekian order. Consequently, Jesus' priesthood is superior and brought an end to the Aaronic priesthood.

If Yahweh sets up Messiah as a priest "forever," the Aaronic order of priests must end as God's appointed order (cf. Heb. 5:6; 6:20; 7:17, 21). As both the Priest and the sacrificial Lamb, Messiah offered himself as a substitute sacrifice on the cross (cf. Heb. 7:27-28; 10:10). Jesus was not of Aaron's line since he descended from the tribe of Judah (cf. Heb. 7:11-18). He is the new eternal High Priest (cf. Heb. 7:21-26, 28), and he mediates the New Covenant that replaces the Old Mosaic Covenant (cf. Heb. 8:13; 9:15).[124]

Blaising however suggests that since King David conquered Melchizedek's former city of Salem, then he would also have obtained Melchizedek's ancient throne; hence he posits that King David was also the "new Melchizedek...[who] restored the wor-

---

www.shasta.edu/admin/userfiles/resourceDocuments/psalm110full.pd> (accessed 1 September 2012), 18.

124 Tom Constable, "Psalm 110," <http://www.soniclight.com/ constable/notes.htm, 200>.

ship of the one true God."¹²⁵ Thereby Blaising concludes, "There should be no doubt that the Melchizedekian priesthood is part of the Davidic covenant."¹²⁶ However, Gunn and Neuman point out that this view would also appear to require that all of David's heirs be of a Melchizedekian king-priestly line, contrary to how Christ is portrayed in his Melchizedekian ministry.¹²⁷ In summary, Christ's current session at the Father's right hand is portrayed in a Melchizedekian King-priestly manner rather than a spiritualized Davidic rule.

Traditional dispensationalists then contend that Jesus is now certainly the Lord of the cosmos and Savior of the church, and he is indeed seated at the right hand of God on a heavenly, priestly throne. Jesus is the anointed Davidic king who has satisfied all requirements to start his Davidic reign and rule. However, that reign and rule will only take place upon his return in establishing the millennial reign.¹²⁸

Most importantly, progressive dispensationalists believe all the biblical covenants are organically connected and share common elements so that initial fulfillment of an aspect of a covenant necessarily involves the realization of the other covenants. Since Christ in his messianic role has satisfied some aspects of the Abrahamic, Davidic, and new covenants, progressive dispensationalists then argue the kingdom age has been inaugurated through their complementary hermeneutic.

They assert that Christ is therefore currently reigning on David's throne in heaven over the church in an already-not-yet form of the messianic kingdom. Progressives, however, do not believe the millennium has started. Consequently, this theological model "does not entail separate programs for the church and Israel that

---

125 Blaising, *Progressive Dispensationalism*, 162.
126 Blaising, 161-62.
127 Gunn and Neuman, "Psalm 110 and Progressive Dispensationalism," 4.
128 House, "Future of National Israel," 482.

are somehow ultimately unified only in the display of God's glory or in eternity."[129]

Some progressives are using this already-not-yet form of the messianic kingdom as a primary theological matrix for social justice, thereby claiming authority that traditional dispensationalists argue is only resident in the millennial kingdom. One apparent insurmountable problem thus far for progressive dispensationalists entails the land promises to Israel. If the church is an already-not-yet form of the messianic kingdom, then how do the land promises to Israel relate to the church today?

While significant differences exist between progressive and traditional dispensational scholars, both groups believe that OT covenantal promises will find literal fulfillment and include (1) a future national kingdom of Israel, ruled by Jesus in Jerusalem according to OT prophecies and (2) that God's unconditional covenants and promises in the OT are irrevocable and will be fulfilled literally for the nation Israel. God promised Israel that they would be gathered to their own land, live in peace in that land, and be ruled by the Messiah as prophesied in Scripture.[130]

Classic or Historic Premillennialism

Historic premillennialists contend for a future earthly reign of Christ, though almost exclusively based upon the NT and in particular based upon Revelation 20:1–6. This view does promote a progressive view of revelation as portraying future-prophetic events such as the tribulation, millennial reign, and eternal state, leading to a postconsummationalist view of Christ's return.

Some historical premillennialists understand the nature of the millennium as a literal one-thousand-year period while others espouse the one-thousand-years reference as hyperbole simply

---

[129] Robert L. Saucy, *The Case for Progressive Dispensationalism* (Grand Rapids: Zondervan, 1993), 27.
[130] House, "Future of National Israel," 482.

expressing a long time period. However, no evangelical historical premillennialist understands the thousand-year reign as only a poetic or allegorical description of the future eternal state or as Christ's current reign in heaven. Most historical premillennialists also affirm the importance of an earthly reign of Christ as reversing the curse of Genesis 3. Blomberg writes, "Premillennialism does best justice to God's determination to vindicate his purposes in creating *this* universe as originally perfectly good, despite the corruption that sin introduced, yet without introducing the unrealistic expectation that Christians can produce the millennium apart from God's supernatural intervention."[131]

Historic premillennialists practice a form of replacement theology (also known as supersessionism) to teach that the church has permanently replaced or superseded Israel. Replacement theologians propose that while Israel was God's chosen, unique people in the OT who did receive promises of a future earthly kingdom, Israel nonetheless forfeited those promises in rejecting their Messiah King. Therefore, the distinctions between Israel and the church in this present age and the millennial age are at best minimized.

Replacement theologians support a future turning of ethnic Jews to their Messiah in the last days of the church prior to the millennial reign, but they exclude national, ethnic Israel as having a distinctive national future in the millennium. Historical premillennialists also argue that the messianic kingdom was inaugurated either during Jesus' life (e.g., Ladd) or at the ascension of Christ; thus they hold an already-not-yet view of the kingdom.[132]

---

131 Craig Blomberg, "The Posttribulation of the New Testament," in *A Case for Historic Premillennialism: An Alternative to "Left Behind Eschatology*," ed. Craig L. Blomberg and Sung Wook Chung (Grand Rapids: Baker Academic, 2009), 69.

132 Ladd further illustrates the key differences between the dispensational model and historical premillennial model as he writes, "The main point...is that many Old Testament passages which applied in their historical setting to literal Israel have in the New Testament been applied to the church. What does all of this have to do with the question of millennium? Just this: The Old Testament did not clearly foresee how its own prophecies were to be fulfilled. They were fulfilled in ways quite unforeseen by the Old Testament itself and unexpected by the Jews. With regard to

Since they exclude the OT depictions of the millennial reign for Israel, they also tend to minimize or exclude how the OT portrays the future great tribulation as a time of God's wrath upon national Israel for discipline and preparation for Israel's national regeneration. Hence historic premillennialists adopt the post-tribulation view of the rapture.

Most importantly in "historical premillennialism the distinction between Israel and the church is not maintained, nor is a consistent literal interpretative method demanded."[133] In support of historical premillennialism, Ladd argued that OT prophecies of Messiah must be interpreted in light of the NT portrayal of the Christ event since "'literal hermeneutics' does not work"[134] when applied to OT Scripture. He describes hermeneutical distinctives of historic premillennialism when he writes, "The New Testament applies Old Testament prophecies to the New Testament church and in so doing identifies the church as spiritual Israel."[135] Thus many historic premillennialists assert that "a millennial doctrine cannot be based on the Old Testament prophecies but should be based on the New Testament alone"[136] and the "only place in the Bible that speaks of an actual millennium is the passage in Revelation 20:1-6."[137] Most historical premillennialists would also agree with Ladd that any "millennial doctrine must be based upon the most natural exegesis of this passage [Revelation 20:1-

---

the first coming of Christ, *the Old Testament is interpreted by the New Testament*. Here is the basic watershed between a dispensational and a nondispensational theology. Dispensationalism forms its eschatology by a literal interpretation of the Old Testament and then fits the New Testament into it. A nondispensational eschatology forms its theology from the explicit teaching of the New Testament. It confesses that it cannot be sure how the Old Testament prophecies of the end are to be fulfilled, for (a) the first coming of Christ was accomplished in terms not foreseen by a literal interpretation of the Old Testament, and (b) there are unavoidable indications that the Old Testament promises to Israel are fulfilled in the Christian church" (George Eldon Ladd, "Historic Premillennialism," in *The Meaning of the Millennium: Four Views*, ed. Robert Clouse [Downers Grove, IL: InterVarsity, 1977], 27).

133 Paul Enns, *The Moody Handbook of Theology: Revised and Expanded* (Chicago: Moody, 2008), 409.
134 Ladd, "Historic Premillennialsim," 23.
135 Ladd, 23.
136 Ladd, 32.
137 Ladd, 32.

6]."[138] Historic premillennialism decidedly assigns the NT as the interpretative lens for the OT.[139]

Concluding Comments

All evangelical premillennialists agree on a future earthly reign of Christ upon his return. Key theological differences arise from varying hermeneutical and theological methodological practices. While significant differences do exist in each model, no evangelical dispensationalist and no evangelical premillennialists denies the future, earthly reign of Christ Who will eradicate the curse and usher in the eternal state.

---

138 Ladd, 32.
139 Don J. Payne, "The Theological Method of Premillennialism," in *A Case for Historic Premillennialism*, 95.

BIBLIOGRAPHY

Bateman, Herbert W., IV. "Dispensationalism Yesterday and Today." In *Three Central Issues in Contemporary Dispensationalism*, ed. Herbert W. Bateman IV. Grand Rapids: Kregel, 1999.

Blaising, Craig A. and Darrell L. Bock, eds., *Dispensationalism, Israel and the Church*. Grand Rapids: Zondervan, 1992.

Bloomberg, Craig. "The Posttribulation of the New Testament," in *A Case for Historic Premillennialism: An Alternative to "Left Behind Eschatology,"* ed. Craig L. Blomberg and Sung Wook Chung. Grand Rapids: Baker Academic, 2009.

Bock, Darrell L. "Covenants in Progressive Dispensationalism." In *Three Central Issues in Contemporary Dispensationalism*, ed. Herbert W. Bateman IV. Grand Rapids: Kregel, 1999.

———. "Evidence from Acts." In *A Case for Premillennialism: A New Consensus*, ed. Donald K. Campbell and Jeffrey L. Townsend. Chicago: Moody, 1992.

Constable, Tom. "Psalm 110," http://www.soniclight.com/ constable/notes.htm, 200.

Dyer, Charles H. "Biblical Meaning of Fulfillment." In *Issues in Dispensationalism*, ed. Wesley R. Willis and John R. Masters. Chicago: Moody, 1994.

Enns, Paul. *The Moody Handbook of Theology: Revised and Expanded*. Chicago: Moody, 2008.

Fruchtenbaum, Arnold. "The Land Covenant." In *Progressive Dispensationalism: An Analysis of the Movement and Defense of Traditional Dispensationalism*, ed. Ron J. Bigalke, Jr. Lanham, MD: Univ Press of America, 2005.

———. *Israelology: The Missing Link in Systematic Theology*. San Antonio: Ariel Ministries, 1993.

Gunn, George and Jerry Neuman, "Psalm 110 and Progressive Dispensationalism," Accessed 1 September 2012. http://www.shasta.edu/admin/userfiles/resourceDocuments/psalm110full.pd.

House, H. Wayne. "The Future of National Israel," *BSac* 166, no. 664 (Oct 2009).

———. In *Dictionary of Premillennial Theology*, ed. Mal Couch. Grand Rapids: Kregel, 1997.

Johnson, Elliott E. "Premillennialism Introduced: Hermeneutics." In *A Case for Premillennialism: A New Consensus*, ed. Donald K. Campbell and Jeffrey L. Townsend. Chicago: Moody, 1992.

———. "Covenants in Traditional Dispensationalism." In *Three Central Issues in Contemporary Dispensationalism*, ed. Herbert W. Bateman IV, 121-55. Grand Rapids: Kregel, 1999.

Kaiser, Walter C., Jr. "The Fallacy of Equating Meaning with the Reader's Understanding," *TJ* 6 (1977).

Ladd, George Eldon. "Historic Premillennialism." In *The Meaning of the Millennium: Four Views*, ed. Robert Clouse. Downers Grove, IL: InterVarsity, 1977.

Mappes, David. "Recalculating: Why We're Still Here After Another Round of Failed Rapture Predictions," *Baptist Bulletin* (May/June 2011).

Payne, Don J. "The Theological Method of Premillennialism," in *A Case for Premillennialism: A New Consensus*, ed. Donald K. Campbell and Jeffrey L. Townsend. Chicago: Moody, 1992.

Ryrie, Charles C. *Dispensationalism: Revised and Expanded*. Chicago: Moody, 1995.

———. *Biblical Theology of the New Testament*. Chicago: Moody, 1959.

Saucy, Robert L. *The Case for Progressive Dispensationalism*. Grand Rapids: Zondervan, 1993.

Stallard, Mike "Progressive Dispensationalism." Accessed 1 September 2012. http://faculty.bbc.edu/mstallard/wp-content/uploads/2009/10/PDChallenge.pdf and http://our-hope.org/blog/2012/05/.

Zuck, Roy. *Basic Bible Interpretation*. Wheaton, IL: Victor, 1991.

CHAPTER FOUR

GOD'S PURPOSE WITHIN HIS OVERALL PLAN FOR A PRETRIBULATIONAL RAPTURE

by Dr. Thomas Ice

"One day, without warning, the Spirit of God will move, the trumpet will sound, the archangel will shout, and the Bible tells us Christ will come and rapture believers home to heaven."[140]

—Ed Hindson

---

140 Ed Hindson, *Future Glory: Living in the Hope of the Rapture, Heaven, and Eternity* (Eugene, OR: Harvest House Publishers, 2021), 28.

God has a plan for history! It is understood that the Bible reveals a divinely orchestrated plan. What is God's purpose for His plan? Most would agree the glory of God is the purpose of history. Romans 11:36 says, "For from Him and through Him and to Him are all things. To Him be the glory forever. Amen." The next question is exactly how God is glorified in history. The well-known Westminster Shorter Catechism begins by saying, "Man's chief end is to glorify God and enjoy him forever."[141] How God works this out in history is best seen through a dispensational understanding of history and eternity. An important aspect within the flow of God's plan, yet future, is the purpose of the pretribulational rapture of the Church.

Israel and the Church

When examining Scripture to determine the purpose and flow of God's overall plan for history, one notices after the Flood the focus is upon the call of Abram and the establishment of God's elect nation—Israel (Gen 12-50). Through Abraham and his descendants, God established a priestly nation through which He will administer His plan for all humanity.

The assurance that God will fulfill His promise is administered through the Abrahamic covenant, which is directed to Abraham, Isaac, Jacob, and their descendants and focuses on God's promise to give the land of Israel to the Jews. The Abrahamic promise has three main aspects: land, seed, and blessing.

The land promise is repeated to them at least twenty times in Genesis alone (12:1-3, 7-9; 13:14-18; 15:1-18; 17:1-27; 22:15-19; 26:2-6, 24-25; 27:28-29, 38-40; 28:1-4, 10-22; 31:3, 11-13; 32:22-32; 35:9-15; 48:3-4, 10-20; 49:1-28; 50:23-25). The covenant or contract was executed in Genesis 15:1-18 when

---

[141] Philip Schaff, *The Creeds of Christendom with a History and Critical Notes*, 4th ed; 3 vols. (Grand Rapids: Baker Book House, 1877), vol. 3, 676.

God sealed the treaty through a unique procedure when He put Abram into a deep sleep and bound only Himself to keep the covenant regardless of Abraham's response. Since God is the only one who swore to keep the covenant, then it is clearly an unconditional covenant dependent solely upon God. Thus, we can be one hundred percent sure He will bring to pass every stipulation of the agreement.

Since the Bible teaches that Israel will play a central role in God's plan throughout all history, its role is continuous through time. How does Israel's historical role relate to the church age?

Israel, as a nation, rejected Jesus as their Messiah at His first coming,[142] resulting in the national dispersion of the Jewish people in AD 70. While the Jewish people are still an elect nation with unfulfilled promises, they have been temporally set aside as the instrument through which our Lord works in the world. This is explained by James at the Jerusalem Council (Acts 15:1-35) who says, "Simeon has related how God first concerned Himself about taking from among the Gentiles a people for His name" (15:14). As proof, James quotes Amos 9:11 from the Septuagint, but prefaces the citation with "after these things." What things? The statement by Peter about "taking from among the Gentiles a people for His name." In the context of Amos, it refers to the restoration of the Davidic dynasty at the second coming of Christ which would be the beginning of the millennium. The current age James refers to before the millennium is a time of worldwide witness we know as the church age. Then after the church age, the Lord will "return, and I will rebuild the tabernacle of David which has fallen, and I will rebuild its ruins, and I will restore it" (15:16). It will be at the second coming, as Paul notes: "and thus all Israel will be saved" (Rom 11:26a).

---

142 I have read that as many as 30% of first-century Jews became believers in Jesus as Messiah. There is always a remnant of Jewish believers who are part of the church during this current dispensation.

The current church age began on the day of Pentecost (Acts 2:1–42). The church age is a temporary period in history in which God has set aside Israel as the vehicle through which He carries out His plan for history. The church is made up of saved Jews and Gentiles who are brought together into a single body known as the Body of Christ. This is explained in Paul's epistle to the Ephesians:

> But now in Christ Jesus you who formerly were far off [Gentiles] have been brought near by the blood of Christ. For He Himself is our peace, who made both groups into one, and broke down the barrier of the dividing wall, by abolishing in His flesh the enmity, which is the Law of commandments contained in ordinances, that in Himself He might make the two into one new man, thus establishing peace, and might reconcile them both in one body to God through the cross, by it having put to death the enmity (Eph 2:13–16).

The church age is the first time God temporarily suspended or set aside the instrument (Israel) through whom He was working to start a new program or dispensation known as the church age. The Jewish people are still a distinct people during the entire church age, but as noted in Ephesians 2, Jewish and Gentile believers have a co-equal status during the present age. Thus, God's instrument through which He works during the church age is the church. It is because of our Lord's future plan for ethnic Israel that He has maintained them as a distinct people during the almost 2,000 years of the church age. A combination of the temporary purpose of the current church age and the future time during the tribulation and millennium when Israel will once again be the primary instrument through which the Lord works provides a reason God has preserved the ethnically distinct Jewish people.

An illustration of the fact that God has preserved the tribal identity of all Jewish people today and will apply this information in the future is illustrated in Revelation 7:1–8. This passage speaks of the 144,000 Jewish evangelists in the first half of the tribulation who will fulfill the Old Testament passage in Isaiah 49:6 to be "a light to the nations." The verse notes that all twelve tribes with tribal representatives from the entire nation of Israel will be involved: "To raise up the tribes of Jacob, and to restore the preserved ones of Israel." Notice they are also called "the preserved ones," which is exactly the state of world Jewry today. They are the ones preserved from the centuries of Gentile anti-Semitism against the Jewish people which has largely prevented them from merging into the masses of Gentile humanity. "I will also make you a light to the nations," the passage continues, "So that My salvation may reach to the end of the earth." During the first half of the tribulation, the Jewish people will fulfill their calling to be a light to the nations through the supernatural involvement of these divinely protected evangelists. They will preach the gospel globally reaping a harvest of "a great multitude, which no one could count, from every nation and all tribes and peoples and tongues, standing before the throne and before the Lamb, clothed in white robes, and palm branches were in their hand" (Rev 7:9).

In addition to the global proclamation of the gospel through the 144,000 witnesses, the Lord will focus on the Jews in Jerusalem and Israel through His two witnesses. "And I will grant authority to my two witnesses, and they will prophesy for twelve hundred and sixty days, clothed in sackcloth" (Rev 11:3). This is in some way a return of Moses (representing the law) and Elijah (representing the prophets) in which the Lord protects them from harm by "fire proceeds out of their mouth and devours their enemies; and if anyone would desire to harm them, in this manner he must be killed" (Rev 11:5). A pre-trib rapture is supported by the clear return to the function of the Old Testament economy in these sections of Revelation (chs. 4–19) in contrast to the current church age. This supports the notion that God temporarily set aside, but preserved, Israel so that the Jewish people reengage as the instrument through which the Lord carries out His plan for history.

The church is currently carrying out the Great Commission: "Go therefore and make disciples of all the nations, baptizing them in the name of the Father and the Son and the Holy Spirit" (Matt 28:19). The Commission is repeated four more times in the New Testament (Mark 16:14-18; Luke 24:44-48; John 20:19-23; Acts 1:6-8). Some think the rapture cannot happen until the Great Commission has been fulfilled. The gospel is available just about everywhere in the world today. Scripture never says that or even hints at such a thing! The Great Commission is being fulfilled in our day like never before. The Bible commissions the church to preach the gospel and make disciples until Jesus returns at the end of the current dispensation at the rapture. The view that Christ cannot return until the whole world is evangelized flows out of a non-dispensational, non-pre-trib viewpoint. The main passage cited for such a view is Matthew 24:14: "And this gospel of the kingdom shall be preached in the whole world for a witness to all the nations, and then the end shall come." In context, it speaks of evangelism in the tribulation, not during the current church age. The preaching of the "gospel of the kingdom" is noted in the book of Revelation.

The book of Revelation documents that global evangelism will take place like never before during the tribulation, after the rapture.[143] Look at all the evangelistic activity after the rapture, including the likely multi-year period before the tribulation even begins. There is normal evangelism by people like we see today, the preaching of the 144,000 Jewish evangelists distributed all over the world, the ministry of the two witnesses in Jerusalem to the Jewish people, and just before the midpoint of the tribulation, after which the antichrist will require the mark of the beast, an angel preaches the gospel to every individual on planet earth.

---

[143] It appears to me that evangelistic intensity increases with the progress of each new dispensation culminating in the completion of Daniel's 70th week, the tribulation.

And I saw another angel flying in midheaven, having an eternal gospel to preach to those who live on the earth, and to every nation and tribe and tongue and people; and he said with a loud voice, "Fear God, and give Him glory because the hour of His judgment has come; and worship Him who made the heaven and the earth and sea and springs of waters" (Rev 14:6–7).

The Purpose in God's Plan for the Rapture of the Church

It is common for anti-pretribulationists to rightly claim that the word rapture does not appear in the New Testament. The English word "rapture" only came into use in the early 1600s.[144] "Rapture" is an English word derived from Latin and the earliest use has the idea of "the act of seizing and carrying off as prey," usually of a captured woman. It also was used as "the act of conveying a person from one place to another, especially to heaven." Probably the most widely used nuance in our day is "a state of passionate excitement."[145] The term came into use for what we call today "the rapture of the church" in the early 1600s in Europe by those who were not advocates of pretribulationism. When these scholars, who spoke various native languages, would gather from many different European countries, they used Latin as their common language to communicate. In those days, most of their writings were in Latin and they all had great facility in Latin. Generally, this is why the term "rapture" is in such common use today even though it is not directly a biblical term. Today, we commonly use some terms not found in the text of Scripture such as Bible, Trinity, Christian, etc.

---

144 "Rapture," *The Compact Edition of the Oxford English Dictionary*, 2 vols. (Oxford University Press, 1971), 2:2417.
145 OED, 2:2417.

Perhaps a reason the term "rapture" developed is because different terminology has been used in various passages that speak of the rapture. It makes sense that such a common word arose to refer to the single event we call the rapture. There are three major passages we focus upon when studying what the New Testament teaches concerning the rapture of the church.

Importantly, the Olivet Discourse does NOT teach the rapture. Instead, it is given a few days before Christ's crucifixion and speaks primarily of prophecy relating to Israel in the future tribulation period relating to our Lord's physical return to earth (Matthew 24; Mark 13; Luke 17:20-37; 21:5-36). This passage is descriptive of issues relating to the second coming, not the rapture.

John 14:1-3

Jesus announces in John 13:33 that He will be with them only a little while longer. Such a shocking statement provokes Peter to want to go with Jesus wherever He was going (John 13:36). Speaking to the eleven Jesus says, "Let not your heart be troubled, believe in God, believe also in Me. In My Father's house are many dwelling places; if it were not so I would have told you; for I go to prepare a place for you. And if I go and prepare a place for you, I will come again, and receive you to Myself; that where I am, there you may be also" (John 14:1-3).

The introduction of the rapture is first revealed by Jesus in His Upper Room Discourse the night before His crucifixion. John's Gospel was written around AD 85-90 and has material in it that is 93% different from the other three Gospels (Matthew, Mark, and Luke). Everything Christ teaches in the Upper Room Discourse (John 13-16 and 17) is new material, never spoken of earlier in His ministry or anywhere else in Scripture. Why? This is the case since He is introducing brand-new church-age revelation.[146]

---

[146] New revelation in the New Testament, not found in the Old Testament, is called a mystery in the New Testament. The major New Testament mysteries include: mysteries of Heaven (Matt 13:10-13, Mark 4:10-12); mystery of Israel's blindness (Rom 11:25); mystery of God (Rom 16:25-27, 1

Charles Ryrie observes: "The Upper Room Discourse serves as a seed-plot of that which is found later in the epistles of the New Testament."[147] An overview of Christ's new teachings includes the following: the rapture (14:1-4); believers will do great works (14:5-14); the New Testament ministry of the Holy Spirit is introduced (14:15-31); the doctrine of the Christian life is taught as abiding in Christ (15:1-17); the warning that the world will hate the followers of Christ (15:18-16:6); the Holy Spirit will aid in evangelism (16:7-15); an outline of the course of the Church age (16:16-24); prayer will now be in the name of Jesus (16:25-33); the intercessory prayer of Christ on behalf of the church (17:1-26).

However, preterists,[148] like Kenneth Gentry, believe the Scripture "teaches that Christ comes...to believers at death (John 14:1-3)."[149] Contrary to Gentry, even most non-premillennialists echo amillennialist Leo Morris' view who says, "The reference to the second advent should not be missed."[150] John 14:3, where Christ tells His disciples, "I will come again, and receive you to Myself," is an expression that is never used of death in the entire Bible. Many times, various biblical texts speak of Christ coming in reference to His Second Advent (Matt 24:27, 30, 37, 39, 42-44, 46; 25:31; John 21:23; Acts 1:9-11; 1 Thess 4:15; 2 Thess 1:10; 2:1, 8, etc.). Interestingly fellow postmillennialist, David Brown, argues strongly against Gentry's view that John 14 speaks of Christ coming at death. Brown argues:

Cor 2:6-8); mystery of the rapture of the church (1 Cor 15:50-53); mystery of God's plan (Eph 1:9-10); mystery of Jews and Gentile in one co-equal body (Eph 3:1-10); mystery of the bride of Christ (Eph 5:25-32); mystery of God, even Christ (Col 1:2-3); mystery of the indwelling ministry of Christ in the church (Col 1:25-27); mystery of lawlessness (2 Thess 2:1-10); mystery of godliness (1 Tim 3:16).

147 Charles Caldwell Ryrie, *Basic Theology: A Popular Systematic Guide to Understanding Biblical Truth* (Chicago: Moody, 1986, 1999), 465.

148 The belief that most, if not all, major prophetic events have already been fulfilled in history.

149 Kenneth Gentry, *The Beast of Revelation* (Tyler, TX: Institute for Christian Economics, 1989), 25-26.

150 Leon Morris, *The Gospel According to John* (Grand Rapids, MI: Eerdmans, 1971), 639.

"And if I go away"—What then? "Ye shall soon follow me? Death shall shortly bring us together?" Nay; but "If I go away, *I will come again and receive you unto myself;*..."[151]

The coming of Christ to individuals at death...is not *fitted* for taking that place in the view of the believer which Scripture assigns to the second advent....

The death of believers, however changed in its character, in virtue of their union to Christ, is, intrinsically considered, not joyous, but grievous—not attractive, but repulsive.....[152] The bliss of the disembodied spirits of the just is not only *incomplete*, but, in some sense, *private* and *fragmentary*, if I may so express myself....

But at the Redeemer's appearing, all his redeemed will be collected together, and perfectly, publicly, and simultaneously glorified.[153]

The Bible never speaks of death as an event in which the Lord comes for a believer, instead, Scripture speaks of Lazarus "carried away by the angels to Abraham's bosom" (Luke 16:22). In the instance of Stephen, the Martyr, he saw "the heavens opened up and the Son of Man standing at the right hand of God" (Acts 7:56). Arno Gaebelein aptly summaries the biblical statements when he says, "This error is clearly refuted by the fact that elsewhere in the New Testament the Spirit of God tells us that the believer's death is not the Lord coming to the dying believer, but the death of a Christian means that he goes to be with the Lord;... For the believer to be absent from the body means "present with

---

151 David Brown, *Christ's Second Coming: Will It Be Premillennial?* (Edmonton, Canada: Still Water Revival Books, [1882] 1990, 21. (emphasis original)
152 Brown, *Christ's Second Coming*, 22. (emphasis original)
153 Brown, *Christ's Second Coming*, 23. (emphasis original)

the Lord,...(2 Cor. v:1-8)."[154] So then, to what does this passage specifically refer?

Further study of John 14:3 provides additional evidence that our Lord's coming again is not only a future coming but is His coming for the church at the rapture. We find that the aorist tense of the verbs "go" and "prepare" "denotes actuality as well as single acts,"[155] which support a second coming view of the passage. "The coming again is the counterpart of the going away; visibly Jesus ascends, visibly he returns, Acts 1:9-11."[156] But note also the language speaks of Christ coming "from heaven to the earth, He describes a coming for His saints to take them to the Father's house."[157] This is a description of the rapture in contrast to the second coming.[158] "This passage, taken literally, indicates that the believer is going to go to heaven at the time of Christ's coming for Him."[159] This will not occur at the second advent since that will be a time in which Christ comes *with* His saints, who are already in heaven, not *for* His saints as John 14:1-3 requires. "I will come back refers here not to the Resurrection or to a believer's death, but to the Rapture of the church when Christ will return for His sheep (cf. 1 Thess 4::13-18) and they will be with Him (cf. John 17:24)."[160] Arno Gaebelein tells us Christ is unveiling a new revelation about the rapture of the Church:

---

154 Arno C. Gaebelein, *The Gospel of John: A complete analytical exposition of the Gospel of John* (New York: Our Hope Publishing, 1925), 266-67.
155 R. C. H. Lenski, *Interpretation of St. John's Gospel* (Columbus, OH: Lutheran Book Concern, 1942), 973.
156 Lenski, *John's Gospel*, 974.
157 John F. Walvoord, *The Rapture Question: Revised and Enlarged Edition* (Grand Rapids, MI: Zondervan, 1979), 194.
158 For a comparison between the Rapture and the Second Coming see Thomas Ice and Timothy Demy, *The Truth About the Rapture* (Eugene OR: Harvest House Publishers, 1996), 26-31. Or Thomas Ice and Timothy Demy, *Prophecy Watch: What to Expect in the Days to Come* (Eugene OR: Harvest House Publishers, 1998), 100-102.
159 Walvoord, *Rapture Question*, 195.
160 Edwin A. Blum, "John" in John F. Walvoord and Roy B. Zuck, eds, *The Bible Knowledge Commentary: New Testament* edition (Wheaton, IL: Victor Books, 1983), 322.

But here in John xiv the Lord gives a new and unique revelation; He speaks of something which no prophet had promised, or even could promise. Where is it written that this Messiah would come and instead of gathering His saints into an earthly Jerusalem, would take them to the Father's house, to the very place where He is? It is something new. And let it be noticed in promising to come again, He addresses the eleven disciples and tells them, "I will receive you unto Myself, that where I am ye may be also." He speaks then of a coming which is not for the deliverance of the Jewish remnant, not of a coming to establish His kingdom over the earth, not a coming to judge the nations, but coming which concerns only His own.[161]

John 14 and 1 Thessalonians 4

A significant number of commentators note that our Lord's statements in John 14:1-3 parallels another New Testament passage—1 Thessalonians 4:13-18[162] the most important rapture passage in the New Testament. Renald Showers points out several similarities between the two passages.[163] However, it was the late Mennonite commentator, J. B. Smith,[164] who demonstrated just how extensive the relationship between these two passages was.[165]

Smith made a word-for-word comparison between the rapture passage (1 Thess 4:13-18) and a clear second-coming text (Rev 19:11-21) and found no significant parallels. "Hence it is impos-

---

161 Gaebelein, *Gospel of John*, 268.
162 Renald Showers cites the following individuals who see a connection between John 14:1-3 and 1 Thess 4:13-18: J. H. Bernard, James Montgomery Boice, Arno C. Gaebelein, Arthur Pink, Rudolf Schnackenburg, F. F. Bruce, R. V. G. Tasker, and W. W. Vine in *Maranatha: Our Lord, Come!* (Bellmawr, N.J.: Friends of Israel, 1995), 162.
163 Showers, *Maranatha*, 161-64.
164 J. B. Smith, *A Revelation of Jesus Christ: A Commentary on the Book of Revelation* (Scottdale, PA: Herald Press, 1961), 311-13.
165 Earl Radmacher first called my attention to Smith's comparison during a debate with Robert Gundry in Long Beach, CA in 1976.

sible that one sentence or even one phrase can be alike in the two lists," observes Dr. Smith. "And finally not one word in the two lists is used in the same relation or connection."[166] He goes on to conclude: "It would be difficult if not impossible to find elsewhere any two important passages of Scripture that are so diverse in the words employed and so opposite in their implications.... We believe the comparison of the words of these two passages... describe different events."[167]

On the other hand, when it comes to a comparison between John 14:1-3 and 1 Thessalonians 4:13-18 we see amazing parallels. That John 14:1-3 is a rapture reference is supported by the progression of words and thoughts when compared to Paul's more extensive rapture passage (1 Thess 4:13-18). Observe the following comparison:

John 14:1-3		1 Thessalonians 4:13-18	
trouble	v. 1	sorrow	v. 13
believe	v. 1	believe	v. 14
God, me	v. 1	Jesus, God	v. 14
told you	v. 2	say to you	v. 15
come again	v. 3	coming of the Lord	v. 15
receive you	v. 3	caught up	v. 17
to myself	v. 3	to meet the Lord	v. 17
be where I am	v. 3	ever be with the Lord	v. 17[168]

---

166 Smith, *A Revelation*, 312.
167 Smith, *A Revelation*, 312.
168 Smith, *A Revelation*, 311.

Dr. Smith notes the following observations as a result of these comparisons:

The words or phrases are almost an exact parallel.

They follow one another in both passages in exactly the same order.

Only the righteous are dealt with in each case.

There is not a single irregularity in the progression of words from first to last.

Either column takes the believer from the troubles of earth to the glories of heaven.[169]

By comparing Scripture with Scripture, it appears obvious that Jesus' teaching in John 14:1-3 and Paul's revelation in 1 Thessalonians 4:13–18 speak of the same event. Smith concludes, "It is but consistent to interpret each passage as dealing with the same event—the rapture of the church."[170] How else does one explain the progression of eight specific words/phrases in the same order, in two different passages, by two different spokesmen? It is clear these two passages refer to a single future event—the rapture of the church under the Divine inspiration of the same Holy Spirit.

1 Thessalonians 4:13-18

The Apostle Paul wrote his first epistle to the Galatians to deal with issues relating to the Jerusalem Council of Acts 15 and the matter of justification by faith alone. His next epistle was 1 Thessalonians and a few months later 2 Thessalonians. In these early letters, Paul introduces and details much of the new eschatology

---

169 Smith, *A Revelation*, 312-13.
170 Smith, *A Revelation*, 313.

relating to the church age, especially the sequence of events. As we have seen previously, Paul borrows language from Jesus' introduction of the rapture in John 14:1–3. Paul follows in 1 Thessalonians 4:13–18 the same thought-for-thought progression Jesus used in John 14 to answer the Thessalonians' concern about fellow believers who died before the Lord's return. It is clear from the "problem" expressed by the Thessalonian believers that they did not expect to go through the tribulation because of their concern that those who had already died would not participate in the Lord's return for the living. Paul alleviates their concern by noting in this passage that all believers, living or dead, will be caught up together to Christ in the air and taken to heaven when this event takes place.

But we do not want you to be uninformed, brethren, about those who are asleep, that you may not grieve, as do the rest who have no hope. For if we believe that Jesus died and rose again, even so God will bring with Him those who have fallen asleep in Jesus. For this we say to you by the word of the Lord, that we who are alive, and remain until the coming of the Lord, shall not precede those who have fallen asleep. For the Lord Himself will descend from heaven with a shout, with the voice of the archangel, and with the trumpet of God; and the dead in Christ shall rise first. Then we who are alive and remain shall be caught up together with them in the clouds to meet the Lord in the air, and thus we shall always be with the Lord. Therefore comfort one another with these words (1 Thess 4:13–18).

As we look at this central rapture passage it is important to realize that at no point in any New Testament epistle does anyone warn believers about going through the tribulation. Instead, Paul comforts believers concerning the tribulation. Paul's exhortation begins with the command to stop being uniformed, since the concern precipitating these epistolary comments was the result of improper thinking on this matter. Paul addresses those believers who have died as ones who are "asleep." In fact, eighty-three times in his epistles Paul refers to the death of believers as one whose body is asleep. We know from 2 Corinthians 5:8 Paul says, "... to be absent from the body and to be at home with the Lord." Even though one's body sleeps in the ground awaiting resurrection, dead believers are fully conscious in the presence of the Lord awaiting resurrection. The logic that flows from these facts provides hope, not grief, in contrast to dead unbelievers who have no hope. The hope Paul likely has in mind is the blessed hope of Titus 2:13: "looking for the blessed hope and the appearing of the glory of our great God and Savior, Christ Jesus."

Paul begins his argument in verse 14 by saying, "For if we believe that Jesus died and rose again." The "if" is a first-class conditional use. Grammarian Dan Wallace explains: "The first class condition indicates *the assumption of truth for the sake of argument.*"[171] Paul certainly believes that Jesus died and rose again, so his statement that follows is equally true. "*Even so God will bring with Him those who have fallen asleep in Jesus.*" The better translation is that God will bring with Him those who have fallen asleep *through* Jesus. Believers who have died before the rapture will return with Jesus when He returns in the air to snatch living believers in the air. This is one of the benefits for a believer in Christ. Tom Constable observes: "Two reasons why Christians should not grieve like unbelievers are that Christians have a revelation from God that gives them hope and they have a glorious future with Christ."[172]

Paul announces that what he is teaching them is the word of the Lord. Isn't the entire Bible the word of the Lord? Yes, of course! However, in this context I believe he is emphasizing this is a truth he received directly, face-to-face from the Lord. "It follows, then," notes John Eadie, "that we accept the clause in its simple

---

171 Daniel B. Wallace, *Greek Grammar Beyond the Basics: An Exegetical Syntax of the New Testament* (Grand Rapids: Zondervan, 1996), 690, 694. (emphasis original)

172 Thomas L. Constable, "1 Thessalonians" in Walvoord and Zuck, eds., *Bible Knowledge Commentary*, 703-704.

significance, as asserting an immediate revelation from Christ to the apostle on this point. Such is the view of the majority of expositors."[173] Paul does speak of a time when he was *caught up* to the third heaven and encountered direct interaction with the Lord Himself (2 Cor 12:24). The rapture is said in this passage to be a coming of the Lord. Yes, He comes in the air, then we go up to meet Him. The second coming is when church-age believers return with Jesus to planet Earth as our Lord touches down on the Mount of Olives. Dead church-age believers in the grave will get about a second head start when the rapture occurs. Tim LaHaye used to say the dead are buried six feet under the ground, thus, they need a head start. Regardless of the reason, we will all meet the Lord in the air, and as Jesus noted, we will return with Him to the Father's house in heaven. John Walvoord says, "When we meet the Lord in the air, we shall assemble in the atmospheric heaven and from there go to the third heaven, which is the immediate presence of the Father."[174]

There are three phases to the single event of the rapture as outlined by Paul in verse 16, all of which most likely take place instantaneously. First, our Lord will descend from heaven with a shout. This threefold process mirrors the passing of a military command down the chain of command to the troops. The commander starts the process by issuing an order. Second, the intermediate agent is the voice or command of the archangel. Third, the general command is then passed along to the troops through the trumpet call leading to the execution of the order. In this case, the event of the rapture begins with the dead in Christ responding with the first movement.

"Then," those believers who are alive when this takes place will be snatched up into the air to meet Christ who is hovering

---

[173] John Eaide, *A Commentary on the Greek Text of the Epistle of Paul to the Thessalonians* (Minneapolis, MN: James and Klock Christian Publishing [1877], 1977), 155.

[174] John F. Walvood, *The Thessalonian Epistles: A Study Guide Commentary* (Grand Rapids: Zondervan, 1976), 45.

in the air where there are clouds. As a result, when we all meet Jesus in the air, we will be transported to the third heaven, which is God's dwelling place. What a meeting it will be! Some commentators note: "It is not said, on the one hand, that they will descend with him to earth, nor, on the other hand, that He will return with them to heaven. What shall follow after His saints meet Him the apostle does not declare."[175] The passage DOES say what follows the action of the command—"thus we shall always be with the Lord" (4:17). In light of Christ's introductory rapture passage, which clearly states we will return with Him to the Father's house and the many dwelling places He prepares for us, "that where I am, there you may be also" (John 14:2-3). We are taken to heaven, which is why Christ comes in the air and we go up to meet Him and return with Him to the Father's house, which is the third heaven.

The final verse in this passage (4:18) draws a comforting conclusion to the narrative. The section starts with a concern and closes with the positive conclusion of comforting one another concerning the Lord's return. "Paul lifts up their eyes to contemplate the coming of the Lord and they were comforted; they were encouraged by the fact that the Lord would come at any time to receive them unto Himself."[176]

Those who merge the rapture and the second coming assume that in 1 Thessalonians 4 Christ meets believers in the air and then continues down to earth for a single coming view. Such a fluctuating "yo-yo" view rapture is not supported in Scripture. We have seen the event introduced and described by Christ in John 14, which pictures Him coming in the air, not all the way to earth, and taking believers to heaven with Him. The 1 Thessalonians 4 passage speaks of believers being caught up in the clouds and meeting the Lord in the air to be forever with our Lord Jesus

---

175 Eaide, *Thessalonians*, 170.
176 Walvood, *Thessalonian Epistles*, 46-47.

Christ. On the other hand, passages that describe the second coming speak of Christ coming to the Mount of Olives in Jerusalem and touching down and splitting the mountain into two (Zech 14:4; see also Matt 24:27-31; 42-44; 25:31; Rev 19: 11-21).

Differences between the Rapture and the Second Coming

If the rapture and second coming are two separate events that can be distinguished, then there must be clear observable differences between them. The rapture is characterized in the Bible as a "translation coming" (1 Cor 15:51-52; 1 Thess 4:15-17) in which Christ comes *for* His church. The second advent is Christ returning with His saints, descending from heaven to establish His earthly kingdom (Zech 14:4-5; Matt 24:27-31). Ed Hindson makes the following observation:

> The rapture (or "translation") of the church is often paralleled to the "raptures" of Enoch (Genesis 5:24) and Elijah (2 Kings 2: 12). In each case, the individual disappeared or was caught up into heaven. At His ascension, our Lord Himself was "taken up" into heaven (Acts 1:9). The biblical description of the rapture involves both the resurrection of deceased believers and the translation of living believers into the air to meet the Lord (1 Thess. 4:16-17; 1 Cor. 15:51-52).[177]

Differences between the two events are harmonized naturally by the pretribulational position, while other views are not able to account comfortably for such distinctions between the rapture and the second coming.

---

177 Edward E. Hindson, "The Rapture and the Return: Two Aspects of Christ's Coming," in Thomas Ice and Timothy Demy, eds., *When the Trumpet Sounds* (Eugene, OR: Harvest House Publishers, 1995), 158.

RAPTURE AND SECOND COMING PASSAGES

RAPTURE

SECOND ADVENT

"Seventieth Week" of Daniel

SEVEN-YEAR TRIBULATION PERIOD

Rapture Passages		2nd Coming Passages	
John 14:1-3	2 Thess 2:3 (?)	Daniel 2:44-45	Acts 1:9-11
Rom 8:19	1 Tim 6:14	Daniel 7:9-14	Acts 3:19-21
1 Cor 1:7-8	2 Tim 4:1	Daniel 12:1-3	1 Thess 3:13
1 Cor 15:51-53	2 Tim 4:8	Zech 12:10	2 Thess 1:6-10
1 Cor 16:22	Titus 2:13	Zech 14:1-15	2 Thess 2:8
Phil 3:20-21	Heb 9:28	Matt 13:41	1 Peter 4:12-13
Phil 4:5	James 5:7-9	Matt 24:15-31	2 Peter 3:1-14
Col 3:4	1 Peter 1:7, 13	Matt 26:64	Jude 14-15
1 Thess 1:10	1 Peter 5:4	Mark 13:14-27	Rev 1:7
1 Thess 2:19	1 John 2:28-3:2	Mark 14:62	Rev 19:11-20:6
1 Thess 4:13-18	Jude 21	Luke 21:25-28	Rev 22:7, 12, 20
1 Thess 5:9	Rev 2:25		
1 Thess 5:23	Rev 3:10		
2 Thess 2:1			

Rapture/ Translation	2nd Coming/ Establish Kingdom
Christ comes in the air for His own Rapture for all Christians	Christ comes with His own to earth
Christians taken to the Father's house	Not one raptured
No judgment on the earth	Resurrected do not see the Father's house
Church taken to heaven	Christ judges inhabitants of the earth
Imminent— could happen any moment	Christ sets up His kingdom on earth
No signs	Cannot occur for at least 7 years
For believers only	Many signs for Christ's physical coming affects all humanity
Time of joy	Time of mourning
Before the "day of wrath" (Tribulation)	Immediately after Tribulation (Matt 24)
No mention of Satan	Satan bound in abyss for 1,000 years
The judgment seat of Christ	No time or place for judgment seat
Marriage of the Lamb	Christ's bride descends with Him
Only His own will see Him	Every eye will see Him
Tribulation begins	1,000-year kingdom of Christ begins [178]

---

[178] Both charts taken and partially modified from Tim LaHaye and Thomas Ice, *Charting the End Times: A Visual Guide to Understanding Bible Prophecy* (Eugene, OR: Harvest House Publishers, 2001), 111-12.

Dr. John Walvoord concludes that these "contrasts should make it evident that the translation of the church is an event quite different in character and time from the return of the Lord to establish His kingdom, and confirms the conclusion that the translation takes place before the tribulation."[179]

1 Corinthians 15:51-54

The third of the three major New Testament passages teaching the rapture is 1 Corinthians 15:51-54. This entire chapter is Paul's great exposition on the resurrection of believers where he focuses on the rapture at the end of this section.

Behold, I tell you a mystery; we shall not all sleep, but we shall all be changed, in a moment, in the twinkling of an eye, at the last trumpet; for the trumpet will sound, and the dead will be raised imperishable, and we shall be changed. For this perishable must put on the imperishable, and this mortal must put on immortality. But when this perishable will have put on the imperishable, and this mortal will have put on immortality, then will come about the saying that is written, "Death is swallowed up in victory."

The previous two verses speak of the fact that "just as we have borne the image of the earthy; we shall also bear the image of the heavenly. Now I say this, brethren, that flesh and blood cannot inherit the kingdom of God; nor does the perishable inherit the imperishable" (15:49-50). These verses presuppose a pre-trib rapture because all church-age believers will enter the millennial kingdom as resurrected people. For this to be the case, all church-age believers will be resurrected at the rapture before the tribulation begins and enter the kingdom with Christ upon His return. If this were not the case, then some church-age believers would likely sur-

---

179 John F. Walvoord, *The Return of the Lord* (Grand Rapids, MI: Zondervan, 1953), 88.

vive the tribulation and enter the kingdom in their current body. Thus, the "flesh and blood" mentioned in this passage only refers to church-age believers to whom Paul is addressing in this passage. Paul says this "cannot" happen. "In the future we believers shall bear the image of the heavenly, the Christ who descended out of heaven, whose resurrection body is the firstfruits and prototype of our resurrection bodies (Phi. 3:21)."[180]

Even though this entire chapter speaks of the resurrection, Paul begins a new subsection with the transitional term "Behold" in verse 51. Paul is informing believers that some will receive a new resurrection body without dying. He is explaining "the fact that some believers would receive a spiritual body apart from death and resurrection."[181] This rapture event will take place at an unknown time in the future, which is why Paul labels this event a "mystery." As a reminder, a mystery in Paul's terminology refers to a new revelation about the Church which God had not revealed previously. The second coming and resurrection were not mysteries since they were spoken of in the Old Testament. When Paul says, "we shall all be changed", it does not mean he thought he would necessarily be alive when the rapture takes place. He is simply using "we" to speak in this context of the cooperate church, of which he is certainly a member.

Once again Paul uses the metaphor "sleep" to refer to church-age believers who died before the rapture event. When the rapture takes place the transformation from this mortal body and the resurrection body will take place in an instant, less than a second. Both the living and those who have died as believers in Christ "shall all be changed, in a moment, in the twinkling of an eye" (verses 51–52). The change for those alive will be an instant change from mortality to immortality as believers will be given a new res-

---

180 Ernest R. Campbell, *A Commentary of First Corinthians: Based on The Greek New Testament* (Silverton, OR: Canyonview Press, 1989), 258.
181 Robert G. Gromacki, *Called to Be Saints: An Exposition of 1 Corinthians* (Grand Rapids, MI: Baker Book House, 1977), 196.

urrection body equipped to live in the millennium and eternity.

Some non-pretribulationists have attempted to identify the phrase "at the last trumpet" with the final trumpet judgment in Revelation 11:15; such a suggestion will not work for several reasons. "And the seventh angel sounded; and there arose loud voices in heaven, saying, 'The kingdom of the world has become the kingdom of our Lord and of His Christ; and He will reign forever and ever'" (Rev 11:15). The Bible is full of trumpet sounds for many different purposes. Like the use of any word or phrase, the context limits a possible meaning. The contexts of 1 Corinthians 15:52 and Revelation 11:15 are very different, like night is from day. First, the trumpet of Revelation is related to the last in a series of divine judgments located somewhere towards the middle of the tribulation. The trumpet call in 1 Corinthians is a heavenly command to rapture the church to heaven and does not involve any statement of judgment. Also, the trumpet sound in 1 Corinthians 15 signals a single event: the rapture. The six successive trumpets in Revelation, concluding with the seventh, signal various judgments upon the earth, but never a catching up of believers to heaven. Walvoord notes,

> The trumpets of Revelation are entirely different from any other series of trumpets in Scripture. They are trumpets sounded by angels. The trumpet at the Rapture is the 'trumpet of God.' The trumpets of Revelation are all connected with divine judgment on sin and unbelief. The trump of 1 Thessalonians 4 and 1 Corinthians 15 is a call to the elect, an act of grace, a command to the dead to rise.[182]

For example, the last trump was commonly understood in Paul's day in connection with the Roman army. H. A. Ironside provides a good explanation of this use. When a Roman camp was about to be broken up, whether in the middle of the night or

---

[182] Walvoord, *The Rapture Question*, 125.

in the day, a trumpet was sounded. The first blast meant, "Strike tents and prepare to depart." The second meant, "Fall into line," and when what was called "the last trump" sounded it meant, "March away." The apostle uses that figure, and says that when the last trump of this age of grace sounds, then we shall be called away to be forever with the Lord.[183]

As Walvoord points out: "The most damaging fact in the whole argument, however, is that the seventh trumpet of Revelation 11 is, after all, not the last trumpet of Scripture. According to Matthew 24:31, the elect will be gathered at the coming of Christ to establish His earthly kingdom "with a loud trumpet call.""[184]

When the rapture event takes place Paul says, "the dead will be raised imperishable, and we shall be changed" (verse 52). The apostle usually uses the term "sleep" in reference to believers who have died. However, in this passage he makes it clear to what he refers by using the term "dead" about believers. In the next verse (53) he explains why the resurrection and the reception of a new body are needed for believers. "For this perishable must put on the imperishable, and this mortal must put on immortality." Our current sin-infected bodies are described as "perishable" and "mortal," which contradicts some elitist pagans who believe that through scientific developments they can figure out how to live forever. All will indeed live forever. Unbelievers will receive a new body for enduring eternal judgment in the lake of fire, forever and ever (Rev 20:11-15).

As Paul continues to speak about believers, he supports the notion that our current perishable bodies will become imperishable at our resurrection. He supports his statement by quoting from Isaiah 25:8, which says, "Death is swallowed up in victory." We see from this passage that church-age believers will receive their resur-

---

[183] H. A. Ironside, *Addresses on the First Epistle to the Corinthians* (New York: Loizeaux Brothers Publishers, 1938), 529.
[184] Walvoord, *The Rapture Question*, 125.

rection bodies at the moment of the rapture. This means all believers from the beginning of the church in Acts 2 until the rapture of the church sometime in the future will receive their resurrection bodies when the church age is completed. All other believers who have died from the time of Adam and Eve to the end of the tribulation will then be resurrected at the second coming of Christ at least seven years later.

Various Rapture Passages

There are about twenty-five other rapture passages in the New Testament, primarily in the New Testament epistles.[185] By this, I mean passages that in some way refer to the rapture. Many of these passages, studied in their contexts, only make sense in relation to a pretribulational rapture understanding.

As noted earlier, Paul speaks of the rapture as a "mystery" (1 Cor 15:51-54)—that is, a truth not revealed until its disclosure by the apostles (Col 1:26), making it a separate event, while the second coming was predicted in the Old Testament (Dan 12:1-3; Zech 12:10; 14:4).

The movement for the believer at the rapture is from earth to heaven, while it is from heaven to earth at the second advent. At the rapture, the Lord comes *for* his saints (1 Thess 4:16), while at the second coming the Lord comes *with* His saints (1 Thess 3:13). At the rapture, the Lord comes only for believers, but His return to the earth will impact all people. The rapture is a translation/resurrection event where the Lord takes believers "to the Father's house" in heaven (John 14:3), while at the second coming believers return from heaven to the earth (Matt 24:30). Ed Hindson says, "The different aspects of our Lord's return are clearly de-

---

185 John 14:1-3; Rom 8:9; 1 Cor 1:7-8; 15:51-53; 16:22; Phil 3:20-21; 4:5; Col 3:4; 1 Thess 1:10; 2:19; 4:13-18; 5:9; 5:23; 2 Thess 2:1-3; 1 Tim 6:14; 2 Tim 4:1, 8; Titus 2:13; Heb 9:28; Jas 5:7-9; 1 Pet 1:7, 13; 5:4; 1 John 2:28-3:2; Jude 21; Rev 2:25; 3:10; 4:1.

lineated in the scriptures themselves. The only real issue in the eschatological debate is the time *interval* between them."[186]

The Scriptures concerning Christ's coming in the air to rapture His church are too distinct to be reduced to a single coming at the end of the tribulation. These biblical distinctions provide a strong basis for the pretribulational rapture.

The Necessary Interval

An interval or gap of time is needed between the rapture and the second coming to facilitate many events predicted in the Bible in a timely manner. Numerous items in the New Testament can be harmonized by a pretrib time gap of at least seven years, while proponents of other views, especially postribulationists, are forced to postulate scenarios that would not realistically allow for normal passage of time. The following events are best temporally harmonized with an interval of time as put forth by pretribulationism.

2 Corinthians 5:10 teaches that all believers of this church age must appear before the judgment seat of Christ in heaven. This event, often known as the "bema judgment" from the Greek word *bema*, is an event never mentioned in the detailed accounts connected with the second coming of Christ to the earth. Since such an evaluation would require some passage of time, the pre-trib gap of seven years nicely accounts for such a requirement.

Revelation 19:7-10 pictures the church as a bride who has been made ready for marriage (with "fine linen," which represents "the righteous acts of the saints") to her groom (Christ). The bride has already been clothed in preparation for her return at the second coming with Christ to the earth (Rev 19:11-18). It follows that the church would already have to be complete and in heaven (because of the pretrib rapture) to have been prepared in the way

---

[186] Hindson, "Rapture and the Return," 157. (emphasis original)

Revelation 19 describes. This requires an interval of time which pretribulationism handles well.

Revelation 4:1–5:14 speaks of the twenty-four elders who are best understood as representatives of the church, as explained by Ryrie:

> In the New Testament, elders as the highest officials in the church do represent the whole church (cf. Acts 15:6; 20:28), and in the Old Testament, twenty-four elders were appointed by King David to represent the entire Levitical priesthood (1 Chronicles 24). When those twenty-four elders met together in the temple precincts in Jerusalem, the entire priestly house was represented. Thus it seems more likely that the elders represent redeemed human beings... the church is included and is thus in heaven before the tribulation begins.[187]

If the elders refer to the church, which they do, then this would necessitate the rapture and reward of the church before the tribulation and would require a chronological gap for them to perform their heavenly duties during the seven-year tribulation.

In contrast, believers who come to faith in Christ during the tribulation are not translated at Christ's second advent but carry-on ordinary occupations such as farming and building houses, and they will bear children (Isaiah 65:20-25). This would be impossible if all saints were translated at the second coming to the earth, as posttribulationists teach. Because pretribulationists have at least a seven-year interval between the removal of the church at the rapture and the return of Christ to the earth, this is not a problem because many people will be saved during the interval and thus be available to populate the millennium in their natural bodies to fulfill Scripture.

---

[187] Charles C. Ryrie, *Revelation* (Chicago: Moody, 1968), 35-36.

It would be impossible for the judgment of the Gentiles to take place after the second coming if the rapture and second coming are not separated by a gap of time. How would both saved and unsaved, still in their natural bodies, be separated in judgment if all living believers are translated at the second coming? This would be impossible if the translation takes place at the second coming, but it is solved through a pretribulational time gap.

Dr. Walvoord points out that if "the translation took place in connection with the second coming to earth, there would be no need of separating the sheep from the goats at a subsequent judgment, but the separation would have taken place in the very act of the translation of the believers before Christ actually sets up His throne on earth (Matthew 25:31)."[188] Once again, such a "problem" is solved by taking a pretrib position with its gap of at least seven years.

A time interval is needed so that God's program for the church, a time when Jew and Gentile are united in one co-equal body (cf. Eph 2–3), will not become commingled in any way with His unfinished and future plan for Israel during the tribulation. Dr. Renald Showers notes: "All other views of the Rapture have the church going through at least part of the 70th week, meaning that all other views mix God's 70-weeks program for Israel and Jerusalem together with His program for the church."[189] A gap is needed for these two aspects of God's program to be harmonized in a nonconflicting manner.

The pretribulational rapture of the church not only allows for the biblical distinction between the translation of church-age saints at the rapture and the second coming, but it also handles without difficulty the necessity of a time gap that harmonizes several future biblical events. This requirement of a seven-year gap of

---

188 Walvoord, *The Rapture Question*, 274.
189 Renald Showers, *Maranatha: Our Lord Come! A Definitive Study of the Rapture of the Church* (Bellmawr, NJ: The Friends of Israel Gospel Ministry, 1995), 243.

time adds support to the likelihood that pretribulationism best reflects the biblical viewpoint.

The Doctrine of Imminency

The New Testament teaching that Christ could return and rapture His church at any moment, without prior signs or warning, called imminency, is such a powerful argument for pretribulationism that it is one of the most fiercely attacked doctrines by pretrib opponents. Non-pretribulationists sense that if the New Testament teaches imminency, then a pretrib rapture is virtually assured.

Dr. Showers describes imminency[190] as something that could take place at any moment without a sign or indication preceding it. Since one does not know when an imminent event will take place, he must always expect it at any moment. This means speculation about the time or season when the rapture will take place is to be avoided. One cannot legitimately say an imminent event will happen "soon," since that would imply a timeframe. However, I do believe that we can see events taking place that are setting the stage for the tribulation that will take place after the rapture and think that we must be near the start of the tribulation. These are not signs for the rapture but are signs for the tribulation which will take place after the rapture.

The fact that Christ could return soon, at any moment (but may not) is a support for pretribulationism. We see imminency supported by the following New Testament passages: 1 Corinthians 1:7, "waiting eagerly the revelation of our Lord Jesus Christ." 1 Corinthians 16:22, "Maranatha." Philippians 3:20, "For our citizenship is in heaven, from which also we eagerly wait for a Savior, the Lord Jesus Christ." Philippians 4:5, "The Lord is near." 1 Thessalonians 1:10, "to wait for His Son from heaven." Titus

---

190 My description of imminency is gleaned from Showers' description of this teaching in his book, *Maranatha*, 127-28.

2:13, "looking [waiting] for the blessed hope and the appearing of the glory of our great God and Savior, Christ Jesus." Hebrews 9:28, "so Christ...shall appear a second time for salvation without reference to sin, to those who eagerly await Him." James 5:7-9, "Be patient, therefore, brethren, until the coming of the Lord...for the coming of the Lord is at hand.... Behold, the Judge is standing right at the door." 1 Peter 1:13, "fix your hope completely on the grace to be brought to you at the revelation of Jesus Christ." Jude 21, "waiting anxiously for the mercy of our Lord Jesus Christ to eternal life." Revelation 3:11; 22:7, 12, 20, "I am coming quickly!" Revelation 22:17, 20, "And the Spirit and the bride say, 'Come.' And let the one who hears say, 'Come.'... He who testifies to these things says, 'Yes, I am coming quickly.' Amen. Come, Lord Jesus."

As we consider the above passages, we note that Christ may come at any moment and that the rapture is imminent. Only pretribulationism can give a full, literal meaning to such an any-moment event. Other rapture views must redefine imminence more loosely than the New Testament would allow. Dr. Walvoord declares, "The exhortation to look for 'the glorious appearing' of Christ to His own (Titus 2:13) loses its significance if the Tribulation must intervene first. Believers in that case should look for signs."[191] If the pretrib view of imminence is not accepted, then it would make sense to look for signs related to events of the tribulation (i.e., the Antichrist, the two witnesses, etc.) and not for Christ Himself. But the New Testament, as demonstrated above, uniformly instructs the church to look for the coming of Christ, while tribulation saints are told to look for signs.

---

191 Walvoord, *The Rapture Question*, 274.

The Nature and Purpose of the Church

God's plan and purpose for the church would naturally relate to whether He will remove His bride before the tribulation or have her go through it. Only pretribulationism can give full biblical import to the New Testament teaching that the church differs significantly from Israel. The church is said to be a mystery (Eph 3:1-13) by which believing Jews and Gentiles are now united into one body in Christ (Eph 2:11-22). This explains why the church's translation to heaven is never mentioned in any Old Testament passage that deals with the second coming after the tribulation, and why the church is promised deliverance from the time of God's wrath during the tribulation (1 Thess 1:9-10; 5:9; Rev 3:10).

The apostle Paul notes in the following passages that the church is not appointed to God's wrath which will be dispensed during the seven years of the tribulation. **Romans 5:9**, "Much more then, having now been justified by His blood, we shall be saved from the wrath of God through Him." **1 Thessalonians 1:9-10**, "You turned to God from idols to serve a living and true God, and to wait for His Son from heaven, whom He raised from the dead, that is Jesus, **who delivers us from the wrath to come.**" **1 Thessalonians 5:9**, "For God has **not destined us for wrath**, but for obtaining salvation through our Lord Jesus Christ." In one of the letters to the seven churches of (**Rev 3:10**), the Lord promises "'Because you have kept the word of My perseverance, I also will **keep you from the hour of testing,** that hour which is about to come upon the whole world, to test those who dwell upon the earth.'"

Believers are promised deliverance from the *hour* of testing. This means the church is absent from the period of this time of testing. It is said to be a worldwide time of testing. The purpose of the testing is to test "those who dwell upon the earth." The single Greek word for "earth dwellers" is used ten other times in Revelation (6:10; 8:13; 11:10 [twice]; 13:8, 12, 14 [twice]; 17:2, 8) as "a company of people constantly in view through the Apocalypse as

objects of God's wrath because of their rebellion against Him....
These are men given up to evil and hatred of God's saints."[192] This
passage provides one of the purposes God has for the tribulation,
which is to test unbelievers and demonstrate that not a single
"earth dweller" ever becomes a believer during the tribulation regardless of the severity of God's judgment. The contrast between
what God has in store for His church and unbelievers could not
be greater. Every aspect of this passage supports pretribulationism.

The godly remnant of the tribulation is pictured as Israelites,
not members of the church. Thus, pretribulationists do not confuse general terms like *elect* and *saints*, which are used in the Bible
of all the saved of the ages, with specific terms like *church* and *those
in Christ*, which refer to believers of this age only.

The nature and purpose of the church is said to be unique
and separate from Israel. The temporary status of the church provides a biblical basis for the removal of the church before God
completes the final seven years leading up to Israel's redemption.
We have seen that specific passages promise the church's removal
before the time of tribulation gets underway. This can only make
sense with a pretrib understanding.

A Few Other Reasons

In addition to the arguments already presented, there are additional reasons to believe in pretribulationism. Some of these reasons are direct points while some are implicative.

Our Lord told His disciples of the possibility of believers escaping the tribulation in Luke 21:36: "But keep on the alert at all
times, praying in order that you may have strength to escape all
these things that are about to take place, and to stand before the
Son of Man." It was later revealed through the apostles that such

---

[192] Robert L. Thomas, *Revelation 1–7: An Exegetical Commentary* (Chicago: Moody, 1992), 289.

a possibility would indeed become a reality for the church.

Divine deliverance is a pattern often exercised by God preceding His judgment. This is clearly illustrated in the cases of Enoch, Noah, Lot, Rahab, etc. (2 Pet 2:5-9). For example, when we look at the story of Enoch, we find an illustration of both deliverance and rapture before judgment. Notice the strong emphasis on physical deliverance from judgment as the New Testament in Hebrew 11:5 comments on the Old Testament event: "By faith Enoch was taken up so that he should not see death; and he was not found because God took him up; for he obtained the witness that before his being taken up he was pleasing to God."

God will call His ambassadors home before declaring war on the world, just as in contemporary international relations a nation calls home its ambassador prior to a declaration or act of war. Dr Hindson notes, "In 2 Corinthians 5:20, believers are called 'Christ's Ambassadors' who appeal to the world to be reconciled to God before it is too late. In biblical times, one's ambassadors were recalled when it was time to make war with the enemy."[193] Such a notion supports only pretribulationism since the rapture is the call home for Christ's ambassadors—the church.

Revelation 4-19 is widely recognized as descriptive of the tribulation. On the other hand, Revelation 2-3 provides instruction relating to the church. The pretrib rapture is reflected in the fact that the apostle John is invited to come up to heaven (Rev 4:1) at the very point in the biblical text (between Rev 3 and 4) where pretribulationists say the rapture will occur. Further, since John is a representative of the *church* in Revelation, it is significant to notice in the first three chapters which are passages directed specifically to the church, the word for *church* is used nineteen times. However, the word *church* is never used again in Revelation, except one time during the closing statements in Revelation 22:16.

---

193 Hindson, "The Rapture and the Return," 161.

This observation supports a pretrib rapture because after chapter three John speaks about events after the church has been taken to heaven. If the church was going through any part of the tribulation, then she would have been referenced on those occasions.

Practical Implications

Belief in pretribulationism is not just wishful "pie-in-the-sky in the by-and-by" thinking. Rather, it is vitally connected to Christian living in the "nasty here and now." Any believer with love in their heart for the coming Savior will want to live a pure and holy life until His return. "Beloved, now we are children of God, and it has not appeared as yet what we shall be. We know that, when He appears, we shall be like Him, because we shall see Him just as He is. And everyone who has this hope fixed on Him purifies himself, just as He is pure" (1 John 3:2-3).

This passage directly links our present Christian conduct to a future event—the rapture. Why? Because our destiny as God's children is not complete in this life, and it is toward that future goal we are moving. At the rapture, when we will receive our resurrection bodies, our character will also be perfected. But in the meantime, we are to be purified in present conduct by fixing our hope on the return of Christ. According to this passage, this should be a motivation to holy living. There are over twenty specific references in the New Testament that link the present conduct of believers to our future destiny.[194] Renald Showers summarized some practical implications of the pretrib rapture when he noted:

> The imminent coming of Christ should have an incredible practical effect on the lives of individual Christians and the church as a whole. The fact that the glorified, holy

---

194 1 Cor 15:58; Phil 3:20; 4:5; Col 3:1-4; 3:4-5; 1 Thess 1:10; 2:19-20; 4:18; 5:6; 2 Thess 2:1-2; 1 Tim 6:14; 2 Tim 4:1; 4:1-5; 4:1-8; Titus 2:12-13; 2:13; Heb 9:28; Jas 5:7-8; 1 Pet 1:13; 5:4; 1 John 2:28; 3:2.

Son of God could step through the door of heaven at any moment is intended by God to be the most pressing, incessant motivation for holy living and aggressive ministry (including missions, evangelism, and Bible teaching), and the greatest cure for lethargy and apathy. It should make a major difference in every Christian's values, actions, priorities and goals.[195]

There is no doubt that in my lifetime[196] belief in the rapture has been stated as the main motive for evangelism and world missions. I have seen this in the Jesus Movement revival in the early 70s, the popularity of books like *The Late Great Planet Earth*[197] and the *Left Behind*[198] series, various movies like *A Thief in the Night*,[199] the many prophecy ministries on both radio and television and many more impactful influences, not to mention the thousands of prophecy conferences. Belief in pretribulationism promotes evangelism when believers are impacted by the fact Christ could return at any moment, without any signs or warning. Wherever those who believe in an any-moment return of Christ have realized the implications of such a view, it has always provided a powerful motive for evangelism and involvement in world missions.

Dr. Timothy Weber, a church historian, has noted that belief in the rapture has been a great incentive for missions in the last 150 years:

> By the 1920s premillennialists were claiming that they made up "an overwhelming majority" of the [missions] movement. Others estimated that believers in the immi-

---

[195] Showers, *Maranatha*, 255-56.
[196] I am currently 73 years old.
[197] Hal Lindsey with C. C. Carlson, *The Late Great Planet Earth* (Grand Rapids, MI: Zondervan, 1970).
[198] Tim LaHaye and Jerry B. Jenkins, *Left Behind: A Novel of the Earth's Last Days* (Wheaton, IL: Tyndale House, 1995).
[199] *A Thief in the Night*, Russell Doughten Films, 1972.

nent second coming made up from 75 to 85 percent of the missionary force worldwide.... American premillennialists were better represented on the mission fields than in the home churches.... Instead of cutting missionary involvement, premillennialism increased it.[200]

Although there is great criticism from many directions within Christendom who say pretribulationism is a negative influence upon Christianity, this teaching is supported by the New Testament and is doctrinally sound. Pretribulationism is a great motivation for many who believe its truth in service to our Lord and Savior Jesus Christ. Ed Hindson says,

Whether our Lord returns today or years into the future, we can face each day of our lives secure in His incredible promises. If we live, we live to the glory of God. If we die, we die to the glory of God. Either way, one day we will hear the angelic shout and the trumpet call of God and *Voosh*! We are on our way to all the rest that God has planned for our amazing future.[201]

---

[200] Timothy P. Weber, *Living in the Shadow of the Second Coming: American Premillennialism, 1875–1925* (Grand Rapids, MI: Zondervan, 1983), 81.
[201] Hindson, *Future Glory*, 48.

BIBLIOGRAPHY

A Thief in the Night, Russell Doughten Films, 1972.

Blum, Edwin A. "John," in John F. Walvoord and Roy B. Zuck, eds., *The Bible Knowledge Commentary: New Testament Edition*. Wheaton, IL: Victor Books, 1983.

Brown, David. *Christ's Second Coming: Will It Be Premillennial?* Edmonton, Canada: Still Water Revival Books, [1882] 1990.

Campbell, Ernest R. *A Commentary of First Corinthians: Based on The Greek New Testament*. Silverton, OR: Canyonview Press, 1989.

Constable, Thomas L. "1 Thessalonians," in in John F. Walvoord and Roy B. Zuck, eds., *The Bible Knowledge Commentary: New Testament Edition*. Wheaton, IL: Victor Books, 1983.

Eaide, John. *A Commentary on the Greek Text of the Epistle of Paul to the Thessalonians*. Minneapolis, MN: James and Klock Christian Publishing [1877], 1977.

Gaebelein, Arno C. *The Gospel of John: A Complete Analytical Exposition of the Gospel of John*. New York: Our Hope Publishing, 1925.

Gentry, Kenneth. *The Beast of Revelation*. Tyler, TX: Institute for Christian Economics, 1989.

Gromacki, Robert G. *Called to Be Saints: An Exposition of 1 Corinthians*. Grand Rapids: Baker, 1977.

Hindson, Edward E. *Future Glory: Living in the Hope of the Rapture, Heaven, and Eternity*. Eugene, OR: Harvest House Publishers, 2021.

——. "The Rapture and the Return: Two Aspects of Christ's Coming," in Thomas Ice and Timothy Demy, eds., *When the Trumpet Sounds*. Eugene, OR: Harvest House Publishers, 1995.

Ice, Thomas and Timothy Demy. *The Truth About the Rapture*. Eugene OR: Harvest House Publishers, 1996.

——. *Prophecy Watch: What to Expect in the Days to Come*. Eugene OR: Harvest House Publishers, 1998.

Ironside, H. A. *Addresses on the First Epistle to the Corinthians*. New York: Loizeaux Brothers Publishers, 1938.

LaHaye, Tim and Thomas Ice. *Charting the End Times: A Visual Guide to Understanding Bible Prophecy*. Eugene, OR: Harvest House Publishers, 2001.

LaHaye, Tim and Jerry B. Jenkins, *Left Behind: A Novel of the Earth's Last Days*. Wheaton, IL: Tyndale House, 1995.

Lenski, R. C. H. *Interpretation of St. John's Gospel*. Columbus, OH: Lutheran Book Concern, 1942.

Lindsey, Hal with C. C. Carlson, *The Late Great Planet Earth*. Grand Rapids: Zondervan, 1970.

Morris, Leon. *The Gospel According to John*. Grand Rapids: Eerdmans, 1971.

Ryrie, Charles Caldwell. *Basic Theology: A Popular Systematic Guide to Understanding Biblical Truth*. Chicago: Moody, 1986, 1999.

———. *Revelation*. Chicago: Moody, 1968.

Schaff, Philip. *The Creeds of Christendom with a History and Critical Notes*. 4th ed. 3 vols. Grand Rapids: Baker, 1877.

———. *The Compact Edition of the Oxford English Dictionary*. 2 vols. Oxford University Press, 1971.

Showers, Renald. *Maranatha: Our Lord Come! A Definitive Study of the Rapture of the Church*. Bellmawr, NJ: The Friends of Israel Gospel Ministry, 1995.

Smith, J. B. *A Revelation of Jesus Christ: A Commentary on the Book of Revelation*. Scottdale, PA: Herald Press, 1961.

Thomas, Robert L. *Revelation 1–7: An Exegetical Commentary*. Chicago: Moody, 1992.

Wallace, Daniel B. *Greek Grammar Beyond the Basics: An Exegetical Syntax of the New Testament*. Grand Rapids: Zondervan, 1996.

Walvoord, John F. *The Rapture Question: Revised and Enlarged Edition*. Grand Rapids: Zondervan, 1979.

———. *The Return of the Lord*. Grand Rapids: Zondervan, 1953.

———. *The Thessalonian Epistles: A Study Guide Commentary*. Grand Rapids: Zondervan, 1976.

Weber, Timothy P. *Living in the Shadow of the Second Coming: American Premillennialism, 1875–1925*. Grand Rapids: Zondervan, 1983.

CHAPTER FIVE

THE NEW HEAVENS AND THE NEW EARTH IN THE ETERNAL STATE

ISAIAH 65:17-25; 66:18-24

by Walter C. Kaiser, Jr.

The key Scriptural passages that speak of the "New Heavens and the New Earth" are Isaiah 65:17-25; 66:18-24; 2 Peter 3:13, and Revelation 21:1-4.[202] The words used in the Hebrew and the Greek script for "new" refer not, as some might suspect, to a total discontinuity between the former universe and the cosmos that is to come. Instead, the word "new" points to a "renewal" of the Heavens and the Earth, represented by the Hebrew figu-

---

202 It is a special delight to dedicate this essay to my former student Dr. Ed Hindson. Our Lord has used his ministry of the Word of God in a most unusual way, for which we give thanks to our Lord for all that our Lord did through his ministry to the glory of God.

rative expression "the heavens and the earth," meaning the whole "universe," for Hebrew has no other term for the "universe." In that sense, then, there are strong lines of continuity, which in this case overcome the radical lines of discontinuity between the old heavens and earth and the "new." We will comment more on the word "new" later.

The doctrine of the renewed universe is an important one, for it sets the record straight on what future life in eternity will be like. Some dislike the Christian hymns that speak of the glories of that life to come in terms similar to the hymn "My Jesus I Love Thee." Believers have sung for years the following words:

"In mansions of glory and endless delight/
I'll ever adore thee in heaven so bright."

But is that hymn beyond (or exceeding) the teachings of the sacred page? Did Jesus not promise in John 14:1–3a that he would go ahead of us to heaven to prepare mansions for us? Therefore, we are taught:

Let not your hearts be troubled…
In my Father's house are many mansions;
if it were not so, I would have told you.
I go to prepare a place for you.

True, heaven is not described in the Bible as some place that is just far off in space, where God's men and women will be wearing white robes, strumming all day long on harps, and singing for all they are worth as they flit and fly from cloud to cloud. What is true, however, is that we who trust in Jesus will be rejoined with our bodies after we die in the coming resurrection. We will have left behind the old remains of our bodies in the graves where we have been buried. We will now be raised from those graves and be given wholly new and improved bodies, much like Jesus' resurrected body, which still had the marks on his hands and feet from the nails on the cross and the mark on his side from the Roman spear driven there to see if he were still alive. But those resurrected bodies will also have properties not seen before until Jesus appeared in his resurrected body. Jesus' new body showed features not seen before, for he easily entered the room where the disciples were gathered after his resurrection, where the doors were carefully shut and locked! This then seems to signal features of our future resurrected body we were unaware.

This doctrine of the renewed heaven and earth is also important because it completes the program of the redemptive plan of God. Ever since the Fall of Adam and Eve, the creation has fallen under the impact of the curse that came on it because of the sin of that first couple. But God will not leave it at that point, for he will usher in a renewed heavens and renewed earth, as Paradise is regained and restored to what God had originally intended it to be at the creation.

This doctrine is important also because it is necessary to clearly demarcate the thousand years when Christ totally rules and reigns on earth during that millennium, beginning when he returns at the time of the second advent. After Yeshua (the Hebrew name for Jesus) has ruled for one thousand years, he will initiate the eternal and everlasting aspects of the covenants, thus completing history. Of course, God will first finish in space and time what he promised in the Abrahamic Covenant (Gen 12:2-3). As with all the other divine promises (e.g., of a coming Seed and the good news of the gospel), God will do in the historical process what he promised to do regarding the "land" also. But this in no way short circuits his commitment to bring a renewal of the heavens and the earth as believers move from history into the new era of eternity itself.

Some have argued, counter to Scripture, that when Abraham was divinely promised in Genesis 17:8 ("I will give as an everlasting possession [the whole land of Canaan] to you and to your descendants after you...") that Abraham understood this promise of the land of Canaan in accordance with Hebrews 11:9-10:

> By faith [Abraham] made his home in the promised land like a stranger in a foreign country; he lived in tents, as did Isaac and Jacob, who were heirs with him of the same promise. For he was looking forward to the city with foundations, whose architect and builder is God.

Of course, many agree that the "city with foundations, whose architect and builder is God" can refer to none other than the future city of Jerusalem. But the key question is this: is that city of Jerusalem to be found on the renewed earth as part of the eternal state, as a-millennialists argue, or is it to be found in the millennial rule and reign of Messiah prior to the eternal state, as pre-millennialists assert? We will contend for the latter view. Scripture repeatedly states that this "everlasting possession" was not addressed to all the people of God, who in the widest sense are the "seed of Abraham," but it is distinctively made first to Israel, as we have argued in our chapters on Zechariah 10:1-12 and Ezekiel 37:1-28 indicate.

However, when it is promised that there will be a "New Heaven and a New Earth," does that mean that the present universe will be annihilated so that a completely new universe will replace the present cosmos? Some interpreters favor such a complete discontinuity between the old and the new universe. However, that view of a complete disjuncture between the condition of the universe in these two views must also be rejected for the following reasons.

The New Testament Greek word for newness is not the Greek word *neos*, but *kainos*. The former Greek word (*neos*) designated "something that was new in time or origin," but the latter word referred to something that was "new in nature or quality." Therefore, what is taught regarding the New Heavens and the New Earth is not the emergence, or creation, of a brand-new universe, but one that has some continuity with the old, yet it is thoroughly renewed.

Moreover, there is an analogy between the newness of the universe as there is between our old bodies and our resurrected bodies. Our resurrected bodies will have both a continuity with our pre-resurrected bodies and as well as a discontinuity with our present bodies. The body we shall receive at our resurrection will exhibit both aspects of continuity and discontinuity with the past. This is precisely what we have seen in the resurrected body of Jesus, for he had some marks on his resurrected body that were carried over from his body laid in the tomb.

One New Testament text that might mislead some to think that this present universe will suffer massive destruction and conflagration is 2 Peter 3:10.

> But the day of the Lord will come like a thief. The heavens will disappear with a roar; the elements will be destroyed by fire and everything in it will be laid bare.

Some manuscripts read for this final verb in 2 Peter 3:10 as if it said: "[the heavens] will be burned up," but the better reading is found in most English texts as is rendered now in the NIV: "[the heavens] will be laid bare." Such a rendering also fits well with the understanding that it is a "renewal" of the universe, and not a "brand new replacement" of the present cosmos, with a complete destruction of the old universe.

The future, then, has both a break with the past as well as a partial connection with it, both continuity and discontinuity. The break is necessitated because there exist the forces of sin that must be broken by Christ and overcome by the power and might of his word and his actions. But we must count on the power of the resurrection forces as being just as active and present in this new work of God. Accordingly, the external "form" (Greek, *schema*) of this world is passing away, but we can be sure also that the same "it" of 1 Corinthians 15:44, that was put into the grave, meaning our old bodies, is the same "it" (i.e., our bodies) that will be raised again to life with enormous improvement by virtue of our resurrection bodies. So let us look more closely at these matters from two important teaching passages in the book of Isaiah.

Text: Isaiah 65:17–25; 66:18-24

Title: "The New Heavens and the New Earth in the Eternal State"

Focal Point: 65:17, "Behold, I will create new heavens and a new earth. The former things will not be remembered, nor will they come to mind."

Homiletical Keyword: DISTINCTIONS. WHAT? (what are the distinctions that will set the new heavens and new earth off from the present universe?)

Teaching Aim: To show that this is a renewed universe by which God inaugurates the eternal state and is not to be confused with the rule and reign of the Lord during the thousand years of the Millennium.

Outline

"Distinctions:"

I. The Sound Of Weeping And Crying Will Be No More—65:17-19

II. The Lives Of Men And Women Will No Longer Be Cut Short—65:20-24

III. The Lives Of Animals Will Be Changed—65:25

IV. The Heavens And The Earth
Will Endure Forever—66:22-24

Exegetical Commentary: Distinctions

The Sound Of Weeping And Crying Will Be No More—65:17-19

As a substantiation for all that has gone on from Isaiah 56:1 up to Isaiah 65:17, this verse begins with "For behold." The NIV has suppressed the translation of the word "For," but this text wants to answer the question: Why "maintain justice and do what is right?" Therefore, to answer this question, this passage will show how mortals are able to fully live out the righteousness of God. There was only one way to do that: if God intervenes and remakes both us and our world as it was before the Fall of Adam and Eve. His divine work is what makes it possible. God must do his work of recreation similarly to his original creation to remove the ruin of our sin.

God can remake this world, for he alone made the whole creation originally by his speaking it into existence the first time when he created the universe. Accordingly, mortals should maintain justice and practice righteousness in anticipation of the time when the power of God will be manifested once again in all its fullness as he renews the heaven and the earth. Just as the language of Isaiah 40-48 used similar ideas when it promised that God would do a "new thing" as he delivered Israel from Babylon, so God would bring a "new thing" into being as he brought forth "a new heaven and new earth," just as he had dealt with sin that had previously so infected and dominated the earth and the heavens after Adam and Eve had sinned.

This promise of God to renew the universe was "in keeping with his [old] promise" (2 Pet 3:13). The former universe would "disappear with a roar" as it was destroyed by fire, thereby laying everything in it exposed and bare (2 Pet 3:10).

"The former things will not be remembered, nor will they come to mind" (Isa 65:17c-d), as God had announced his word to the prophet Isaiah. In its place, God would "create Jerusalem to be a delight and its people a joy" (18c-d). No longer would weeping and crying be heard (19c-d), for God would wipe away both the effects and the memory of sin and its stains (Rev 21:4).

Such news was unprecedented, for all too long sin had left in its trail shame and sorrow. This would all be exchanged for joy and delight, because of what God would create in his renewal of the heavens and the earth. So significant is this note of rejoicing and gladness that it is repeated three times in verses 18–19, therefore we must make special note of it.

God would adopt Jerusalem for himself. That is why Revelation 21:1 depicts a new Jerusalem coming down out of heaven. It would be from this city of Jerusalem that the teaching by the Lord Jesus himself would go forth as the nations of the world would gather annually in Jerusalem to be instructed and to worship the Lord and receive his teaching from his lips (Isa 2:1-4). The fact that it came down from heaven was to indicate that God would be the source of the nature and culture of this renewed city.

Some biblical texts call for the perpetuity of the earth, for example, Psalm 104:5, which reads: "He set the earth on its foundations; it can never be moved." Psalm 148:6 also teaches: "He set [the sun, moon, stars, and the heavens] in place forever and forever; he gave a decree that will never pass away." It is for reasons similar to these texts that the better reading in 2 Peter 3:10 should be to say that the heavens and the earth "will be laid bare," but not that they "will be [totally] destroyed."

The Lives Of Men And Women Will No Longer Be Cut Short — 65:20-24

These verses are generally regarded as some of the most difficult to interpret. They should not be read as a contradiction to Isaiah 25:6-9; 26:18-19, for the general sense is clear, even if the precise nuances of each word may not be understood in their entirety. The point is that in the future one may disregard any thoughts of an untimely death.

It may well be that the "Jerusalem" of verses 17-19 is altogether different from the "Jerusalem" of verses 20-24. If that assumption (an unusual assumption to be sure) is true, then this later Jerusalem is the Jerusalem of the millennial kingdom, which exists one thousand years before the new heavens and new earth appear. The reason we take this view is that when the universe is renewed in its eternity, sin, sorrow, and death will no longer appear, while all of these briefly appear in the millennial kingdom. Death, sin, and sorrow do appear in the millennial kingdom, for Satan is released for a short period at the end of the thousand years before he is once and for all cast into the Lake of Fire to abide there forever. Yet during the millennium, death is so rare that it can be said that "Never will there be an infant who lives only a few days" (20a-b). Moreover, "an old man who does not live out his years, [or]...who dies a hundred will be thought a mere youth; [or] he who fails to reach a hundred will be considered accursed" (20c-g). This seems to indicate that Isaiah is teaching that death during this time will be extremely rare and exceptional. Even the presence of one who might be "accursed" raises the question as to whether that one has not been cursed for a good reason to face the natural results of his sin.

But none of this death occurs during the time of the renewed universe in the eternal state. On the other hand, one wonders why God would even allow this, even this small amount of evil to be present when he, the Lord, is present. One reason may be that with the Devil out of the way and in prison for most of the thousand years, it will show what a lame excuse some have given to our Lord for their sinning in the present era. All too frequently we hear, "I sinned because the Devil made me do it." But that excuse will be shown for what it is when Satan is bound up in prison during those years. Instead, so strong will the call for obedience to divine things be evidenced that the old excuses will plainly be passé.

The joy of life will consist of building houses and living in them; planting vineyards and eating the fruit that comes from them (21–22b). This is what had been promised as long ago as the times under the laws of Moses in Deuteronomy 28:1–14.

So enduring and secure will the people of God be in those days that they will last as "the days of a tree" (22c). The staples of life, then, will be long life and joyful appreciation for life and all it has to offer.

Even more promising is the fact that no labor or toil will be regarded as "in vain" (23a). With all frustration and futility removed from the earth, all of living will at once be a joy and a source of great satisfaction. Children born during the millennium (if we are right in regarding this section as speaking of those thousand years, instead of the eternal state) will not be "doomed to misfortune" (23b), for they too will be blessed by the Lord (23c).

One more gift is added from God: God will answer our prayers before we call upon him, or even while we are still speaking (24). No longer will sin block access to our Lord, for he will promptly respond to all our requests that are made to him.

The Lives Of Animals Will Be Changed – 65:25

Isaiah had already raised this topic in 11:6-9. In the Messianic age, the effects of God's new creation work would be seen in the way that the carnivorous animals, such as the lion and the wolf, would no longer bother such domesticated animals as lambs (25a). All these animals would now be able to feed together. What is more, the lion would also need to have some type of gastronomical change, for it too would eat straw just like an ox (25b).

The surprising part of this text is that "dust will be the serpent's food" (25c). Does this text allude to Genesis 3:14, where in the Garden of Eden the Serpent was cursed and wrecked by sin so that his defeat was put in terms of being fed with dirt, or is it placed here just as we say metaphorically in an athletic contest, "Let the opponents bite the dust"? There is no doubt that "the Serpent" was condemned to crawl on his belly and to bite the dust in defeat, just as we today use a similar expression to indicate the defeat of our opponents in athletic contests!

The Heavens And The Earth Will Endure Forever – 66:22-24

Once again, the prophet reverts to the topic of Isaiah 65:17-25, where he spoke of "the New Heavens and the New Earth." Even though Israel will suffer a diaspora (i.e., a scattering) among the nations of the world (66:18-19), God will gather all the nations to see what he will do for them by his divine glory (18). But God will bring both Israel and "[their] brothers" forth "from all the nations to [his] holy mountain in Jerusalem" (20a). Even more astounding is the fact that God would select some of these Gentile nations to be "priests and Levites" in his kingdom (21). This must have shocked some of Israel's theological and liturgical instincts for sure! "All mankind" (23) will come up to Jerusalem month after month and Sabbath after Sabbath (Zech 14:16–21) to worship the Lord. The redeemed of the Lord will encompass men and women from every race, tribe, and language!

God will also make the renewed heavens and earth to "endure" before him just as he will make the name of those who believe in him as well as their descendants "endure" (22). Therefore, the destiny of the remnant of Israel who believed will be the grounds not only for their sure return to the land of Israel; it will also be the grounds for the blessings that will come to the Gentiles as well.

This passage ends with the horrific destiny of the ungodly. The godly "will go out and look upon the dead bodies of those who rebelled against [God]." This may seem to be somewhat crude and offensive, but recall how long the redeemed have had to watch goodness, justice, truth, and righteousness be handed defeat after defeat in their past lifetimes on earth! This examining what God had done was not to gloat over the destruction of the wicked, but it was instead to see that both sides of the promise-plan of God were true. God's threats are just as true and secure as his promises of blessing.

The picture of the end of the wicked is the basis for the most frequently cited description of hell most often given by Jesus during his time on this earth in the Gospels. The imagery came from the "Valley of Hinnom," later known as *Ge Hinnom* or "Gehenna." This was the site just outside of Jerusalem, where the Israelites unmercifully offered as a sacrifice their firstborn to gods such as Molech, to be burnt alive as sacrifices to these idols. However, so despicable was this practice, as it was later realized, that this same spot became the city dump, a place where "the worm did not die [as it fed on the garbage in the dump]; nor was the fire quenched [as the wind would frequently stir up the smoldering embers back into full flame]" (24). Thus, the God-rejecting group will be subject to everlasting torment throughout all eternity as a contrast to the saints fulfilling God's purpose and living righteously.

Conclusions

1. As history concludes with the thousand-year rule and reign of Christ on this earth (the millennium), eternity will commence as God reworks the renewed heavens and renewed earth.

2. Even though evil may raise its ugly head briefly during the millennium, so rare will be death, sorrow, and sin that a person who dies at age one hundred will seem like a young child who dies before his time.

3. In the eternal state, people will be able to enjoy the homes they have built along with the fruit of the vineyards they also have planted.

4. The Renewed Heavens and the Renewed Earth will not fade away, but they will endure forever along with Israel and all the Gentiles who have also believed on the Name of the Lord.

CHAPTER SIX

WHERE IS THE KINGDOM OF GOD IN THE SOCIAL GOSPEL?

by David Mappes, PhD

Dr. Ed Hindson was a man who committed himself to glorifying and serving our Lord Jesus Christ through careful exegesis of the Scriptures, consistent quality theological reflection, and a controlled method of contextualization. He submitted himself and his pursuits to working underneath the Scriptures through the ministry of the Spirit—not above the Scriptures, not apart from the Scripture, nor even beside the Scriptures. He practiced a consistent hermeneutical historical-grammatical-literal method of interpretation to discern the intention of the human author by examining what the author affirmed in the historical context of his writings. And then once he discerned the meaning of Scripture, he did not alter its meaning in contextualization for the sake of relevancy or peer approval. I am indebted to Ed for his scholarship, his godly treatment of others, and how he exemplified the true meaning of a Christian scholar.

Introduction[203]

The social gospel movement of the eighteenth and nineteenth centuries eradicated any biblical notion of the Kingdom of God motif in Scripture through their liberal-rationalized hermeneutic and reframed eschatology to exclude any future catastrophic intervention in human affairs by God. Rather, many viewed the Kingdom of God only in an ethical, progressive sense of human-centeredness. Leading proponents of the social gospel also used such terms as *humility*, *tolerance*, and *charity* as a rhetorical whip to solicit and frame the views of others. There is no biblical view of the Kingdom of God in the social gospel.

The modernist-fundamentalist debate of the latter nineteenth and early twentieth century surfaces divergent approaches to doctrine, theology, theological method, contextualization, and notably views of eschatology; the Kingdom of God motif in Scripture was reduced to human-centeredness and measured by human benevolence. The modernist portrayed the Kingdom of God as only ethical in nature, here and now in history, and denied any future catastrophic intervention in human affairs by God as portrayed by Scripture. This reinterpretation of eschatology became an all-pervading, thoroughgoing, and controlling motif. Hence the issue of eschatology became a hotbed of discussion within the liberal-conservative controversy. This protracted debate also illustrates how each group portrayed the virtues of humility, tolerance,

---

[203] All material copyright to Dr. David Mappes, PhD (2024, all rights reserved). Partially adapted from "Overview and Analysis of the Modernist-Fundamentalist Debate and their View of Humility, Tolerance and Charity in their Theological Method and Contextualization," presented to the Southeastern Evangelical Theological Society Annual meeting at the Columbia International University, 7435 Monticello Road, Columbia, SC 29203 on February 24, 2023.

and charity in advancing their theological positions.[204]

Notably, most modernists employed a classic liberal-rationalized hermeneutic that viewed the Old and New Testament as written in supernatural imagery which the modernists summarily rejected. They argued that this New Testament first-century supernatural imagery was mythological in nature (myth understood as stories embedded in culture) and needed to be demythologized for contextualization to occur in the modern area. In general, their demythologization rejected the miraculous events in Scripture including futurism. Particularly, they redefined eschatology by excluding the miraculous and redefined the Kingdom of God as referring to human, non-supernatural benevolent deeds. For the modernist, the phrase Kingdom of God became a catchall phrase characterized by humankind's benevolence. The fundamentalists emphasized literal-contextual interpretation and defended the Scriptural view of the second return of Christ. The modernists used such virtues as humility, tolerance, and charity to promote their human-centered view of the Kingdom of God and contextualization while the fundamentalists used humility, tolerance, and charity in a far different manner.

By the 1920s the liberal-fundamentalist conflict had reached a fever pitch, and the social gospel was well entrenched in the religious fabric of America. Both groups had coalesced into well-supported movements. Many schools and denominations were controlled by modernists (also known as liberals) during this time. The phrase *social gospel* first appeared in the late 1870s and gained popularity with many of the social reformers of the day. Promoters of the social gospel sought to provide ethical and benevolent solutions to the horrible social abuses brought about

---

204 See David Mappes, "Two Sermons of Major Impact" in, *Inspire: The Cedarville University Alumni Magazine* (Winter 2005), 17; "Humility and Tolerance: Exploring their Biblical, Theological, and Cultural Expression" presented by David Mappes at the Faculty Forum of Baptist Bible Seminary, Clarks Summit, PA, October 25, 2010, and "The Relationship of Theological Method and Cultural Engagement: A Biblical and Theological Overview of Dating," presented by David Mappes at the Faculty Forum of Baptist Bible Seminary, Clarks Summit PA., November 14, 2014.

by the Civil War and the Industrial Revolution. Some within this movement also sought to create a kind of *economic social reform gospel* directed towards economic inequities hence they promoted governmental and social reform along with other institutional and corporate reform.

The social gospel movement was not monolithic and did not have theological boundaries or parameters, so a concise definition is difficult. However, the movement emphasized the immanence of God, an overly optimistic view of humanity, depreciated (or denied) individual sin, the need for personal salvation, and prioritized General Revelation asserting that God reveals Himself through history over and against Special Revelation

In April of 1907, Walter Rauschenbusch (1864-1917) published one of the most influential books of that time to promote the social gospel entitled, *Christianity and the Social Crisis*. Later in 1917, Rauschenbusch sought to further solidify the social gospel movement by publishing *A Theology of the Social Gospel*. Importantly, Rauschenbusch was deeply influenced by the liberal views of Schleiermacher (1768-1834), Immanuel Kant (1724-1804), Albrecht Ritschl (1882-1889), and Horace Bushnell (1802-1876). Each of these aforementioned men who influenced Rauschenbusch viewed the Kingdom of God as a human-centered progressive event that was not brought about through any type of cataclysmic miraculous event such as the second return of Christ.

Rauschenbusch embedded and popularized views of German higher criticism and theological liberalism from these scholars amongst the social reformers of his day. Rauschenbusch is generally viewed as the father, chief founder, or chief exponent of the social gospel movement.

Views of Contextualization and the Essence of Christianity

The essential issue that fueled the modernist-fundamentalist debate during this time entailed the nature and role of doctrine with respect to contextualizing Christianity into a new, modern scientific era. Contextualization here refers to consciously communicating and embedding the biblical message into a culture (or sub-culture) so that the meaning of the message can be properly understood by that culture.

Historical fundamentalists argued that Christian orthodoxy entailed a non-reducible doctrinal core or center, hence there were fundamental, essential, primitive doctrines that could not be altered nor further reduced. If these core doctrines were altered, then Christianity would cease to be Christian. Notably, the term "fundamentalist" most likely came from or at least was popularized by ninety essays referred to as "The Fundamentals: A Testimony to the Truth." These twelve paperback volumes were published between 1910-15 and distributed free of charge. Lyman Stewart and his brother Milton endowed $300,000 for the publication and distribution of these paperback volumes. In today's vernacular, the fundamentalists believed part of being *missional* and *promoting the mission of the church* entailed preserving orthodox doctrine and truth and not just engaging and connecting to meet the social challenges of the day.

These essays served as a defense of historical, classic Christianity against liberalism and were written by academic and well-trained ministry leaders such as B. B. Warfield, W. H. Griffith Thomas, H. C. G. Moule, A. T. Pierson, C. R. Erdman, J. Orr, A. C. Gaebelein, and many others. The fundamentalists sought to defend five fundamentals of the Faith that were being challenged: the miracles of Christ, the virgin birth, the substitutionary atonement of Christ, the bodily resurrection and return of

Christ, and the inspiration of Scripture.[205] These ninety essays not only addressed the "Fundamentals of the Faith"[206] but also addressed related topics that the modernists were denying such as the historical authenticity of Scripture, literary unity and authorship of individual books in the Bible, and the uniqueness of the canonical books.

Modernists appealed to supposed new knowledge obtained through general revelation such as scientific, literary, and archeological discoveries as a lens to reinterpret and redefine the core doctrines of Christianity; this new knowledge provided the nexus for contextualization. Authors of Scripture were viewed as men having deep human insight and commitment to humanity albeit conditioned by the culture of their day. This approach to Scripture reduced Christianity to an ethical system to combat social injustices hence the phrase, social gospel.

The modernists argued for a full contextualization of Christianity into the modern culture without the need for any core, historical, non-provisional verbal doctrines that defined Christianity. The modernists insisted that knowledge through science was the final arbiter and lens to interpret and demythologize Scripture. The modernist viewed truth as constantly changing with each new generation and truth in each generation was measured by love. Je-

---

205 While other lists of fundamentals existed, those lists generally included the five fundamentals included in "The Fundamentals: A Testimony to the Truth."

206 The Scripture often identifies a basic framework of doctrinal truths and apostolic traditions referred to as "the faith" which the fundamentalists sought to preserve. The use of an article such as "the" has the intrinsic ability to identify and definitize or distinguish something as unique. When a word such as "faith" is made definite by the article "the" a writer often is emphasizing a body of objective and knowable truth (e.g., Acts 6:7; Gal 1:23; 3:23-25; Jude 3). This framework entails both doctrinal orthodoxy (correct belief) and orthopraxy (upright and godly biblical conduct). Other terms are also used in the New Testament. The term traditions (2 Thess. 2:15) focuses on truth handed down from the New Testament apostles or apostolic delegates to the churches. Sound doctrine denotes a fixed body of doctrine—a fixed, orthodox confession of faith that believers receive and are responsible to preserve against heresy. Paul reminds Timothy to guard the "sound words" (2 Tim. 1:13, 14) and "sound doctrine" (2 Tim. 4:3), which he refers to as "the truth" in 2 Timothy 4:4. Jude reminds his readers to contend for "the Faith." Adapted from David Mappes, "The Nobility and Knowability of Truth: Part 1," in *The Journal of Ministry and Theology* 12 (Spring 2009): 64-105; David Mappes, "What is Faith in Luke 18:1-8" *BibSac* (July-September 2010), 292-306, and David Mappes, "Prioritizing and Revising Articles of Faith," *The Baptist Bulletin* (July/August 2016), 16-22.

sus was viewed *not as the incarnated perfect Son of God who added humanity to Himself to save humanity from their sins. Rather, Jesus was viewed more as the incarnation of the ultimate human spirit and good teacher who should be imitated.*

The Use of Humility, Charity, and Tolerance and Integration of Truth Claims

One major contention in this conflict entailed how truth claims from General Revelation were validated and integrated with Special Revelation. The earlier Fundamentalists insisted that Scripture was the final arbiter and they repeatedly appealed to the objective teaching of Scripture regarding its own nature of inspiration to validate their truth claims. They were not opposed to integrating truth from General Revelation nor were they opposed to dialogue and discussion. However, they insisted that discussion and dialog always start and end with the pursuit of first using Scripture when the Scripture intersects with other competing truth claims.

When the Princetonians and early Fundamentalists spoke of objective knowledge of truth and reality, they did not refer to knowing truth and reality that was completely objectively neutral apart from bias of any kind. Rather they spoke of a knowledge that did not originate within themselves but a knowledge that was revealed by God. They spoke of knowledge "outside of our minds, the reality that is independent of our preferences and desires... the Princetonians [and fundamentalists] affirm that we can have knowledge of objective reality...they do not necessarily affirm that we know this reality objectively."[207] Paul Helm concurs as he writes, "The recognition that the revealed mysteries are truth

---

207 Paul Kjoss Helseth, *Right Reason and the Princeton Mind: An Unorthodox Proposal* (Puritan & Reformed), 2010, ch. 1 n. 39. This book is a scholarly refutation that Princetonians were committed rationalists and provides extensive interaction with the conservative and post-conservative debate regarding the nature of objectivity and truth.

has a long pedigree in Christian theology [and this] objectivity of knowledge may have been a part of the Enlightenment *quest*, but it is most certainly not an Enlightenment *invention*) [and this] knowledge is common to the disciples [of Christ]."[208]

While some Fundamentalists retreated from the culture and created a kind of anti-intellectualism, many leading fundamental scholars of the day such as Macartney, Machen, Gaebelein, and others argued for active engagement with the culture. They sought to engage this new modern knowledge through the lens of Scripture though they did so with a hermeneutical literary certainty of the historical doctrines of Christianity.

The liberals often used the terms *humility, charity, unity, and tolerance* to support their project of contextualizing Christianity into the modern culture. These terms were used like a rhetorical whip to shape the views of others and to disparage the fundamentalists. Dillenberger and Welsh assert that central to the liberal project of modernization was the "spirit of open-mindedness, of tolerance and humility, of devotion of truth wherever it might be found [and] theological differences were insignificant [and they gave great] respect for science and the scientific method [while espousing] skepticism as to the possibility of achieving certain knowledge of ultimate reality."[209] They insisted that the fundamentalists accept their re-interpretation of truth and accept their open, tolerant methodology of contextualization; when the fundamentalists refused, they were accused of being arrogant, bigoted, intolerant, non-loving people who worshipped the Bible and not the God of the Bible.

In 1924 the Presbyterian Church in the United States of America (PCUSA) sought to galvanize unity among its members through the much-debated Auburn Affirmation. The Auburn Af-

---

208 Paul Helm, "No Easy Task," in *Reforming or Conforming: Post-Conservative Evangelicals and the Emerging Church*, ed. Gary L. W. Johnson and Ronald N. Nash (Wheaton, IL: Crossway Books, 2008), 108.
209 John Dillenberger and Claude Welch, *Protestant Christianity* (New York: Scribner's, 1954), 211-16.

firmation sought to reverse the Presbyterian General Assembly declaration that every Presbyterian ordination candidate affirm the five fundamentals of the faith. The Auburn Affirmation specifically denied the inerrancy of Scripture and denied any call for fundamental doctrinal absolutes. Rather, the declaration called for unity and prompted Spirit-led interpretations rather than any stated theological dogma. The document further alleged that "to believe such [fundamental] doctrines, or to obey such commandments out of conscience, is to betray true liberty of conscience [and] the requiring of an implicit faith, and an absolute and blind obedience, is to destroy liberty of conscience, and reason also." (Conf. XX, ii).[210] Princeton Theological Seminary was reorganized to reflect the spirit of the Auburn Affirmation. This reorganization eventually led the noted New Testament Scholar John Gresham Machen (1881–1937) and several of his seminary teaching colleagues to found Westminster Theological Seminary in 1929. Ultimately the conservatives formed the Orthodox Presbyterian Church in 1936.

The fundamentalists also used the terms *tolerance, unity, humility, and charity* though they used these terms very differently. As the fundamentalists evaluated and integrated truth assertions from General Revelation, they sought to evaluate all these new claims through the lens of Scripture. While core doctrines were held at a non-provisional level of contextual literary certainty (not open to re-interpretation), the fundamentalists did not hold all doctrines at this non-provisional level. They based their literary certainty of core doctrines (often referred to as "the Faith") upon the contextual and literary evidence in Scripture and argued that the contextual and literary evidence was adequate to remove interpretative justifiable doubt. *The fundamentalists spoke of exercising humility, charity, tolerance, etc. towards others, especially in discussing*

---

[210] https://www.pcahistory.org/documents/auburntext.html, accessed, March 5, 2024.

non-essential doctrines of Christianity. Their use of humility, charity, and tolerance then was governed by the amount of Scriptural evidence on a matter. They generally called for humility, charity, and tolerance in discerning the meaning of Scripture when Scripture alone was the sole interpretive context or when addressing non-essential doctrinal issues.

Perhaps the two most famous and insightful sermons of the fundamentalist-liberal controversies were entitled, "Shall the Fundamentalist Win?" preached in May of 1922 by Harry Emerson Fosdick (a noted liberal spokesman and pastor raised in a Bible-believing home, 1878-1969)[211] and the respondent "Shall Unbelief Win?" by Clarence E. Macartney (1879-1957)[212] who was an ordained, conservative Presbyterian Minister.

During this period many newspapers published parts of famous sermons, so these sermons were widely read. A layman named Ivy Lee published "Shall the Fundamentalist Win?" under a different title, "The New Knowledge and the Christin Faith" in both *The Christian Century* and *The Christian Work* and he sent 130,000 copies of the sermon to ministers and friends throughout the nation. There was some earlier debate about whether Fosdick gave permission for this sermon to be initially published. Apparently, later in life, Fosdick did admit he permitted the publication. There is also debate and conjecture about where Ivy Lee obtained the money to reprint and distribute the sermon. Some scholars believe that John D. Rockefeller, Jr. provided the funds.

Fosdick had hoped to build a bridge between liberal churches and conservative churches through his sermon. He continually cited discoveries in science and literature as products of modern-

---

211 Fosdick graduated from Colgate College in Hampton New York (1900) and Union Theological Seminary in New York (1904) and had over 40 publications; his brother Raymond Fosdick was a key administrator of philanthropy for John D Rockefeller.

212 Macartney attended several colleges and eventually graduated from the University of Wisconsin in Madison, Wisconsin (1901). After briefly attending Harvard and Yale, he graduated from Princeton Theological Seminary (1905) and had over 40 publications.

ism, which he argued should be used as a lens to reinterpret Scripture so the church could be effective and relevant in the modern anti-supernatural era.[213]

Fosdick and other modernists were convinced the church's historic and certain position on essential verbal doctrinal matters of truth was just a matter of first-century contextualization. He argued that the authors of Scripture reflected the views of supernaturalism of their period so the first-century church could be relevant. As stated earlier, he and other modernists asserted doctrines in Scripture such as the virgin birth, the substitutionary atonement, the return of Christ and at times the resurrection of Christ were just products of first-century contextualization for a supernatural era and needed to be reinterpreted in contextualization.

According to Fosdick and other modernists, the New Testament authors' insights were obscured and veiled behind ancient mythological and cultural baggage. Interpretation and transference into the modern age required demythologization since the modern age denied much of the supernatural events described in biblical accounts. Fosdick argued that insights and knowledge from his modern age must be used to re-interpret Scripture and separate the myth from the true insights that Scripture's authors possessed. Fosdick's sermon reveals he, like other modernists, denied that any fundamental or primitive doctrinal truth existed at a textual, verbal, indisputable, non-provisional level.

Fosdick's major hermeneutical presumption centered on *intelligibility* (defined by modernism's anti-supernaturalism hence his need to demythologize) and *practicality* (hence his view social gospel). He writes, "Two questions today face every proposition and custom of religion: first, is it intelligently defensible; second, does it contribute to man's abundant life?"[214]

---

213 See David Mappes, "Two Sermons of Major Impact" in *Inspire: The Cedarville University Alumni Magazine* (Winter 2005), 17.
214 Harry Emerson Fosdick, *Adventurous Religion: And Other Essays* (New York: Harper & Brothers, 1926), 18.

Fosdick portrayed himself and other moderates as open-minded, tolerant, intellectual inquirers, who promoted true Christian fellowship as he and his followers contextualized the gospel into the modern culture. As Fosdick preached this sermon, he equated the historical foundational doctrines advocated by the fundamentalists as *opinions* and removed any doctrinal centering of Christianity:

> It is interesting to note where the Fundamentalists are driving in their stakes to mark out the deadline of doctrine around the church, across which no one is to pass except on terms of agreement. They insist that we must all believe in the historicity of certain special miracles, preeminently the virgin birth of our Lord; that we must believe in a special theory of inspiration...that we must believe in a special theory of the Atonement—that the blood of our Lord, shed in a substitutionary death, placates an alienated Deity and makes possible welcome for the returning sinner; and that we must believe in the second coming of our Lord.... If a man is a genuine liberal, his primary protest is not against holding these opinions, although he may well protest against their being considered the fundamentals of Christianity.... The question is—Has anybody a right to deny the Christian name to those who differ with him on such points and to shut against them the doors of the Christian fellowship?[215]

Macartney responded to Fosdick in a sermon of his own, though he argued from the context of Scripture. He believed that the Scripture possessed the necessary clarity and a type of self-witness of its own nature to adjudicate and counter these new truth

---

[215] Harry Emerson Fosdick, "Shall the Fundamentalists Win?" *Sermons in American History: Select Issues in the American Pulpit 1630–1976*, ed. Dewitte Holland (Nashville: Abingdon Press, 1971), 340-41.

assertions from modernism. His sermon reveals a form of doctrinal taxonomy and theological stratification entailing a distinction between first order objective doctrinal truths and secondary theological synthesis—he distinguished the essential vs. the non-essential doctrines of Christianity based upon the literary, contextual evidence in Scripture and not upon discoveries through General Revelation.[216]

His sermon also reveals modernists' allegations against conservatives. Macartney writes, "The greatest need of the church to-day is a *few men of ability and faith* [emphasis mine] who are not afraid of being called 'bigots,' 'narrow,' 'mediaeval' in their religious thought."[217] When referring to "a few men of ability," Macartney is calling for biblically trained individuals to contend for "the Faith" using their biblical expertise, and when referring to "a few men of faith" he is referring to those who not only possess biblical literacy but also who "by faith" are embracing biblical truth for which they contend. Macartney is calling for fundamentalists to "Contend for the Faith" without being contentious.

When referring to the debate between the modernists and fundamentalists, Macartney dissuades the modernists' call for unity and humility at the expense of truth and doctrine:

> Whatever the Church is to do or not to do [according to the modernists], it is not to defend the faith, it is not to point out the errors and inconsistencies of those who stand as the interpreters of Christianity. This amazing agreement would have struck the Christian believer of almost any age in Church history, save our own, as a very extraordinary one...one of the greatest contributions that

---

216 See David Mappes, "How to Think about and Practice Theology," *The Journal of Ministry and Theology* (Spring 2014), 65-85 for further discussion of doctrinal taxonomy and theological stratification.

217 Clarence E Macartney, "Shall Unbelief Win?" *Sermons in American History: Select Issues in the American Pulpit 1630-1976*, ed. Dewitte Holland (Nashville: Abingdon Press, 1971), 350.

a man can make to the success of the Gospel is to contend earnestly and intelligently and in a Christian spirit, but nevertheless, CONTEND, for the faith.[218]

Macartney's sermon reveals that he, like other historical fundamentalists, believed that the Scripture provided a kind of objective literary criteria which both defined and confined Christianity by Scriptural, doctrinal absolutes. He concludes his sermon by stating that Fosdick's modernism "is slowly secularizing the Church, and if permitted to go unchecked and unchallenged, will ere long produce in our churches a new kind of Christianity, a Christianity of opinions and principles and good purposes, but Christianity without worship, without God, and without Jesus Christ."[219]

Machen expressed similar concerns in 1925 in his book, *What is Faith* when discussing the modernists' denial that the New Testament provided objective, real truth. He writes,

> It makes very little difference how much or how little of the creeds of the Church the Modernist preacher affirms, or how much or how little of the Biblical teaching from which the creeds are derived. He might affirm every jot and tittle of the Westminster Confession, for example, and yet be separated by a great gulf from the Reformed Faith. It is not that part is denied and the rest affirmed; but all is denied, *because all is affirmed merely as useful or symbolic and not as true* [emphasis mine].[220]

In his sermon, Fosdick pled for an *intellectually hospitable, tolerant, liberty-loving church*. However, as he concludes his sermon, he himself appears intolerant and not so hospitable:

---

218 Mccartney, 351.
219 Mccartney, 364.
220 J. Gresham Machen, *What Is Faith?* (1925; reprint, Edinburgh: Banner of Truth, 1991), 34.

I do not even know in this congregation whether anybody has been tempted to be a Fundamentalist. Never in this church have I caught one accent of intolerance. God keep us always so and ever increasing areas of the Christian fellowship; intellectually hospitable, open-minded, liberty-loving, fair, tolerant....[221]

Interestingly, Fosdick believed he needed to decode and demythologize such important doctrines as the atonement, the deity of Christ, the second return of Christ, and other doctrines. However, he did not feel the need to decode or demythologize the notions of humility or tolerance or love but rather appealed directly to Scripture to promote his own views. Additionally, he rarely if ever differentiates how he knew what portions of Scripture needed to be demythologized and what portions did not.

Professor Charles R. Erdman (1866–1960), who taught at Princeton Theological Seminary, illustrates how some early fundamentalists differentiated first order (or fundamental) doctrines from other less clear doctrines which required more theological syntheses. His article in 1915 entitled "The Coming of Christ" demonstrates the importance of church history and theological taxonomy in their theological method. Most importantly, he allows the full canon of Scripture to validate the basis for his interpretative certainty. He addresses the second coming of Christ as an essential or fundamental doctrine marked by historical creeds, hymns, and most importantly, *clearness, emphasis, and prominence in the Scripture*. Erdman's comments regarding the *clearness, emphasis, and prominence of the Scripture* help illustrate the historical fundamentalists' hermeneutical process and theological method. Erdman writes:

---

[221] Fosdick, "Shall the Fundamentalists Win?," 348.

The return of Christ is a *fundamental doctrine* of the Christian faith. It is embodied in hymns of hope; it forms the climax of the creeds; it is the sublime motive for evangelistic and missionary activity; and daily it is voiced in the inspired prayer: "Even so: Come, Lord Jesus." It is peculiarly a *Scriptural doctrine*. It is not, on the one hand, a dream of ignorant fanatics, nor, on the other, a creation of speculative theologians; but it is a truth divinely revealed, and recorded in the Bible with marked *clearness, emphasis and prominence* [emphasis mine]. Like the other great truths of revelation, it is a *controverted doctrine*. The essential fact is held universally by all who admit the authority of Scripture; but as to certain incidental, although important, elements of the teaching, there is difference of opinion among even the most careful and reverent students. Any consideration of the theme demands, therefore, *modesty, humility, and abundant charity* [emphasis mine].[222]

Erdman differentiates between the doctrinal, objective fact of the second coming of Christ as held by all who admit the authority of the Scripture while calling for *modesty, humility, and abundant charity* in relation to the incidental albeit important elements surrounding the second coming of Christ. This doctrinal taxonomy allowed Presbyterian fundamentalists, Baptist fundamentalists, Anglican fundamentalists, and non-denominational fundamentalists to work together in promoting the fundamentals of the gospel truth. As he concludes his booklet and discusses these incidental events surrounding the coming of Christ, he writes:

> This is therefore a time, not for unkindly criticism of fellow Christians, but for friendly conference; not for disputing over divergent views, but for united action; not for dog-

---

[222] Charles R. Erdman, "The Coming of Christ," rev. and ed. Gerald B Stanton in *The Fundamentals for Today*, ed. Charles L. Feinberg (Grand Rapids MI, 1958), 637.

matic assertion of prophetic programs, but for the humble acknowledgment that "we know in part...."[223]

The call for *modesty, humility, and abundant charity* by the historical fundamentalists was governed by the amount of Scriptural testimony given to a particular doctrinal truth. The greater amount of Scriptural testimony described as *clearness, emphasis, and prominence in the Scripture*, the greater their commitment to the Scriptural teaching and to their contending for that truth. They allowed the Scriptural evidence to adjudicate their sense of humility and modesty in theological constructs and theological advocacy.

Howard Crosby's (1826-1891) article, entitled "Preach the Word," reveals a fascinating allegation by the modernists against the fundamentalists who were using Scripture as a lens to critique all forms of knowledge. The modernists alleged the fundamentalists were Bibliolaters- asserting that fundamentalists worshipped the Bible and not the God of the Bible. Interestingly that same term is used today by some post-conservatives against conservative evangelicals.[224] Crosby's comments here reveal how the early fundamentalists allowed God's self-disclosure of Himself in Special Revelation (i.e., the Scripture) to serve as the final authority. He writes:

---

223 Erdman, 645.

224 For articles addressing post-conservative views of truth and related issues see the following by David Mappes: "A New Kind of Christian: A Review" in *BibSac* 161 (July–September, 2004): 289-303; "The Nobility and Knowability of Truth: Part 1," in *The Journal of Ministry and Theology* 12 (Spring 2009): 64-105 and "The Nobility and Knowability of Truth: Part 2," in *The Journal of Ministry and Theology* 13 (Fall 2009): 1-22; "Current Trends in Hermeneutics and Theology: Certainty and Simplicity," *Paraklesis* (Summer 2010), 1, 6; "What is Faith in Luke 18:1-8" *BibSac* (July–September 2010), 292-306; "*Love Wins* by Rob Bell: A Biblical and Theological Critique," *The Journal of Ministry and Theology* (Spring 2012) 87-121; "Prioritizing and Revising Articles of Faith," *The Baptist Bulletin* (July/ August 2016), 16-22; "Literal Interpretation and Theological Method: What Is It and How to Do It?" *Ariel Ministries*, December 2017, 18-23; "A Biblical and Theological Critique of Stanley's Irresistible: Reclaiming the New that Jesus Unleashed from the World" in *The Journal of Ministry and Theology* (Winter 2019), 8-22; Ἐν ἀρχῇ "What Should Christian do with Andy Stanley's Irresistible?" interview with Dr. David Mappes in *The Journal of Ministry and Theology* (Winter 2019), 3-7.

> It is a favorite charge of the advocates of this looseness [modernism] that we are worshipping a Book. 'Bibliolatry' is the formidable word that they cast at us; But we worship no book. We do worship God who sent the Book, and it is no true worship of God that slights the Book which He gives. If we honor God, we shall honor the Word He has sent..."[225]

One example of integration between General and Special Revelation occurs in an article written in 1910 by A. W. Pitzer. In his brief article entitled "The Wisdom of the World," he posits there is no real conflict between Christianity and science. He argues for an integrated approach to truth from general and special revelation while allowing the Scripture to serve as the final arbiter of the integrated whole:

> The Christian does not look with dismay upon these researches into Nature, these discoveries of Science; on the contrary, he hails with joy each new discovery as affording additional evidence of the wisdom, power, and goodness of God. Full well does he know that the facts written on the rock-leaves beneath, the star depths above, and the pages of Inspiration, when properly understood and interpreted, will be found to be in exact and perfect accord, showing forth the glory of the Infinite Writer of them all. There is no controversy between the man of faith and the man of wisdom, provided each one acts in his proper sphere. There is not, and never has been, any real conflict between Religion and Science. There may be conflicts between interpretations of Scripture and interpretations of the facts of Nature; but what God has written in His Word never conflicts with what God has written in His creation.... We

---

[225] Howard Crosby's "Preach the Word," *The Fundamentals for Today*, 419-20.

have the right to demand of the Wisdom of this World by what authority it asserts that there is nothing above and apart from Nature, nothing in all the boundless universe except matter and force. Why shall we give up all that man holds dear at the bidding of the Wisdom of this World whose highest, and best, and latest revelation is "a grave without a resurrection, and a universe without a God."[226]

James Orr's article, "Science and Christian Faith" advocates an integration of special and general revelation through careful examination of both spheres of truth. He advocates looking for inconsistencies either in interpretations of Scripture or inconsistencies in scientific conclusions when apparent disagreement surfaces; he writes, "this alleged conflict of Christianity with science should be carefully probed, and that it should be seen where exactly the truth lies..."[227] Orr later asserts that "mistakes are often made on both sides—on the side of science in affirming contrariety of the Bible with scientific results where none really exists...[and] on the side of believers in demanding that the Bible be taken as a text-book of the newest scientific discoveries, and trying by forced methods to read these into them."[228] Pitzer and other historical fundamentalists allowed the authority of Scripture to function as a final arbiter to critique the anti-supernatural assumptions and sentiments the modernists were imposing upon the Scripture while still respecting general revelation.

As the fundamentalist-modernist debate intensified, the fundamentalists and modernists separated. In some cases, the fundamentalists were driven out of the modernist churches and schools while in other cases Fundamentalists actively separated from the

---

226 A. W. Pitzer, "The Wisdom of this World," *The Fundamentals: A Testimony to the Truth*. Vol. IV (The Bible Institute of Los Angeles, CA, 1917), 41-43.

227 *The Fundamentals: A Testimony to the Truth*, Volume IV, Compliments of Two Christian Laymen. Testimony Publishing Company (Chicago, IL, 1910), 93.

228 Orr, "Science and Christian Faith," *The Fundamentals: A Testimony to the Truth*, Volume IV, 97.

modernist churches and schools to start new churches and new schools. Many of the early fundamentalists were biblical scholars who were well trained in logic, history, philosophy, theology, Greek, Hebrew, etc., and could easily debate the modernist scholars. However, later generations of fundamentalist pastors were not as well trained since so many colleges embraced modernism and those colleges were not welcoming to the fundamentalists. Hence the fundamentalist movement began to be overshadowed and eventually dominated by anti-intellectualism including depreciation of higher education, *ad hominem* arguments, strong militant personalities, and a spirit of rancor dominated the movement. In contending for *the Faith*, many became contentious about *the Faith* and matters outside *the Faith*.[229]

Additionally, the later fundamentalists drifted from a balanced taxonomy of doctrine. They began to over-emphasize their systematized theology rather than the biblical doctrines derived from exegesis that initially formed systematized theology. In some cases, their systemized theology was popularized by strong personalities through colloquial, popular phrases lacking quality exegesis. They broadened "The Faith" over which the early fundamentalists separated to include their entire system of theology. A kind of social fundamentalism evolved where the idea of "separation" became the defining mark of the movement rather than doctrinal fidelity over which the historical fundamentalists separated; it was during

---

229 Earlier critics of the fundamentalists sought to portray the modernist-fundamentalist controversy as part of a larger societal urban-rural conflict in America while critics in the 1950s portrayed the early fundamentalists as shallow anti-intellectuals; however, neither of these earlier criticisms are widely held today. Certainly, the Fundamentalist movement did later become shallow and anti-intellectual. Significant works detailing fundamentalist-modernist controversy include the following: David Beale, *In Pursuit of Purity: American Fundamentalism Since 1850* (1986); John Dillenberger and Claude Welch, *Protestant Christianity* (1954); George Dollar, *History of Fundamentalism in America* (1973); J. Falwell, ed. *The Fundamentalist Phenomenon* (1981); J. Gresham Machen, *What Is Faith?* (1925); J. D. Hunter, *American Evangelicalism* (1983); George Marsden, *Reforming Fundamentalism*; George Marsden, ed., *Evangelicalism and the Modern Mind* (1980), George Marsden, *Fundamentalism and the American Culture: The Shaping of the Twentieth-Century Evangelicalism 1870-1925* (1980); Walter Rauschenbusch, *Christianity and the Social Crisis* (1907); Walter Rauschenbusch, *Theology of the Social Gospel* (1917); E. R. Sandeen, *The Roots of Fundamentalism: British and American Millenarianism, 1800-1930* (1970); D. F. Wells and J. D. Woodbridge, eds., *The Evangelicals* (1977).

this time when fundamentalism lost its historical moorings and became identified with anti-intellectualism, divisiveness, and loss of social conscience.

Concluding Personal Summary Comments

In today's climate almost every aspect of Christianity is challenged, including the Kingdom of God. Believers should maintain a balanced theological method and prayerful mindset as they defend *the Faith* and engage a hostile culture with the gospel. Theological method here is simply the interpretative process starting with exegesis to determine the meaning and application of the Scriptures. A correct theological method is necessary to bring the full voice of Scripture to a subject since the Scripture is progressively revealed and no one topic is fully addressed by any one author in any one-time era.

As Christ-followers, we are all called to pursue God's truth humbly and responsibly as presented by the biblical authors as our final guide and standard for life. The goal of interpretation is to discern the intention of the human author by examining what the biblical author affirms in the historical, contextual, and textual parameters of his writing. In both our theological method and then contextualization, we should not simply identify with the views of previous generations, nor should we conform to the culture's agenda. Our theologizing should be driven by strong exegesis, our systemized theology should be framed within a balanced taxonomy, and our ministry should emphasize the gospel by demonstrating the love and truth of Christianity.

BIBLIOGRAPHY

Dillenberger, John and Claude Welch. *Protestant Christianity*. New York: Scribner's, 1954.

Erdman, Charles R. "The Coming of Christ," revised and edited by Gerald B. Stanton in *The Fundamentals for Today*, edited by Charles L Feinberg. Grand Rapids MI, 1958.

Fosdick, Harry Emerson. *Adventurous Religion: And Other Essays* (New York: Harper & Brothers, 1926.

———. "Shall the Fundamentalists Win?" *Sermons in American History: Select Issues in the American Pulpit 1630–1976*, edited by Dewitte Holland. Nashville: Abingdon Press, 1971.

Helm, Paul. "No Easy Task," in *Reforming or Conforming: Post-Conservative Evangelicals and the Emerging Church*, ed., Gary L. W. Johnson and Ronald N. Nash. Wheaton, IL: Crossway Books, 2008.

Helseth, Paul Kjoss. *Right Reason and the Princeton Mind: An Unorthodox Proposal*. Puritan & Reformed, 2010.

Macartney, Clarence E. "Shall Unbelief Win?" *Sermons in American History: Select Issues in the American Pulpit 1630–1976*, edited by Dewitte Holland. Nashville: Abingdon Press, 1971.

Machen, J. Gresham. *What Is Faith?* 1925; reprint, Edinburgh: Banner of Truth, 1991.

Mappes, David. "A Biblical and Theological Critique of Stanley's Irresistible: Reclaiming the New that Jesus Unleashed from the World" in *The Journal of Ministry and Theology* (Winter, 2019), 8-22.

———. "A New Kind of Christian: A Review" in *BibSac* 161 (July–September 2004): 289-303.

———. "Current Trends in Hermeneutics and Theology: Certainty and Simplicity," *Paraklesis* (Summer 2010.

———. "How to Think about and Practice Theology," *The Journal of Ministry and Theology* (Spring 2014), 65-85.

———. "Humility and Tolerance: Exploring their Biblical, Theological, and Cultural Expression" presented Mappes at the Faculty Forum of Baptist Bible Seminary, Clarks Summit PA., October 25, 2010.

———. "Literal Interpretation and Theological Method: What Is It and How to Do It?" Ariel Ministries, December 2017, 18-23.

———. "Love Wins by Rob Bell: A Biblical and Theological Critique," *The Journal of Ministry and Theology* (Spring 2012), 87-121.

———. "Prioritizing and Revising Articles of Faith," *The Baptist Bulletin* (July/ August 2016), 16-22.

———. "The Relationship of Theological Method and Cultural Engagement: A Biblical and Theological Overview of Dating" presented at the Faculty Forum of Baptist Bible Seminary, Clarks Summit PA., November 14, 2014.

———. "The Nobility and Knowability of Truth: Part 1" in *The Journal of Ministry and Theology* 12 (Spring 2009): 64-105.

———. "The Nobility and Knowability of Truth: Part 2" in *The Journal of Ministry and Theology* 13 (Fall 2009): 1-22.

———. "Two Sermons of Major Impact" in *Inspire: The Cedarville University Alumni Magazine* (Winter 2005).

———. "What is Faith in Luke 18:1-8" *BibSac* (July-September 2010), 292-306.

———. Ἐν ἀρχῇ "What Should Christians Do with Andy Stanley's, Irresistible?" interview with Dr. David Mappes in *The Journal of Ministry and Theology* (Winter, 2019), 3-7.

Orr, James. "Science and Christian Faith" *The Fundamentals: A Testimony to the Truth*. Volume IV. Compliments of Two Christian Laymen. Chicago, IL: Testimony Publishing Company, 1910.

Pitzer, A. W. "The Wisdom of this World," *The Fundamentals: A Testimony to the Truth*. Vol. IV, 41-43. The Bible Institute of Los Angeles, CA, 1917.

PREMILLENNIALISM AND THE DEAD SEA SCROLLS

by J. Randall Price, PhD

Dr. Ed Hindson was a close friend and colleague for over four decades. He was a great encouragement in my life personally and academically and our last shared work was the *Evangelical Study Bible*. His *first* published work was in the academic field and the subject of biblical archaeology. His subsequent academic and popular works focused in large part on biblical prophecy, especially in the defense of premillennial eschatology. For this reason, I felt it would be fitting to honor his memory with an academic study that combined both disciplines. May his memory be blessed.

The Qumran Sect and the Significance of the Dead Sea Scrolls

The sectarian Dead Sea Scrolls reveal the way a Jewish sect existing before and during the time of Jesus and the formation of the early church interpreted the prophetic scriptures. Examining their methodology and their commentary on prophetic passages relating to the end time war, the advent of the Messiah, the restoration of national Israel, and the establishment of the messianic Kingdom, their timeline and details align closest with the eschatological school of interpretation known as Premillennialism.

The more than 1,000 documents discovered in caves in the vicinity of the Dead Sea have been commonly referred to as the Dead Sea Scrolls.[230] This material is composed of biblical texts (every book of the OT is represented, except Esther, though allusions to it are present in other texts), commentaries on biblical texts, apocryphal and pseudepigraphical texts, sectarian and ritualistic documents, and apocalyptic literature.[231] The community that preserved this collection[232] represented a type of Messianic

---

230 Although other unrelated written material, generally contemporaneous, was discovered in other places in the Judean Desert (e.g., Jericho, Wadi Murabba'at), the designation is still proper since the largest representation among the scroll discoveries, although fragmentary, is from Qumran situated on the western shore of the Dead Sea. But cf. Shemaryahu Talmon, who for this very reason prefers the designation "Qumran Scrolls," *The World of Qumran from Within* (Jerusalem: Magnes Press, 1989), 274, n. 2. For an evangelical treatment of the subject of the Scrolls see *Secrets of the Dead Sea Scrolls* (Oregon: Harvest House Publishers, 1996).

231 It may be that even these extensive finds do not represent the majority of that originally preserved. Some believe that Cave IV, where the largest accumulation of scroll material was discovered (15,000 fragments), was merely a Genizah (archive for worn-out documents), and that vast numbers of intact scrolls were removed from antiquity through modern times by Bedouins, monastic orders, or others. Many were destroyed, being used e.g., as fuel or incense, but others were preserved, re-copied, and passed on through the Jewish community and others (e.g., the Saint Katherine Monastery, Cairo Genizah, and Karites). Many collapsed caves still unexplored yet contain ancient manuscripts.

232 Some of the Scrolls were undoubtedly written by members of the Qumran Community themselves, but others (such as the Temple Scroll) pre-date the community and were most likely brought to the site by those who joined the sect. It was a practice for families to have their own torah scroll, and, although costly, many of these Jews may have possessed personal libraries that became a part of the collection. Norman Golb believes that all the Scrolls represent a Temple library that was carried from Jerusalem and hidden in the desert before the AD 70 destruction, cf. N. Golb, *Who Wrote the Dead Sea Scrolls? The Search for the Secret of Qumran* (New York: Scribner, 1995).

Judaism more closely related to early Jewish Christianity than the sects of the Pharisees and Sadducees familiar from the pages of the New Testament.[233] The majority of scholars identify the Jewish community at Qumran with the Essene sect (see Josephus' and Philo's description of this group),[234] although the term "Essene" does not appear in the scrolls themselves and dissenting scholars see more differences than similarities with the Essenes and note that neither Josephus or Philo locate them in a desert setting. However, the Roman historian Pliny the Elder appears to locate them at Ein-Gedi.[235] In my opinion, they occupied a unique place within Judaism, calling themselves the *Yahad*, the Community of the Renewed Covenant. With regards to their eschatology, they have been classified as the most decidedly millenarian or chiliastic movement in Second Temple Judaism and possibly in antiquity altogether, Christianity included.[236] Their fairly extensive apocalyptic literature presents not only the eschatological perspective of the community, but perhaps also that of an earlier post-exilic community as well.[237] As such, it offers us an unparalleled glimpse into the eschatological setting of Jesus and the New Testament writers, who while not dependent upon such literature, wrote within a context that was familiar with this worldview.

---

233 The Scrolls have enabled us to see that there was no normative Judaism during the Second Temple period. For a good discussion of the similarities and differences between the Dead Sea Scrolls and the New Testament cf. James Charlesworth, ed., *Jesus and the Dead Sea Scrolls*. The Anchor Bible Reference Library (New York: Doubleday, 1993), 8-40.

234 See Flavius Josephus, *The Jewish War* 2.8.2:119-21; 8.3:122-23; 8.4:124-27; 8.5:128-133; 8.6:134-36; 8.7:137-42; 8.8:143-44; 8.9:145-49; 8.10:150-53; 8.11:154-58; 8.12:159; 8.13:160-61 and Philo, *Every Good Man is Free* 12, 75-87. It should be noted that Josephus does not identify the Essenes he describes with the Jewish community at Qumran (see Steve Mason, "Did the Essenes Write the Dead Sea Scrolls? Don't Rely on Josephus," *BAR* (November/December 2008).

235 Pliny, *Natural History* 5.73. There is a debate whether his Latin term refers to a place north of Ein-Gedi (possibly Qumran) or south, Ein-Gedi itself, see Hershel Shanks, "Searching for Essenes at Ein Gedi, Not Qumran," *BAR* 28:4 (July/August 2002).

236 S. Talmon, *The World of Qumran from Within*, 278.

237 Some apocalyptic documents, such as the Temple Scroll (which are themselves copies) predate the mid-second-century BC occupation of Qumran.

The Eschatological Context of the Dead Sea Scrolls

To understand the eschatology of the Dead Sea Scrolls, we must first have an understanding of the wider context of the post-exilic or Second Temple period, since it was during this time that apocalyptic writing and its eschatological content developed.[238] Today, more than in any previous century since the time of Christ, we have an increasingly abundant supply of intertestamental documents to assist our study of the New Testament. Too often, these primary source materials from the Second Temple Period have been neglected by evangelicals.[239] However, as Julius Scott, Jr. observes, "without due regard to the original historical and cultural context of the text, every exegete is suspectable to eisegesis, interpreting according to his own historical, cultural context, or controlled (even unintentionally) by his own subjective concerns, relational goals, or philosophical presuppositions."[240] By disregarding those extra-biblical texts that permit us to properly view the authorial context, we may modernize the text in a way not dissimilar to higher-critical interpreters who reject the divine intent.

---

[238] For a good overview see J. Julius Scott, Jr., *Customs and Controversies: Intertestamental Jewish Backgrounds of the New Testament* (Grand Rapids: Baker Book House, 1995), 283-95 (eschatology). For a good survey of the theology of the Scrolls cf. Helmer Ringgren, *The Faith of Qumran: The Theology of the Dead Sea Scrolls*. Expanded Edition (New York: Crossroad, 1995), 152-98 (eschatology). For a good source of selected original sources see George W. E. Nickelsburg, *Jewish Literature Between the Bible and the Mishnah* (Philadelphia: Fortress, 1981) and George W. E. Nickelsburg and Michael E. Stone, *Faith and Piety in Early Judaism: Texts and Documents* (Philadelphia: Fortress, 1983), and the now standard collection of Intertestamental Literature in *The Old Testament Pseudepigrapha*. 2 vols. ed. James H. Charlesworth (New York: Doubleday, 1983, 1985).

[239] The reasons for this neglect range from simple unconcern and/or unfamiliarity with the content, to prejudice against the use of non-canonical writings, and the fear of aligning themselves with critical scholars who have used these sources to buttress their attacks of evangelical doctrines.

[240] J. Julius Scott, Jr., "On the Value of Intertestamental Jewish Literature for New Testament Theology," *JETS* 23:4 (December 1980): 316.

The Eschatological Framework of the Dead Sea Scrolls

From about the fourth century BC onwards,[241] the Prophetic Literature takes on the genre of apocalyptic.[242] It is this genre that is characteristic of the eschatological material of the Dead Sea Scrolls. Among the works discovered at Qumran are commentaries on the books of the Prophets and the Psalms which scholars refer to as *Pesher* ("interpretation"). The Qumran *Pesher* developed through the prophetic influence of Daniel as a special means of reconstructing the hidden history revealed to the prophets concerning the end of time. It is based on the interpretive assumption that the biblical prophetic texts held clues for fulfillment to their generation, which they believed was the final generation upon whom the end would come. The apocalyptic vision of Qumran's *pesher* literature is derived from its understanding of human history as being built up in stages determined by God and linked together to move toward an inevitable goal, the eschaton.[243] John Collins referred to this as patterns projected into the eschatological future which disclosed the dominance of the hostile order of Belial (desecration motif) and the affirmation of an alternative

---

241 Research into the development of apocalyptic has provided evidence of its developmental link with prophetic eschatology. Edwards has concluded: "What, then, marks the transition from prophecy to apocalyptic?...it is the combination of spiritual readiness and historical events. So the visions of the prophets become extended, elaborate and literary, as their symbolic acts are turned into symbols. The close relationship of these writers is seen in their concentration on the two focal points of time: the historical event of the fall of Jerusalem and the despair it brought; the historical fall of Babylon and the hope it brought. And between, the picture of the reactions of a displaced people." Grace Edwards, "The Historical Background of Early Apocalyptic Thought," *Scripture in History & Theology: Essays in Honor of J. Coert Rylaarsdam*. ed. A. L. Merrill and T. W. Overholt (Pennsylvania: Pickwick, 1977), 202.

242 The term "Apocalyptic" is used commonly to signify the sudden catastrophic intervention of God in the affairs of earth to right all wrongs and to terminate human history. In general, the term has come to designate a literary genre "apocalypse" (derived from Greek term for "revelation, disclosure"), and the special type of eschatology contained therein, separating from prophetic literature in only minor respects, cf. H. H. Rowley, *The Relevance of Apocalyptic: A Study of Jewish and Christian Apocalypses from Daniel to the Revelation* (New York: Association Press, 1963), 23.

243 Cf. for discussion O. Betz, "Past Events and Last Events in the Qumran Interpretation of History," *Proceedings of the Sixth World Congress on Jewish Studies in Jerusalem 1976* (Jerusalem: The World Union of Jewish Studies, 1977) 1:27-34.

order (restoration motif), at present eclipsed, though practically experienced by the Elect, but yet to be completely revealed in the future.[244] David Flusser argues that

> This is not an evolutionary approach containing the concept of progress, for in this view, it is precisely before the end that the worst time will come, troubles of a kind not seen since the beginning of the world. History and its stages have been predetermined, one after another, by God. And after the final crisis (the War of Gog and Magog, or an invasion of monstrous enemies, or...of a terrible and wicked king, who corresponds with the Christian Antichrist), after all this, the final peace will come; men will live a thousand generations, evil will be destroyed, and an ideal world will come about.[245]

In concluding his study of the use of the Old Testament at Qumran, which primarily consisted of the Torah and the Prophets,[246] George Brooke has shown that one cannot approach this usage without presupposing that such use was guided by an overall eschatological perspective.[247] This eschatological perspective was drawn from the book of Daniel, whose pervasive influence on the community needs to be briefly considered.

---

244 John J. Collins, "Patterns of Eschatology at Qumran," *Traditions in Transformation*, ed. Baruch Halpern and Jon Levenson (Winona Lake, Indiana: Eisenbrauns, 1981), 375.

245 David Flusser, *The Spiritual History of the Dead Sea Sect*, trans. Carol Glucker (Tel-Aviv: MOD Books, 1989), 75.

246 CD 16:2 speaks of the Torah as that wherein "all things are strictly defined," and 1QS 1:1-3 outlines the aim of the covenanteers as "to seek God with a whole heart and soul, and to do what is good and right before Him, as He commanded by the hand of Moses and all His servants the Prophets." We have also seen(above) how 1QHab. 7:4-5 declares that the "Teacher of Righteousness" can interpret all the words of the Prophets.

247 Cf. George J. Brooke, *Exegesis at Qumran: 4QFlorilegium in its Jewish Context*. JSOTSup 29 (Sheffield: JSOT Press, 1989), 356.

The Influence of the Book of Daniel on Qumran

Noel David Freedman has pointed out: "From Daniel it is a relatively short distance to Qumran. Not only was the book admired or at least copied and preserved in the Essene community...but there may be an historical link between the book and the community."[248] The Aramaic cognate of *pesher* appears thirty-one times in Daniel (along with *raz*) in reference to Daniel's "interpretation" of dreams.[249] In keeping with Daniel, in the Qumran prophetic literature, both *pesher* and *raz*, are given by divine revelation, however, *raz* is the first stage of the revelation (that imparted to the biblical writer), which remained "hidden" until the second stage when the *pesher* was imparted to the "Teacher of Righteousness" and through him to the community.

Daniel was explicitly told concerning his prophetic revelation to "conceal these words and seal up the book until the end of time; many will go back and forth, and knowledge (of the prophetic interpretation of the predicted events) will increase" (Dan 12:4). The Qumran Community appears to have believed that the visions of Daniel, which had not been completely fulfilled in the persecutions of Antiochus IV Epiphanes, were to be fulfilled in their own day. In this light, they saw themselves as the embodiment of the "discerning teachers" and Daniel's "holy ones" (Dan 4:17) who sat on high and watched over Israel, announcing, and interpreting the events of the end-time.[250] One of the clearest explanations of this occurs in *1QpHab*. 7:1-5 on Habakkuk 2:1-2 (cf. Dan 9:10) which says:

---

248 N. D. Freedman, "The Flowering of Apocalyptic," in Apocalypticism, ed. Robert W. Funk. JTC 6 (New York: Herder and Herder, 1969), 170.

249 Daniel uses other terms to convey the same idea as *pesher* as the Hebrew noun only appears once in the Bible (Eccl 8:21: "who knows the *interpretation* of a matter?").

250 Cf. for a discussion of this perspective among the Community, F. F. Bruce, *Biblical Exegesis in the Qumran Texts*, rev. ed. (Grand Rapids: Eerdmans, 1959), 27, 63-67, 70.

And God told Habakkuk to write down the things that will happen to the last generation, but the consummation of time He did not make known to him... The interpretation of [Habakkuk 2:2] concerns the Teacher of Righteousness to whom God made known all the secrets of His servants the prophets.

The crucial touch point for the Qumran Community is seen in the clause "all the mysteries of the words of His servants the prophets." With this statement, the history of the present community was joined with that of the past, and a prophetic continuum was established through divine revelation to the "Teacher of Righteousness," the supposed founder of the sect.[251] It appears that this individual, as well as others in Israel at this time, believed the role of the Prophet had not yet ceased.[252] This fundamental principle of Jewish interpretation—of a perceived relationship between the past and the present—forms the basis of Danelic exposition in explaining the mysteries of past divine revelation with a view to historic interpretation. In other words, not until the two parts of the revelation: *raz* and *pesher* are joined is the meaning made plain, a revelation which is predominately concerned with the end days, the eschaton.[253]

Just as Daniel reinterpreted Jeremiah's prophecy of the seventy-year exile (Jer 25:1) to encompass the greater "seventy weeks

---

[251] Cf. Kurt Elliger, *Studien zum Habakkuk-Kommentar vom Toten Meer* (Tübingen: Mohr-Siebeck, 1953), 118-64.

[252] Alex P. Jassen, "Prophecy after 'the Prophets': The Dead Sea Scrolls and the History of Prophecy in Judaism," *The Dead Sea Scrolls in Context*. 2 vols. (Leiden: Brill), 577-93. For a discussion of this issue see F. E. Greenspahn, "Why Prophecy Ceased," *JBL* 108 (1989): 37-49; B. D. Sommer, "Did Prophecy Cease? Reevaluating a Reevaluation," *JBL* 115 (1995): 31-47. T. Overholt, "The End of Prophecy: No Players without a Program," in The Place Is Too Small for Us: The Israelite Prophets in Recent Scholarship, ed. R. P. Gordon. SBTS 5 (Winona Lake: Eisenbrauns, 1995), 527-38. For full bibliography, see A. P. Jassen, *Mediating the Divine: Prophecy and Revelation in the Dead Sea Scrolls and Second Temple Judaism*. STDJ 68 (Leiden: Brill, 2007), 11-19; A. P. Jassen, "Prophets and Prophecy in the Qumran Community," *AJSR* 23 (2008): 299-334.

[253] Cf. further, George W. E. Nickelsburg, "Reading the Hebrew Scriptures in the First Century: Christian Interpretations in Their Jewish Context," *W & W* 3:3 (Summer 1983): 238-50, esp. 239-46.

of *years*" (Dan 9:24-27), so the "Teacher of Righteousness" reinterpreted various prophetic passages from the Old Testament by reapplying them to the situation of his day which he believed was on the threshold of the eschaton. This was understood in the Hasmonean period as they beheld religious defection among Israel's leaders (kings and priests) and defilement of the holy Temple (i.e., Israel moving toward the time of Jacob's trouble, Jer 30:7). This was further confirmed when the Roman army invaded, appointed politically compliant kings and priests and Herod the Great rebuilt the Second Temple with pagan (Roman) architectural features and allowed pagan images (emblems of the Roman Emperor) within the Temple complex. They identified these end-time enemies of Israel with the general term for foreign invaders, the *Kittim*, and saw their presence in the Land as signaling the War of Gog of Magog (Ezek 38-39) and/or end-time invasion (Zech 12-14).

In keeping with the observation of inter-textual usage, whereby we may note how the biblical authors, and especially the prophets, understood and built upon the revelation previously received, we can observe how the Qumran Community understood and used the revelation of the biblical prophets to develop a linear eschatology. Moreover, we can observe how an important eschatological text like Daniel 9:24-27 was used by the Community,[254] to discern their place in history and to even expect from this passage (vv. 25-26) the arrival of the Messiah between 3 BCE and 2 CE.[255]

---

254 For example, the Damascus Rule offers the first of a long line of commentaries on this text, the allusion to Dan 9:20-24 in the "tenth Jubilee" of 11QMelch, the underlying influence of Dan 9.25-27 on 11QPsa, and the 4Q liturgical text "The Words of the Luminaries." For discussion on these texts cf. respectively, A. Mertens, *Das Buch Daniel im Lichte der Texte vom Toten Meer* (Würzburg: Echter, 1971), 87; J. A. Fitzmyer, "Further Light on Melchizedek from Qumran Cave 11," JBL 86 (1967): 251; M. Balliet, "Un recueil liturgique de Qumrân, grotte 4: 'Les paroles des luminaries'," *RB* 68 (1991): 247.

255 Cf. R. T. Beckwith, "Daniel 9 and the Date of Messiah's Coming in Essene, Hellenistic, Pharisaic, Zealot, and Early Christian Computation," *RevQ* 19 (1979-81): 521-42.

The Prophetic History in the Dead Sea Scrolls

The Scrolls depict a defined order of the ages that unfolds progressively and successively in predetermined periods or in keeping with biblical usage of "generations" in the sect's defining document, *Community Rule* (*1QS* 4:13; cf. Deut 32:7; Isa 41:4 *et. al.*). This "prophetic history" according to *4Q180* (*The Ages of Creation*) consecutively enumerates these periods beginning with the time before the creation of man (cf. *CD* 2:7; *1QS* 3:15-18; *1QH* 1:8-12). The history of mankind is traced from the Creation (*1QS* 4:15-17) and leads up to the eschaton or the "latter generation" or the "end-time" (*4Q169* 3-4 iii. 3; 173 1, line 5), finally culminating in the "latter days" (*1QpHab* 4:1-2, 7-8, 10-14; cf. 2:5-7). This culminating period also looks forward in its description of this age ending the era of wickedness as "the decreed epoch of new things" (*1QS* 4:25; cf. Dan 9:26-27; 11:35-36; Isa 10:23; 28:22; 43:19). The dividing point of this order of the ages is the destruction of the First Temple (586 BC), with the ages preceding it termed "the generations of wickedness" and those that follow (the post-destruction/post-exilic period) as "the generations of the latter days."[256]

Historically we may understand how those who penned the apocalyptic literature of the Scrolls came to this position. The First Temple had been destroyed because of Israelite unfaithfulness to the covenant (Dan 9:5-17), and Temple-related laws (Ezek 5:11-17). Those who returned to Judah after the destruction and exile to rebuild the Temple expected a national restoration and spiritual revival according to the prophecies of Jeremiah (31-33) and Ezekiel (33-48) that were re-enforced by the post-exilic Prophets, especially Haggai (2:4-9), Zechariah (14:9-21) and Malachi

---

[256] This division is similar to that of the biblical post-exilic era, cf. Zech 1:4; 7:7, 12 where the prophets of this era are called "the latter prophets" and Hag 2:3-9; cf. Ezra 3:12, which refer to the Second Temple (of Zerubbabel) as "the latter Temple."

(4:4). But these prophecies also contained prior conditions of repentance with the coming of the Messiah (Haggai; Zech 12:10-13:6; Mal 3:1-7) as well as a final war (Hag 2:20-23; Zech 12:2-9; 14:1-8, 12-15; Mal 4:1-3). Moreover, the historical reality was that the Persian authorities granted the Judean Remnant only limited autonomy in the sphere of Temple-building and ritual maintenance (cf. Ezra 1:1-4; 4:8-23; 5:3-5), an act which both reduced the status of their government while it enhanced the status of their priesthood (cf. Ezra 7:11-26). The ideal government (i.e., the Messianic Kingdom) envisioned by the prophets combined the offices of king and priest, typified at the beginning of this period by the Davidic descendant Zerubbabel and the High Priest Joshua. Their union of monarchy and priesthood, guided by "a counsel of peace," was the insignia of the Messiah, who would build the ideal, eschatological Temple with the help of the Gentile nations, a sign of a complete restoration (Isa 56:6-7; 60:10-14; Zech 6:13-15).

But neither the messianic advent nor the promised national and spiritual restoration (Ezek 36:25-27; 37:1-28) was realized by the post-exilic community, nor did the Temple built by Zerubbabel achieve the glory the prophet Haggai had predicted for the First Temple's successor (Hag 2:7-9), much less the grand design of that predicted by Ezekiel (Ezek 40-48). The Qumran Community explained that Jeremiah's seventy years exile did not technically end His discipline of the Nation and understood that Ezekiel's predicted Judean exile (Ezek 6:4-6, 9) would be 390 years (vv. 5, 9), and only after this time elapsed would the end come and the restoration begin (CD 1:3-8).[257] At the conclusion of this period, in what they termed "the age of wrath" (CD 1:5), they believed God would again "plant" a righteous remnant (i.e., the Qumran

---

257 Ezekiel's prophecy took on the same meaning as had Jeremiah's and was regarded by Talmon as an example of "millenarian arithmetic" or "messianic numerology," *The World of Qumran from Within*, 282 (text) and n. 18.

Community). Subtracting 390 years from 586 BC (the beginning of the Babylonian exile) yields the date 196 BC. Subtracting another 20 years (which *CD* 1:8-11 reveals was a preparation period before the Community's establishment) gives a date of 177 BC, the approximate time for the beginning of the settlement at Qumran.[258] This correlates generally with the time when the Jewish People experienced liberation from foreign rule with the Hasmonean revolt (167 BC) and the subsequent establishment of an independent Jewish kingdom (Maccabean period).

From the beginning of this period, they interpreted the forty days of Ezekiel 6:4 as one generation (forty years) and expected the eschatological war of Gog of Magog to take place at its conclusion. For the first twenty years they "groped" along (their term) searching for direction, until a Teacher of Righteousness (*Moreh ha-Tzedek*) arose to properly interpret the prophecies. The next twenty years were devoted to his instruction in the desert (*CD* 1:8–11) and it was at this time that they most likely applied to themselves the role of Isaiah's messianic preparer "a voice crying in the wilderness" (Isa 40:3; *1QS* 8:12–16). This wilderness—Egypt and Babylon in one—was also viewed as a typological "Damascus," since Amos 5:27 had predicted that God would take Israel into exile "beyond Damascus" (cf. *CD* 7:13–14), and Zechariah 6:8 had predicted from there they would escape in the time of God's visitation of judgment [upon the wicked], (*CD* 7:20-21). This forty-year period is the same as that given by them in their *War Scroll* for the duration of the climatic war between the "Sons of Light" and the "Sons of Darkness" (*1QM* 2–3). At this time, they were to conquer all the non-aligned (i.e., non-New Covenant) Jews, all foreign nations, and especially the *Kittim*, who embodied the end-time oppressors who followed Belial (Satan). Believing their

---

258 So Ben Zion Wacholder has reasoned, cf. *The Dawn of Qumran: The Sectarian Torah and the Teacher of Righteousness*. Monographs of the Hebrew Union College 8 (Cincinnati: Hebrew Union College, 1983), 177ff; cf. James C. Vanderkam, *The Dead Sea Scrolls Today* (Grand Rapids: Eerdmans, 1994), 100.

chronology was divinely ordained, they waited patiently during this period for the appointed day.[259]

When this period ended without the expected fulfillment, the Community seems to have not attempted further calculations. However, some feel that the "seventy years of wrath (desolation)" in Daniel 9:2 (mentioned often in the *War Scroll*) could have been employed as a means to determine the end of the Roman oppression of Judea (cf. 4Q243-45).[260] However, this chronological failure seems to have forced them not only to reformulate their earlier expectations to accommodate a divine postponement or delayed judgment but also to adopt a new militaristic posture that saw the urgent need for intervention to bring about the next age. They were expecting a messianic intervention "imminently," since the date indicated by their chronology had passed. This application of their eschatological perspective reveals that it arose from a literal interpretation of prophetic texts. It also shows that they utilized a numerological calculation of temporal indicators from the prophetic texts and incorporated a divinely ordained postponement of the final age. After Jesus' resurrection His disciples, apparently based on their understanding of the order of messianic predictions (suffering then glory, humiliation then rule), had the imminent expectation of the Lord's restoration of national Israel (Acts 1:6). However, they were instructed by their Teacher of Righteousness to accept a postponement of that promised fulfillment so that the full number of Gentiles could be brought into the Church (Acts 1:7-8; Rom 11:25-32).

---

259 On the predestinarian position of the Community in relation to eschatology see Eugene H. Merrill, *Predestination at Qumran: A Theological Study of the Thanksgiving Hymns* (Leiden: Brill, 1975), 51-54.

260 Eisenman and Wise suggest that they applied this figure to the first outbreak of revolutionary activity at the time of Herod's death in 4 BC and looked for the end in AD 66, the time of the Jewish uprising, which they believed would usher in the final battle of the End of Days, Eisenman and Wise, *The Dead Sea Scrolls Uncovered* (Massachusetts: Element, 1992), 64.

The Attitude Toward the Temple

Since the prophetic program for the Temple essentially structured the eschatological order revealed in the Scrolls, it is necessary to consider how the Temple, and especially the Second Temple (from which the Qumran Community had separated in terms of their calendar and ritual) was perceived. There has been considerable debate concerning the issue of the attitude of the Qumran Community toward the Second Temple. First, spiritual analogies in the Dead Sea Scrolls to the Qumran Community as a "temple" have been interpreted by some scholars in the same manner that New Testament references to the Christian community as a "temple" (Eph 2:21; 2 Cor 6:16; cf. 1 Cor 3:16-19) have been interpreted as a rejection and replacement of the Jerusalem Temple. Gärtner is among those who make this mistake, believing that the community calling itself *a* temple meant a substitution for *the* Temple.[261] There are many references in the sectarian scrolls to the historic Temple, often with respect to its holiness and concern for its defilement, but one text, *1QS* 8:5 states: "Then shall the party of the *Yahad* truly be established, (*vacat*) an 'eternal planting' (cf. Jubilees 16:26), a temple for Israel, and—mystery!—a Holy..." This has been thought to imply the Community rejected the Jerusalem Temple and saw themselves as a "new temple." However, nomenclature referring to the Qumran Community as a "new temple," is questioned by E. S. Fiorenza on the grounds of the anti-cultic implications of the term "new." He prefers rather to speak of the concept at Qumran as that of "transference" or "reinterpretation."[262] Other scholars have used terms such as a "spiritualiza-

---

[261] Bertil Gärtner, *The Temple and the Community in Qumran and the New Testament* (Cambridge: At the University Press, 1965), 4-46, interprets such passages as 1QS 5:6; 8:8, 11 in this manner. Cf. R. J. Mckelvey, *The New Temple: The Church in the New Testament*. Oxford Theological Monographs (London: Oxford University Press, 1969), as an example of those who use the concept at Qumran to argue for the Church as replacing the Temple from the New Testament metaphor.

[262] Cf. E. S. Fiorenza, "Cultic Language in Qumran and in the New Testament," *CBQ* 38 (1976): 159-77.

tion of the temple," or a "spiritualized temple,"[263] however, these terms also fail to understand the full-orbed concept of the Temple as it existed at Qumran. We prefer to speak of the Community as a "symbolic temple," since in our opinion, they continued to reverence the sacred distinction held by Jerusalem and the Temple Mount. The overwhelming number of references to the Temple respect it as God's sole Sanctuary and its unique holiness was the basis for the Community deriving their concepts of representative sanctity as a holy priesthood. A positive example of the Community's esteem for the Second Temple may be had from several lines in the document called *The First Letter on Works Reckoned as Righteousness* (4Q394–398):

> (34) We reckon that the Temple [is the Tent of Witness, while] Jerusale[m] (35) is the camp outside the camp [meaning outside Jerusalem] (It refers to) the camp...(38) [He chose] from among all the tribes of Israel, to establish His Name there as a dwelling...] Because (from 67-68) Jerusalem is the Holy camp—the place (69) that He chose from among all the tribes of Israel. Thus Jerusalem is the foremost of (70) the ca[m]ps of Israel.

From this text we can see that the Temple sanctified Jerusalem as the place where YHWH's Name had been caused to dwell. It is preferable to view the Qumran Community as drawing an analogous relationship from Temple sanctity to express their role as an elect remnant. This understanding argues for Paul describing the Church (as well as believers' bodies) as "holy" and as a "spiritual temple." It is clear from other New Testament references that Jesus, Jesus' disciples, and Paul regarded the Jerusalem Temple as God's (and Israel's) legitimate Sanctuary (Matt 21:13; Luke 2:49;

---

263 Cf. e.g., H. Wenschkewitz, *Die Spiritualisierung der Kultusbegriffe Tempel, Priester, und Opfer im Neuen Testament*, Angelos. Beiheft 4 (Leipzig: Pfeiffer, 1932), and Yves M.-J. Congar, *The Mystery of the Temple or the Manner of God's Presence to His Creatures from Genesis to the Apocalypse*, trans. R. E. Trevett (Newman, 1962).

24:53; Acts 3:1; 21:26; 22:17; 25:8). Nevertheless, the Qumran Community did criticize the existing polluted state of the Temple and priesthood and positioned itself *outside* Jerusalem. Furthermore, the Temple Scroll (*11Q19*), which the Qumran sect revered, instructed Israel to construct its own purified Temple once the final battle between the "Sons of Darkness" and the "Sons of Light" was concluded. This demonstrates their high view of the Temple as a legitimate institution, albeit a corrupted one in their time. This, however, agrees with Jesus' attitude toward the Temple (John 2:13-17). The only replacement of the Temple they envisioned was with a new purified Temple; not with their community temporarily serving in the wilderness as a "spiritual temple." This Temple was to be built by men (*4QFlor 107-10*),[264] after the plans laid out in The Temple Scroll, but it would be eclipsed at the end of days, in the new Creation by the Temple built by God Himself (*11Q19 29:9; 4QFlor 107*), with gigantic dimensions as described in *The New Jerusalem* document (*4Q554*) within a rectangular city 13 x 18 miles with twelve gates for the twelve tribes and guarded by 1,500 towers 100 feet high. This agrees with Ezekiel's prophecy of Israel's final (Messianic) Temple (Ezek 40-48).

The Eschatology of the Dead Sea Scrolls

The eschatological perspective of the Scrolls is seen in its terms to describe its expectation of the days about to arrive on the historical scene: "the latter days," "the end of days," "the appointed time," "the new Creation," and the "visitation," i.e., divine retributive judgment, intervention. The eschatological scheme of the Scrolls[265] was a two-stage eschatology (*now* and *then*), with the past being the condition of exile imposed by the destruction of the

---

264 Some would translate the key phrase μda vdqm ("a Sanctuary of men") as "a Sanctuary *consisting of* men," however, this symbolic interpretation is unnatural and the natural "a Sanctuary *of* men," [i.e., built by them] is preferred.

265 See supplemental chart "Eschatology of the Dead Sea Scrolls."

First Temple, and the present characterized by a non-restoration of the proper spiritual order with the Second Temple, hence, an age of wickedness that served as a time of trial and testing (i.e., refining) for the Elect Remnant (the Qumran Community), cf. *4QCantena*^{a} 2:9-10; *4QFlor* 2:1. This age was to see the visitation of Elijah as the percursor of Messiah (*4Q521*) and the advent of the Messiah(s), who would slay the wicked (the correct interpretation of *4Q285*) in the great Gog and Magog war (cf. *1QM*; *4QpIsa*^{a} 7-10; 22-25; *4QpIsa*^{b} 2:1; *4Cantena*^{b} 3:7-8), at the Day of the Lord (4Q558). Then would follow the promised age of Messianic rule and righteousness (cf. *1QSa* 2:14; *4Q554* 11:20-22). This, however, was not the final age, for with Daniel (12:1-2) it was held that the righteous would be resurrected (*4Q521* 1:1, line 12; cf. *1QH* 4:18-21; 11:12; *1QS* 4:7-8).

Several of these themes, especially of the interim period preceding the advent of the Messiah to atone for Israel and establish its kingdom, will be interesting for comparison with New Testament eschatology.

The Eschatological Age of Evil

The characteristic of the post-exilic age is that of wickedness that will escalate until the final conflict between the "sons of darkness" and the "sons of light." According to the War Scroll the final age was to be preceded by a period of tribulation or "birth pangs [of the Messiah]" (*1QH* 3:7-10),[266] which "shall be a time of salvation for the People of God..." (*1QM* 1). Central to this coming age of conflict is the image of eschatological evil rulers and deceivers (counterfeits of the true Messiah). The Dead Sea

---

266 This expression appears also in the New Testament (cf. Matt 24:8; Mark 13:8) and especially in rabbinic literature in which it became a technical term for the Tribulation (e.g., Babylonian Talmud, tractate *Sanhedrin* 97a). The origin of the phrase is the Old Testament prophetic teaching on the judgment of Israel (cf. Isa 13:8; 26:17; 66:7-9; Jer 4:31; 22:23; 49:22; 50:43; Hos 13:13; Mic 4:9-10). For a study of this phrase and the related concept see the author's "Old Testament Tribulation Terms," in *When the Trumpet Sounds* (Oregon: Harvest House Publishers, 1995), chapter 3.

sect saw a cosmic dualism[267] between the "Angel/Spirit of Truth/ Holiness"/Prince of Light," hence the members of the sect were the "sons of light" (*1QS; 1QM*) or "sons of truth," (*1QS; 1QH; 1QM*), and the "Angel of Darkness/Spirit of Perversity/of the Pit," hence, their opponents, the "sons of darkness" (*1QS; 1QM*) or "sons of perversity," (*1QS; 1QH*) or even "sons of the Pit," (*CD*).[268] This conflict between the forces of light (good) and darkness (evil) has been declared by J. Daniélou as "nothing else but the *leitmotif* of Qumran."[269] These cosmic eschatological desecrators were mirrored by the conflict between the sect and two figures: the "Wicked Priest/priests," and the "Man of Lies." We will first consider this earthly dualism and then proceed to the negative element of this cosmic dualism.

The Wicked Priest and the Man of Lies

Neither the "Wicked Priest/priests" nor the "Man of Lies" are identified by name, like the "Teacher of Righteousness" with whom they principally contend, however, the "Wicked Priest" was apparently a non-Zadokite High Priest (or a group of Hasmonean priests),[270] who were considered illegitimate priests, while

---

267 This dualism most likely may be traced to the division of light from darkness in Gen 1:3-5.

268 The terminology in this light-versus-darkness motif has long been considered synonymous and interchangeable, cf. G. R. Driver, *The Judean Scrolls, The Problem and a Solution* (Oxford: Blackwell, 1965), 545; F. Nötscher, "Geist und Geister in den Texten von Qumran," *Mélanges bibliques: rédigés en l'honneur de André Robert*. Trauvaux de l'Institut Catholique de Paris 4 (Paris, 1956): 305-16. James Charlesworth, "A Critical Comparison of the Dualism in 1QS 3:13-4:26 and the 'Dualism' Contained in the Gospel of John," *NTS* 15 (1968-69): 400, observes that the probability of these terms being synonymous is strengthened by the fact that YHWH is also is given various names. He also notes that *rwa* or *'vwh* denote origin and qualify the actions of the respective beings.

269 J. Daniélou, *The Dead Sea Scrolls and Primitive Christianity* (Baltimore: Helicon, 1963), 107. This motif, however, is a unique paradigm to Qumran, and its contrast with other sects of Judaism, e.g., Christianity, has been demonstrated by H. Kosmala, "The Parable of the Unjust Steward in the Light of Qumran," *Annual of the Swedish Theological Institute*, ed. H. Kosmala (Leiden: Brill, 1964) 3:114-21.

270 The Wicked Priest may not be a single individual. A. S. van der Woude, "Wicked Priest or Wicked Priests? Reflections on the identification of the Wicked Priest in the Habakkuk Commentary," *JJS* 33 (1982): 349-59, and W. H. Brownlee, "The Wicked Priest, the Man of Lies, and the RighteousTeacher—The Problem of Identity," *JQR* 83 (1982): 4, argue that there six different individuals called by the name "Wicked Priest" in the text of the Habakkuk Commentary, prob-

the "Man of Lies" was seemingly a traitor who was formerly an ally of the Zadokite "Teacher" (the legitimate High Priest), but subsequently betrayed him. J. Murphy-O'Connor has suggested that the "Man of Lies" became the opponent of the "Teacher" as the result of a schism within the sect in Jerusalem that forced it to withdraw to Qumran.[271] As a non-Zadokite, he was not only considered an illegitimate priest but was also said to be guilty of terrible desecrations of the Temple. According to the *Pesher Habakkuk*, the "Wicked Priest" instituted ritual practices that defiled the Temple of God (*1QpHab* 8:12-13 and 12:7-12) as well as profaned (through violence) the Land (*1QpHab* 12:9; cf. 2:17).[272]

Other violations listed for the "Wicked Priest" are his abuse of power, his drunkenness, his violence and arrogance, his greed (in the accumulation of wealth), and especially, his persecution of the "Teacher." The "Wicked Priest" also violated the divine order by substituting a lunar for a solar calendar. Since the calendrical order was a rule expressive of divine creation and the preservation of the universe, and *therefore the basis for regulating* the festivals and daily Jewish practice, its alteration or modification was a crime against the ritual that supported the Temple and Jewish life.[273] The "Teacher" and the Qumran sect believed that the dates on which the festivals were held at the Jerusalem Temple were "those in which all Israel was in error" (*CD* 3:14), while to them were revealed the true times of "the Sabbaths of His holiness and the

---

ably revealing a series of conflicts between the Qumran sect and the Hasmonean rulers.

271 Cf. J. Murphy-O'Connor, "The Essenes and Their History," *RB* 81 (1974): 215-44; "The Essenes in Palestine," *BA* 40 (1977): 94-124.

272 Cf. text and comments, George Wesley Buchanan, *RQ* 53:14.1 (June 1989): 44-45, and "Eschatology and the 'End of Days,'" *JNES* 20 (1961): 188-93.

273 S. Talmon, "The Calendar Reckoning of the Sect from the Judean Desert," *Scripta Hierosolymitana* IV (Jerusalem: Magnes Press, 1965), 167; for studies on the origin of the sectarian calendar, cf. A. Jaubert, "Le Calendrier des Jubilés et de la Secte Qumrân: Ses origines bibliques," *VT* 3 (1955): 250-64; J. C. VanderKam, "2 Maccabees 6, 7a and Calendrical change in Jerusalem," *Journal for the Study of Judaism* 12 (1981): 52-74; "The Origin, Character, and Early History of the 364-Day Calendar: A Reassessment of Jaubert's Hypothesis," *CBQ* 41 (1979): 390-411; P. R.. Davies, "Calendrical Change and Qumran Origin: An Assessment of VanderKam's Theory," *CBQ* 45 (1983): 80-89. For a general overview of the problem, cf. Neil S. Fujita, *A Crack in the Jar: What Ancient Jewish Documents Tell us about the New Testament* (New York: Paulist Press, 1986), 45-46.

festivals of His glory" (CD 3:15-16). Thus, the "Wicked Priest" in the Habakkuk Commentary was basically a rebel against God, who was due divine punishment.[274] These figures prepare us for their cosmic counterparts around whom the predestined end-time conflict will revolve: the "Angel of Darkness" and/or "Belial."

The Angel of Darkness

There is still debate as to whether the "Angel of Darkness" and "Belial" are one figure or two.[275] Many scholars have assumed this is the case and have identified Belial with the "Devil," as the Angel of Darkness, as opposed to Michael, the "Angel of Light."[276] On the other hand, while the consensus of scholarly opinion has been that 1QS 3:13-4:26 (the most representative text for the dualism concept, and the possible influence for other such texts) reveals an eschatological cosmic conflict of two warring spiritual forces, it has been contended that at times this dualism approaches the "psychological" arena.[277] The arguments in favor of this position have been predicated on the use of the Hebrew term *ruach* ("spirit") in the Old Testament, where it is thought the idea of incorporeal entities is never meant. However, A. A.

---

274 On the verdict of divine punishment for calendrical offense in the Habakkuk Commentary, cf. Lawrence H. Schiffman, *The Halakha at Qumran, and Sectarian Law in the Dead Sea Scrolls: Courts, Testimony and the Penal Codes* (Chico, CA: Scholars Press, 1983).

275 The noun "Belial" is entirely absent from early compositions such as the *Hodayot*, though it is peculiar to later texts. For example, "Belial" occurs as a *nomen proprium* in the Damascus Document six times, and since this scroll was composed later than the earliest portion of the rule, it is thought that "Belial" is a substitute for "Angel of Darkness." In the War Scroll, the term appears twelve times, and since it is the latest of the major sectarian scrolls, it strengthens the probability of the term becoming a surrogate for "Angel of Darkness." Further, "Belial" is found only in the preface (1QS 1:18, 24; 2:5, 19) and the concluding hymn (1QS 10:21) of the Rule, again, sections probably added at a later date.

276 The primary motive for this association has been the Christian tradition of Lucifer as the leader of the fallen angels and the archangel Michael as the leader of the Elect angels, although this idea was certainly influenced by Tanach (cf. Dan 10:13, 21; 12:1) and the apocalyptic literature (cf. *I Enoch* 6:1-6; 7:1; 10:8-9; *Jubilees* 5:1-2).

277 P. Wernberg-Møller, "A Reconsideration of the Two Spirits in the Rule of the Community (1QSerek 3:13-4:26)," *RQ* 11 (1961): 423, who argues entirely for the psychological interpretation. In this case, the two spirits are equivalent to the rabbinic notion of the "good inclination" and the evil inclination."

Anderson has correctly pointed out that in the scrolls this term is used frequently to denote *supernatural beings* or *angels*, as an apocalyptic development in comparison with the usage in the Old Testament.[278] Therefore, what approaches the "psychological" may be simply a reflection of the ethical power exerted over men by these beings, a thought certainly in harmony with the predestinarian idea scrolls.[279] Further, the distinctions drawn between *malak* ("messenger") and *ruach*, as well as statements (e.g. *1QS* 3:24) depicting the spirits under the command of (in this case) the single Angel of Darkness, seem to make the equivocation of angel with spirit impossible.[280]

The influence of the Angel of Darkness was explained as one that had produced desecration historically and would continue to do so until the final conflict. The language of cultic pollution, and particularly Temple pollution, runs throughout the whole of Qumran literature (e.g., the Damascus Document), and one means of assuring the eventual restoration of the Temple and the Remnant to a purified state was to see this as the resolution to a cosmic enmity that was greater than any one religious sect or political regime. It appears that the author of *1QS 3:13-4:26* felt

---

278 Cf. A. A. Anderson, "The Use of '*Ruah*' in *1QS, 1QH* and *1QM*," *JSS* 7 (1962): 298. He argues that where this terminology differs, it is the result of differences in authorship, date, and nature of the writings. It also appears that the Johannine meaning of the terms "Spirit of Truth" (John 14:17; 15:26; 16:13), and "sons of light" (John 12:36), have been read back into the Qumran text. Frank Moore Cross, Jr., *The Ancient Library of Qumran & Modern Studies* (New York: Doubleday, 1961), 213, has noted: "The "Spirit of Truth" in *1QS* is an angelic creature who is at a greater distance from God than the "Spirit of Truth," who in John is God's own Spirit."

279 The source of evil in *1QS* is *external* to men and not as Werberg-Møller has suggested "created by God to dwell in man." Rather, in *1QS* 3:18 the text says that God allotted the spirits unto man." Furthermore, *1QS* suggests that men are divided into two mutually exclusive camps ("sons of light" or "sons of darkness"). W. D. Davies, "The Dead Sea Scrolls and Christian Origins," *RL* 26 (1957): 246-64, has pointed this out saying, "that [these spirits] are not merely inherent properties of man, as such, emerges from the use of the term 'angel' to describe the two spirits: this preserves the 'otherness' of the two spirits even when they appear to be immanent." Therefore, U. Simon, *Heaven in the Christian Tradition* (London, 1958), 173, concludes: "The struggle in the heart of man is inseparable from the cosmic array of powers (*1QS* 4:18)."

280 Cf. A. R. C. Leaney, *The Rule of Qumran and Its Meaning* (Philadelphia: Fortress, 1966), 43 notes: "The tendency to personify as angels the powers which control the stars and to identify God himself with the *Urlicht* may be paralleled by the identification of the two spirits with personal supernatural beings."

that the recognition of the existence of an "Angel of Darkness" resolved the problem of the failure of the post-exilic community to attain proper purification and holiness and to receive the promised restoration: "And through the Angel of Darkness all the sons of righteousness stray and all their sins, their faults, their defilements and their acts of disobedience are caused by his rule" (*1QS* 3:22). Thus, if the problem of desecration was part of a predestined plan (under the rule of evil forces), so must also the resolution through restoration (under godly forces) be the expected climax of that plan. In this theology, therefore, greed, falsehood, pride, deceit, hypocrisy, lust, and all other evils in the world were seen to be caused by this entity, also called appropriately, the "Spirit of Perversity."

Since a similar role of seduction to evil is given to Belial (see below) we perhaps should not distinguish the two, however, it may be possible that the Angel of Darkness functions primarily as a pervasive evil influence,[281] much like the Angels of Mastemoth, in conjunction with Belial, whose figure has supernatural proportions, but is better defined as an evil adversary to the Community and their Teacher of Righteousness, and ultimately the Messiah. On this basis, it is probable that the figure refers to Satan.

One of the primary characteristics of Qumran dualism is the eschatological dimension, and we must always keep these figures of desecration and destruction in the eschatological perspective. Indeed, the oldest form of dualism found at Qumran is represented by the *War Scroll* which has as its focus the final dualistic battle (*Endkampfdualismus*). The decisive apocalyptic intervention of God and the triumph of the "sons of light" was always a future act. In this context, the ultimate outcome for the Angel of Darkness as well as for Belial and the "sons of darkness," is "destruction" or

---

281 However, if these two are one entity, then the Angel of Darkness may be construed as the deceptive functioning of Satan, much as in the New Testament, cf. Satan "appearing as an angel of light" (2 Cor 11:14), and "deceiving the whole world" (Rev 12:9; 13:14; 20:3).

"annihilation" at the final judgment stated in the scrolls as "the time of decreed judgment" (*1QS* 4:14, 19b-20a; *1QM* 1:4-7).

The Figure of Belial

The figure of "Belial" ("worthlessness") in the New Testament has been considered a cognomen of Satan (2 Cor 6:15; cf. 2 Pet 2:15; Jude 11; Rev 2:14), and on this parallel usage, the term has been said to be used for the figure of the Devil at Qumran. Since Temple pollution is one of the three "nets of Belial" according to the Damascus Document (column iv), this figure is as central in the use of the desecration motif at Qumran as it was in other apocalyptic literature (e.g., 3 *Sibylline Oracles* 63-74).

As with the influence of the Angel of Darkness over the post-exilic community, the rule of Belial was in accord with the predestined plan of God which included his evil actions in bringing about the sin of Israel. This is evident from the statement in 1QM 13:9-11: "And from former times You [YHWH] appointed the Prince of Light to help us...and You made Belial to corrupt..." We also find that the desecration of the cultus by religious syncretism and violations of the purification laws were the result of Belial's corruption of the Nation: "And the Levites shall recite the iniquities of the sons of Israel and all their guilty rebellions and their sins, accomplished under the power of Belial" (*1QS* 1:22-24). Conversely, the righteous man is the one who resists the power of Belial and thereby will be rewarded at the Restoration. For example, we read in a Qumranic psalm called *The Second Letter on Works Reckoned as Righteousness* (*4Q397-399*): "...and to keep you far from evil thoughts and the counsel of Belial. Then you will rejoice at the End Time..." (lines 32-33). Thus, the desecration of the Temple, land, and exile was part of the cosmic conflict, with the movement being toward an eschatological restoration at the eschaton, the day of deliverance for the righteous, when the rule of Belial would be terminated by the "People of God" (*4Q246* 1:7-9; 2:1-8; *1 QM* 1:5-10).

Belial also follows in the developmental progression of foreign oppressors of God and Israel. In *CD* 5:17ff Belial is portrayed as a ruling angel in opposition to the Law of God: "At the beginning Moses and Aaron arose through the hand of the prince of light, but Belial, in his wickedness, raised up Jannes and his brother..." In this instance, Belial is equated with Pharaoh as a type of divine opponent of God's agents and therefore of God Himself. Additionally, in the Damascus Document, it is stated that the "Prince of Lights" is directly opposed by Belial (CD 5:18). Thus, the adversarial position of Belial places him in continuity with Satan whose name itself means "adversary" and appears in the Old Testament as one (as well as his fallen angel agents) influences evil acts (1 Kgs 22:20-23; 1 Chr 21:1; Ezek 13:9; Zech 3:1-2) as well as directly opposing YHWH (Job 1-2).

The "Antichrist" in the Dead Sea Scrolls

While Belial may be generally equated with the figure of Satan, his role as an evil spiritual influence appears in many texts to become focused in the end time through a human opponent of God and Israel. In some texts this figure appears as an evil oppressor named "Malkiresha" in contrast to the royal/priestly figure "Melchizedek." In *Second Ezekiel* (4Q385-389) this individual is called the "son of Belial" and a "blasphemous/boastful king" who will "arise and oppress the Jewish People" (cf. 4Q246). This resembles the New Testament description of the Antichrist as the "man of sin and lawlessness" (2 Thess 2:3) and the first Beast who follows the dragon (Satan), gains global worship and has a mouth full of "arrogant words and blasphemies against God" (Rev 13:1-6). Consequently, Jewish scholars have also identified him as the Antichrist. The terms in *Second Ezekiel* occur in fragmentary texts within a context alluding to the national regathering and restoration of Israel based on a reference to the vision of the valley of dry bones (Ezek 37:4-6), immediately followed by a prayer concerning the end-time regathering. The lines that follow describe the "son of Belial" and the "blasphemous king" during the time these individuals function:

> And YHWH sai[d]: "A *son of Belial* will plan to oppress My People, but I will not allow him to do so (4Q386 f1ii:3). His rule shall not come to pass, but he will cause a multitude to be defiled [and] there will be no seed left... [In] those [days] a *blasphemous king* will arise among the Gentiles, and do evil things [ ] Israel from [being] a People. In his days I will break the Kingdom" (4Q388a f7ii:1-4; 4Q389 f8ii:10).

This text describes this future ruler as a Gentile king who will attempt to annihilate the People of Israel but will be destroyed by God. In the same context are references to Babylon, to God's hiding His face until Israel has filled up the measure of its sins, and of a period of apostasy, characterized by breaking the Abrahamic Covenant (4Q388a f7ii:2; 4Q389 f8ii:8). There is also an interesting comment concerning the wicked before they are taken into judgment: "Just as they will say, 'Peace and quiet is ours', so they will say 'The Land rests quietly'" (cf. Jer 6:14; 8:11; 1 Thess 5:3). All of this is reminiscent of passages concerning "the coming prince" of Daniel 9:26-27 and the deceptive security before the War of Gog of Magog in Ezekiel 38:8-16. Eisenman and Wise suggest that these terms may have parallels in *Pseudo-Daniel* (4Q243-45) in the terms ("Kings of the Peoples") and ("Kingdom of the Peoples"), which appear in a similar context during which time "ev]i[l] has led astray..." and "the called ones will be gathered," (lines 33-34, cf. line 51-55).[282]

---

282 Eisenman and Wise, *DSSU*, 65.

Other texts at Qumran also appear to be referring to this "son of Belial" by different descriptive terms. In CD 6:10; *1QpHab* 5:7-8, texts which depict a period of great spiritual declension on the part of Israel, this apostasy is said to be spearheaded by a figure called "son/man of sin" (cf. CD 6:15; 13:14; *1QS* 9:16; 10:19). This expression is quite similar to the New Testament term "the son of destruction," an expression found in the Pauline description of the eschatological desecrator, the Antichrist (2 Thess 2:3b). It is complemented by another term "son of iniquity" (*1QS* 3:21), which is also comparable to another New Testament phrase "the man of lawlessness." In addition, the New Testament *hapax legomena* "the mystery of lawlessness," found only in the Pauline Antichrist context (2 Thess 2:7), has an almost identical corresponding expression at Qumran: "mystery of wickedness" (*1Q20* 1:2).[283] Dupont-Sommer also claimed to have found a parallel in this Pauline text to the cryptic term "restrains" (2 Thess 2:6, 7) in the term "detain" (*1Q27* 1:7), translated the complete line of the text: "And all of those who detain [unjustly] the marvelous mysteries..."[284]

David Flusser claimed to identify another Qumran "Antichrist text" in a late first-century BCE Aramaic *4Q Pseudo-Daniel* fragment.[285] He has argued that it describes the superhuman hubris of the Antichrist, and therefore reveals that the idea of an antichrist

---

283 Cf. Joseph Coppens, "'Mystery' in the Theology of Saint Paul and its Parallels at Qumran," *Paul and the Dead Sea Scrolls*, ed. Jerome Murphy-O'Connor and James H. Charlesworth (New York: Crossroad, 1990), 141.

284 A. Dupont-Sommer, *The Essene Writings from Qumran*, trans. Geza Vermes (Oxford: Blackwell, 1961), 327.

285 This fragment from Cave IV was bought from Kando the antiquities dealer on July 9, 1958, and officially assigned to J. T. Milik of Harvard. Milik's failure to publish the text or his translation motivated the Jesuit priest Joseph A. Fitzmyer to publish an unauthorized translation of part of the text in "The Contribution of Qumran Aramaic to the Study of the New Testament," *NTS* 20 (1973-74): 391-94. First credit for full publication goes to Emilé Peuch, "Fragment d'une apocalypse en araméen (4Q246 = pseudo-Dand) et le 'royaume de Dieu'", *RB* 99 (1992): 98-131, who succeeded Milik as the officially designated editor. Following the release of a photograph of the text by the Huntington Library of San Marino, California, Fitzmyer published his own complete translation with commentary, cf. "4Q246: The "Son of God" Document from Qumran," *Biblica* 74:2 (1993), 153-74.

(or anti-messiah) is Jewish and pre-Christian.[286] Here we may have a remarkable, though contested, allusion to Daniel 9:27, which may have served as the original seedbed for apocalyptic Antichrist imagery. This text, formerly classified with the *4Q Pseudo-Daniel* fragments, was later designated as the *Messianic Apocalypse* or *The Son of God* text (4Q246).[287] Emile Puech, who was the official translator of this text, also interpreted this so-called "son of God" as a negative figure, though he identified him with a past, rather than future king. Let us first consider the text and its translation, and then the arguments of Flusser and his opponents concerning the interpretation of this controversial text:

> **Q246 f1i:1** [...a spirit from God] rested upon him, he fell before the throne. 2[...O ki]ng, wrath is coming to the world, and your years 3[shall be shortened...such] is your vision, and all of it is about to come unto the world. 4[... Amid] great [signs], tribulation is coming upon the land. 5[...After much killing] and slaughter, a prince of nations 6[will arise...] the king of Assyria and Egypt 7[...] he will be ruler over the land 8[...] will be subject to him and all will obey 9[him. Also his son] will be called The Great, and be designated by his name.
>
> **4Q246 f1ii:1** He will be called the Son of God, they will call him the son of the Most High. But like the meteors 2that you saw in your vision, so will be their kingdom. They will reign only a few years over 3the land, while people tramples people and nation tramples nation [*vacat*]

---

286 David Flusser, "The Hubris of the Antichrist in a Fragment from Qumran," *Immanuel* 10 (Spring, 1980): 31-37.

287 It was originally entitled Pseudo-Daniel, with the sigla *4Q psDanAa* or *Dan^d* 209, because of the mention of "Daniel" in column 1, line 2, although this Daniel only appeared as a man falling before the throne, yet there was also an allusion to the eternal kingdom of Dan 2:44, which warranted this signification. However, the exceptional appearance of the term "S/son of God" and the interpretation of this text as an allusion to Dan 7:13, has become the basis for the title and sigla.

> 4Until the people of God arise; then all will have rest from warfare. 5Their kingdom will be an eternal kingdom, and all their paths will be righteous. They will judge 6the land justly, and all nations will make peace. Warfare will cease from the land, 7and all the nations shall do obeisance to them. The great God will be their help, 8He Himself will fight for them, putting peoples into their power, 9overthrowing them all before them. God's rule will be an eternal rule and all the depths of...

This account reveals common apocalyptic traits. A seer (roughly following the interpretation of the vision in Dan 2:40-44) interprets for the king a mystery concerning the last days, which he has received either in a dream or a vision. The vision is of a time of wars and great distress during which a wicked kingdom will rule over the world. This end-time condition is described as "one nation shall trample another..." (cf. *Sibylline Oracles* 635-36: "nations ravage nations;" *4 Esdras* 13:31: "city against city...kingdom against kingdom"; and Matt 24:7; Mark 13:8; Luke 21:10: "nation shall rise against nation") sets the tone for this text of a conflict between opposing kingdoms and a militant, nationalist king who is extremely war-like.[288] This ruler will be served by all nations and he will claim to be the son of the Most High. His reign will continue until Israel ("the People of God") will be restored ("rise"). Then all war will end, and universal peace will be established. In concert with biblical prophetic literature and Jewish apocalyptic, the wicked are deposed by divine intervention and Israel is exalted in the Messianic Kingdom. It should also be noted that this peace will come only *after* the cataclysmic [Messianic] war, indicating the tone of conflict that characterizes this text.

What Flusser saw in this text is the self-enthronement of a wicked ruler to be worshipped as, in some-sense, divine. He argues

---

288 Cf. Eisenman and Wise, *DSSU*, 69.

that we should identify this figure, who either claims or demands from others that they acclaim him with the title "'son of God," and "son of the Most High" as the king or leader of an oppressing kingdom.[289] Although Flusser's translation does not differ significantly from those who disagree with his interpretation, what controls his understanding of the text is the *vacat* (intentional break) in the middle of column 2 before the phrase "until the people of God arises." If this break is taken as an indication of the beginning of a new topic, which is viewed positively, then by contrast, what precedes it would be viewed negatively. Accepting this as an intentional hermeneutical key, Flusser, and Milik before him, interpreted what preceded the *vacat* as a description of the wicked ruler of the oppressive kingdom which brought distress and war, and also demanded divine worship from his subjects. Milik saw in this figure the Syrian king Alexander Balas (150-145 BCE, son of Antiochus IV Epiphanes who had persecuted the Jews in 167-164 BCE), whose image on coins is accompanied by the Greek inscription *theos epiphanou* ("god-manifest") or the Latin *Deo patre natus* ("born of a divine father").[290] However, as F. García Martíñez has pointed out, since it was Alexander Balas who appointed Jonathan as high priest (cf. Josephus, *Antiquities* 13. 2. 2 § 45), he could not have been regarded as an oppressor of Israel.[291]

Flusser observes that the text does not say that this usurping figure will *be* the son of the Most High, only that he, and/or

---

289 There is, however, ambiguity in the Aramaic wording as to whether he is self-designated or designated by others. In 2 Thess 2:4 the Antichrist figure designates himself, but in Rev 13:4 his worshippers so designate him. As Flusser (33) points out, the difference is minimal: "if others 'shall call him son of the Most High' they will do it at his behest." Perhaps both could be understood in this manner: he designates himself by his actions (in 2 Thess 2:4 by seating himself in the Temple), his worshippers designate him by their acclaim (by "crowning" his actions with the self-sought title).

290 Cf. F. Imhoof-Blumer, *Monnaies grecques*. Koninklijke Nederlandse Akademie van Wetenschappen, Afdeeling Letterkunde, Verhandelingen 14 (Amsterdam, 1883), 433-34 (§ 102, pl. H 13).

291 Cf. F. García Martínez, "4Q246: ¿Tipo del Anticristo o Libertador escatológico?," *El misterio de la Palabra: Homenaje a L. Alonso Schökel*, ed. V. Collado -E. Zurro (Madrid, 1983), 235; in English: "The Eschatological Figure of 4Q246," in *Qumran and Apocalyptic: Studies on the Aramaic Texts from Qumran*. STDJ 9 (Leiden: Brill, 1992), 169.

others shall *call* him such. Flusser conjectures that the claim of this Antichrist may be even greater than the available text reveals. Since the beginning of line 9 of the first column is missing, we can only read: "...[g]reat...he shall be called, and by his name shall he be designated." The phrase "by his name" may mean that the person shall be designated by his *own* name, but here it seems it is understood to have been called the name *of God*. Flusser argues that the parallelism "son of God"/"Son of the Most High" has an affinity with other apocalyptic texts: (1) the *Ascension of Isaiah* 4:2–16, which speaks of the incarnation of Beliar in whom all the peoples will believe and to whom they will sacrifice, (2) the *Oracles of Hystaspes*, which describes a king who will arise from Syria (as in *4Q246* column 1, line 6) as a destroyer of mankind, who "will constitute and call himself God and order himself to be worshipped as the Son of God,"[292] and (3) the *Assumption or Testament of Moses* 8:1–5, in which an end-time king of supreme authority persecutes the Jewish People, blasphemes God, violates the Law, and desecrates the Temple by forcing entrance to the Holy of Holies and offering pagan sacrifices on the altar.[293] He likewise compares 2 Thessalonians 2:4-5, where the end-time ruler called the "man of sin," has an investiture with divinity by seating himself in the Temple and proclaiming himself God.[294]

The chief argument in opposition to Flusser is that while the *vacat* does mark the transition to the final stage of the drama, it does not require that everything preceding it be understood as negative because repetition is a general characteristic of apocalyptic and thereby vitiates the assumption of sequential order neces-

---

292 Preserved in Lactantius, *Divinae Institutiones* 7. 17. 2-4 in CSEL 19: 638-39.

293 The term in this text in both Mishnaic Hebrew (e.g., *TJ* Shabbat 7:10a) and Aramaic signifies "the Person of God," thus, the blasphemy was directed toward God, cf. R. H. Charles, APOT 2:420, n. 5. Charles also suggests that "the innermost sanctuary" referred to may be that "of the heathen temples which the Jews were compelled to build (cf. I Macc. i. 47; Joseph. Ant. xv. 5.4)," while J. H. Charlesworth (OTP 1:931) translates it neutrally as "secret place." It seems preferable in light of the references to the Person of God, the Law, and the altar to see here the Holy of Holies, which Charles list as an alternative.

294 See Dan 9:27.

sary for this interpretation. However, if repetition is the literary device employed here, one must ask why the figure identified as "Son of God" only appears in column 1. John Collins, addressing this problem, answers that: "The figure who is called the Son of God is the representative, or agent, of the people of God. That is why he is not mentioned again after the rise of the people of God in column 2. His career and the rise of the people of God are simply two aspects of the same event."[295] However, just as repetition often is employed in apocalyptic, so also may sequential order appear, and the literary structure of the narrative must best decide whether this is the case in each context. However, in fragmentary texts, such as this, the decision is difficult. Collins's argument depends upon the prior acceptance that the Son of God has a reference to the Messiah, or at least is used in a positive sense, so that he can be viewed as the representative of the people of God.

Fitzmyer and Collins both object that this text could not be the "Antichrist" because this is a Christian idea and unattested in pre-Christian Judaism.[296] However, while the concept of the figure as a "mirror-image of Christ" (Collins's words) does not appear in Judaism, nearly every trait associated with the Antichrist depicted in the New Testament has a corollary in pre-Christian apocalyptic, especially in the "son of Belial" and "blasphemous king" texts. However, there appears no reason why, as Flusser contends, that this text might not be *the* exceptional example of such a pre-Christian anti-Messiah. This is in fact what Collins claims for this text as an example of a pre-Christian reference to the Messiah as "Son of God,"[297] a concept lacking clear parallels in Jewish apocalyptic. It is for this reason that Fitzmyer hesitates to make this identifica-

---

295 John J. Collins, "A Pre-Christian 'Son of God'" Among the Dead Sea Scrolls," *BR* 9:3 (June 1993): 36.
296 Cf. Fitzmyer, *op. cit.*, 169; Collins, *op. cit.*, 57, n. 5.
297 *Ibid.*, 35. Collins, "A Pre-Christian 'Son of God'" Among the Dead Sea Scrolls," notes (57, n. 4) that the messianic interpretation was first proposed by Frank Moore Cross.

tion.[298] While some of Flusser's exegesis and reconstruction of the text may be questionable, his argument for an Antichrist figure in this text does appear valid.

Based on the foregoing survey, including that of Flusser, some observations from Jewish apocalyptic literature about the specific nature of the Antichrist figure can be noted:

(1) The idea of "Antichrist" is Jewish and pre-Christian. It should be recognized that while this figure may well be anti-Messiah, the Greek preposition *anti* can also mean "in place of," and indicate one who *substitutes* himself for or *counterfeits* the claims of another, as in 4Q246.

(2) As a Jewish apocalyptic motif, it grew and developed within the apocalyptic *Weltanschauung*—the dualism between the cosmic and earthly forces of good and evil. The Antichrist became the human exponent of the evil forces that oppressed the people of God and desecrated the cult by which God was represented. 2 Thessalonians 2:4 pictures the Antichrist seating himself in the Temple to proclaim (and authenticate) his divinity, a blasphemous act that may certainly be described as an "abomination of desolation" (Dan 9:27; Matt 24:15; Mark 13:14).

(3) The eschatological desecration/restoration setting of this fragment makes it clear that the interpretation of "mystery," both in the context of Daniel 9 and, in this instance, at Qumran, was in view of a future revelation of a "mystery of lawlessness" which involved the unveiling of a human antagonist who usurps divine authority (his reign) and title (His Name). The defeat

---

298 *Ibid.*, 170-73.

of this epitome of human arrogance and defiance of the divine will along with concomitant acts of human rebellion (foreign invasion of Israel), will usher in the restored kingdom of Israel with its glorified Temple.

Thus, at Qumran, we have an eschatological figure (whether "Wicked Priest," "Belial," "son of Belial," "Malkiresha," or "son of God/son of Most High" = "Antichrist") is responsible for the desecration of the Temple, Land, and the oppression of the people of God. This figure leading "the sons of darkness" in a final war with the "the sons of light" will be destroyed by YHWH and His agents. This order of events, which has been interpreted literally, fits the eschatological timeline of tribulation before the advent of a messianic figure to wage a final battle with evil in order to establish his righteous kingdom.

The Eschatological Messiah

The Messiah of the Dead Sea Scrolls is clearly eschatological. His coming is at "the end of days," and is royal, priestly, and prophetic in nature. The Hebrew term *mashiach* ("anointed") is only found in about seventeen Qumran manuscripts[299] and in only eleven of these is there an unambiguous technical reference to a messianic figure. The remaining six employ a non-technical sense of "anointing." This number (in my opinion)[300] could be raised to twenty-one if we also include messianic terminology such as *nasi'* (Prince), *shevet* (Scepter), and *tzemach David* (Branch of David),[301]

---

299 CD 2:12; 6:1; 12:23; 14:19; 19:10; 20:1; 1QS 9:11; 1QSa 2:12, 14, 20; 1QM 11:17; 1Q30 1 2; 4Q252 1 v. 3; 4Q266 [Da] 18 iii. 12; 4Q267 [Db] 2 6; 4Q270 [De] 9 ii. 14; 4Q287 10 13; 4Q375 1 i. 9; 4Q376 1 i. 1; 4Q377 2 ii. 5; 4Q381 15 7; 4Q458 2 ii. 6; 4Q521 2 ii. 4 1; 8 9; 9 3, 6Q15 [D] 3 4; 11QMel 2:18.

300 Some would include 4Q246 ("Son of God") and 4Q534 1 i. 10 ("Elect of God"), however, I do not believe these are messianic. In the first instance I identify the figure with an evil eschatological ruler (Antichrist), and in the second the reference is to Noah.

301 1QSb 5:20, 27; 4Q161 5-6 3; 4Q174 1:11; 4Q175 12; 4Q285 4 2; 5 3, 4; 4Q369.

and perhaps a reading *ben bekor* (Firstborn).³⁰² All of these occurrences are in eschatological or apocalyptic contexts.³⁰³ The overriding theme is one of royal messianic expectation. The support for this expectation is built upon citations or allusions from Genesis 49:10 and Isaiah 11:1-4 and two of the aforementioned biblical messianic titles: "Prince" (cf. Ezek 34:24; 7:25), and "Branch of David" (cf. Jer 23:5; 33:15).

Most interpreters of the Messianic figure in the Scrolls conclude that not one, but two (and even three) messiahs are understood, each with their own office as king and priest (and prophet). This assumption rest upon one reference in the plural to the "Messiahs of Aaron and Israel," although this same construction is normally found elsewhere only in the singular. Rather than see this one instance of the "Messiahs of..." as a defective spelling (the *yodh* alone makes the construct plural) in light of the many and consistent examples of the singular "Messiah of...," interpreters have continued to follow the early theory made in consideration of CD (the Damascus Document, discovered in the Cairo synagogue genizah in 1896) that the singular was defective for the plural.³⁰⁴ Despite the later discovery of this one plural spelling in 1QS (Manual of Discipline), no case of such defective spelling was attested in the genizah manuscript of CD or among any of the Dead Sea Scrolls. This led Kuhn to suggest that the medieval scribes who had copied CD corrected the text to bring it into conformity with their theology.³⁰⁵ Nevertheless, there still seems to

---

302 4Q369 f1ii:6. Lines 6-8 read: "in everlasting light, and You appointed him as Your firstbo[rn] son. [There is none] like him, as a prince and ruler in all Your inhabited world [...] the c[rown of the] heavens and glory of the clouds You have laid [on him...]"

303 For a detailed study of these terms in their contexts see John J. Collins, *The Scepter and the Star: The Messiahs of the Dead Sea Scrolls and Other Ancient Literature*. The Anchor Bible Reference Library (New York: Doubleday, 1995).

304 This was first proposed by Louis Ginzberg in 1922 in his German publication *Eine Unbekannte Jüdische Sekte*, later translated in English as *An Unknown Jewish Sect* (New York: The Jewish Theological Seminary of America, 1976), 257-73.

305 H.-W. Kuhn, "The Two Messiahs of Aaron and Israel," in *The Scrolls and the New Testament*, ed. Kristal Stendahl (New York: Harper & Row, 1957). This is at least as reasonable an argument as that of Ginzburg, who seeing affinities between CD and the pseudepigraphal Testaments of the

be more than one messianic figure in the Dead Sea Scrolls. Such interpretive confusion is understandable in light of the difficulty of the Old Testament texts, and the Scrolls, spanning the period from the mid-second century BC to the latter half of the first-century AD, may reflect a developing theology in Second Temple messianism.[306] Nevertheless, the application of Old Testament Messianic texts in the Scrolls appears to have predominately combined the messianic offices in one person, and this is the Jewish theology reflected in the Gospels (cf. Matt 2:4-6; 22:42; Mark 14:61; Luke 2:25-38; 3:15; John 6:14; 7:27, 31; 12:34).[307] The New Testament clearly regards Jesus as the King Messiah after the Davidic dynasty (Matt 1:1; Luke 1:32; 3:31; cf. Acts 2:29-31) and as a Priest, though not Levitical, but after the order of Melchizedek (Heb 10:12-14).

Conclusion

The Dead Sea Scrolls are the earliest documentation of the eschatological views of an Orthodox Jewish sect during the late Second Temple period (late Hellenistic–early Roman periods). Rabbi Lawrence H. Schiffman summarizes the sectarian eschatological perspective when he writes:

Twelve Patriarchs and recognizing later Christian redaction from earlier two-Messiah versions, determined that CD also maintained a two-Messiah theology.

306 The Karaite commentators on the Twelve Prophets (Daniel al-Qumisi and Yefeth ben 'Ali) reveal that they understood Zechariah and Malachi to teach two Messiahs (Davidic and Priestly). Their affinities with the Essenes may indicate that their interpretations reflect a Qumran two-Messiah theology, or it may simply reflect the development of the messianic concept that may have become theologically separate in the later Second Temple period due to political imposition on the priesthood, an imposition that affected the Hasidean division that gave rise to the sects of both the Pharisees and the Essenes, cf. Emile Puech, "Messianism, Resurrection, and Eschatology," *The Community of the Renewed Covenant*, ed. Eugene Ulrich and James Vanderkam. Christianity and Judaism in Antiquity Series 10 (Indiana: University of Notre Dame Press, 1993), 237-40.

307 For a further study of this issue cf. Martin G. Abegg, Jr., "The Messiah at Qumran: Are We Still Seeing Double?," *Dead Sea Discoveries* 2:2 (June 1995): 125-44.

The Dead Sea Sect expected that the end of days would inaugurate an era of perfection in which they would see the culmination of the rituals and regulations practiced in the present pre-messianic age... The author of the [Rule of the Congregation (1QSa)] looked to the end of days for the restoration of the ancient glories of Israel. The monarchy, the true high priesthood, the tribal organization, all these were to be relived in the end of days. At the same time, he looked for a level of sanctity and purity impossible in the present age... The coming cataclysm would inaugurate both a return to the past and a new previously unachievable future observance of the law, ritual purity and perfection. It is this combination of trends which made possible the messianic fervor and immediacy which characterized the Dead Sea sect.[308]

The Dead Sea Scroll Community therefore had an imminent expectation of the coming of the Messiah, the end-time battle, and the era of Messianic Rule in which Israel would be restored politically and spiritually and conditions of ideal ritual purity would be established and enforced. With this background, the Dead Sea Scrolls also offers us a window into the eschatological worldview of Jesus and the New Testament. While some differences exist, especially with respect to the time of fulfillment and its realization by the Qumran Community, their concept of a linear development of eschatology within Israel as formulated by the biblical prophets correlates well with the premillennial timeline found in the early Jewish Christianity from the Apostles.[309] This

---

308 Lawrence H. Schiffman, *The Eschatological Community of the Dead Sea Scrolls: A Study of the Rule of the Congregation*, Society of Biblical Literature Monograph Series 38 (Atlanta, GA: Scholars Press, 1989), 68, 70.

309 Premillennialism is documented as the earliest view of the Church, for which see Philip Schaff, *History of the Christian Church* (Grand Rapids: Eerdmans, 1973), 2:614 and the statement of Justin Martyr, Dialogue with Trypho, 80, *Ante-Nicaean Fathers*, 1:239. Premillennialism was also part of the early Church's polemic against Gnosticism, see Donald Fairbairn, "Contemporary Millennial/Tribulational Debates," in *A Case of Historic Premillennialism: An Alternative to "Left Behind"*

can be reviewed via the diagram below that charts the eschatological views of the Qumran Community.

With this understanding, it cannot be said that premillennialism does not represent the earliest, and most consistent, prophetic interpretation. Certainly, it reflects the original eschatological context of the biblical Judaism into which Jesus was born which defined for national Israel and the Gentile nations the kind of Messiah that was expected and the religious and political conditions that would precede His rule from Israel over the world. Further, this understanding argues against a New Testament reinterpretation of national Israel as spiritual Israel (e.g., Christian supercessionism) and of a reinterpretation of the First Covenant (Old Testament) from a wholly typical or allegorical hermeneutic (e.g., amillennialism, postmillennialism).[310] The hope of Israel in a Messiah that would come to defeat Israel's enemies (Gentile nations) and death itself (resurrection) and would subsequently reign in His earthly Kingdom was a hope shared by believers in Israel and among the nations at the beginning of the Church. It is the hope that the Church today will return to its eschatological roots and again embrace the coming Messiah Who will appear and fulfill His good word to both Israel and the nations through His Kingdom (Acts 1:6–7a; 3:18–21; 2 Tim 4:1; Rev 11:15).

Eschatology, ed. Craig L. Blomberg and Sung Wook Chung (Grand Rapids: Baker, 2009), 129.

310 For a review of this hermeneutic see Michael Vlach, "The Hermeneutics of Non-Dispensationalism" (Paper for the 32nd Annual Pre-Trib Study Group Conference, Sheraton Hotel, Irving, TX, December 4-6, 2023, posted at MichaelJVlach.com).

Eschatology of the Dead Sea Scrolls

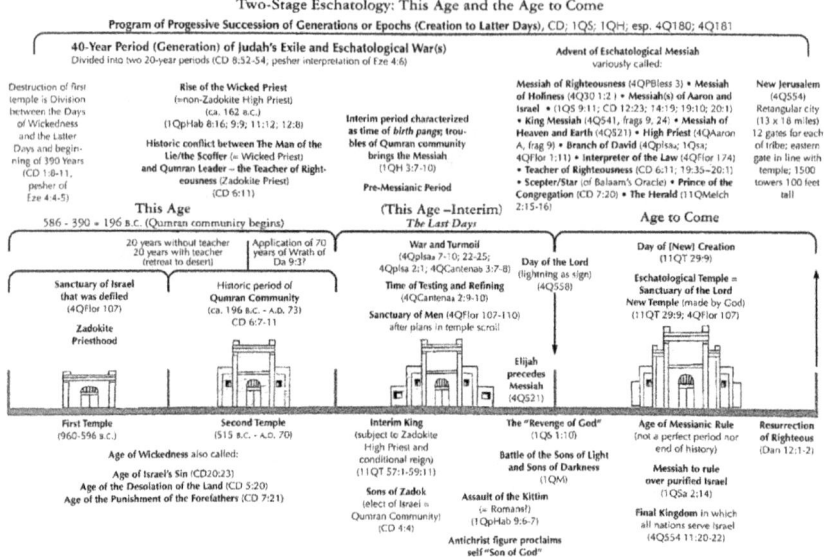

Chart 20 (used by permission) H.W. House, Randall Price, *Charts of Bible Prophecy* (Zondervan, 2003), 40.

BIBLIOGRAPHY

Abegg, Martin G., Jr. "The Messiah at Qumran: Are We Still Seeing Double?," *Dead Sea Discoveries* 2:2 (June 1995): 125-44.

Anderson, A. A. "The Use of '*Ruah*' in *1QS, 1QH* and *1QM*," *JSS* 7 (1962).

Balliet, M. "Un recueil liturgique de Qumrân, grotte 4: 'Les paroles des luminaries,'" *RB* 68 (1991).

Beckwith, R. T. "Daniel 9 and the Date of Messiah's Coming in Essene, Hellenistic, Pharisaic, Zealot, and Early Christian Computation," *RevQ* 19 (1979-1981): 521-542.

Betz, O. "Past Events and Last Events in the Qumran Interpretation of History," *Proceedings of the Sixth World Congress on Jewish Studies in Jerusalem 1976*. Jerusalem: The World Union of Jewish Studies, 1977.

Brooke, George J. *Exegesis at Qumran: 4QFlorilegium in its Jewish Context*. JSOTSup 29. Sheffield: JSOT Press, 1989.

Brownlee, W. H. "The Wicked Priest, the Man of Lies, and the Righteous Teacher—The Problem of Identity," *JQR* 83 (1982).

Bruce, F. F. *Biblical Exegesis in the Qumran Texts*. Revised ed. Grand Rapids: Eerdmans, 1959.

Buchanan, George Wesley, "Eschatology and the 'End of Days'," *JNES* 20 (1961): 188-93.

Charlesworth, James, ed. *Jesus and the Dead Sea Scrolls*. The Anchor Bible Reference Library. New York: Doubleday, 1993.

———, ed. *The Old Testament Pseudepigrapha*. 2 vols. New York: Doubleday, 1983, 1985.

———. "A Critical Comparison of the Dualism in 1QS 3:13-4:26 and the 'Dualism' Contained in the Gospel of John," *NTS* 15 (1968-1969).

Collins, John J. "A Pre-Christian 'Son of God' Among the Dead Sea Scrolls," *BR* 9:3 (June 1993).

———. "Patterns of Eschatology at Qumran," *Traditions in Transformation*. Edited by Baruch Halpern and Jon Levenson. Winona Lake, IN: Eisenbrauns, 1981.

———. *The Scepter and the Star: The Messiahs of the Dead Sea Scrolls and Other Ancient Literature*. The Anchor Bible Reference Library. New York: Doubleday, 1995.

Congar, Yves M.-J. *The Mystery of the Temple or the Manner of God's Presence to His Creatures from Genesis to the Apocalypse*. Translated by R. E. Trevett. Newman, 1962.

Coppens, Joseph. "'Mystery' in the Theology of Saint Paul and its Parallels at Qumran," *Paul and the Dead Sea Scrolls*. Edited by Jerome Murphy-O'Connor and James H. Charlesworth. New York: Crossroad, 1990.

Cross, Frank Moore, Jr., *The Ancient Library of Qumran & Modern Studies*. New York: Doubleday, 1961.

Daniélou, J. *The Dead Sea Scrolls and Primitive Christianity*. Baltimore: Helicon, 1963.

Davies, P. R. "Calendrical Change and Qumran Origin: An Assessment of VanderKam's Theory," *CBQ* 45 (1983): 80-89.

Davies, W. D. "The Dead Sea Scrolls and Christian Origins," *RL* 26 (1957): 246-64.

Driver, G. R. The Judean Scrolls, *The Problem and a Solution*. Oxford: Blackwell, 1965.

Dupont-Sommer, A. *The Essene Writings from Qumran*. Translated by Geza Vermes. Oxford: Blackwell, 1961.

Edwards, Grace. "The Historical Background of Early Apocalyptic Thought," *Scripture in History & Theology: Essays in Honor of J. Coert Rylaarsdam*. Edited by A. L. Merrill and T. W. Overholt. Pennsylvania: Pickwick Press, 1977.

Eisenman, Robert and Michael Wise, *The Dead Sea Scrolls Uncovered*. Massachusetts: Element, 1992.

Elliger, Kurt *Studien zum Habakkuk-Kommentar vom Toten Meer*. Tübingen: Mohr-Siebeck, 1953.

Fairbairn, Donald. "Contemporary Millennial/Tribulational Debates," in *A Case of Historic Premillennialism: An Alternative to "Left Behind" Eschatology*. Edited by Craig L. Blomberg and Sung Wook Chung. Grand Rapids: Baker, 2009.

Fiorenza, E.S. "Cultic Language in Qumran and in the New Testament," *CBQ* 38 (1976): 159-77.

Fitzmyer, J. A. "Further Light on Melchizedek from Qumran Cave 11," *JBL* 86 (1967).

Flusser, David. "The Hubris of the Antichrist in a Fragment from Qumran," *Immanuel* 10 (Spring, 1980).

———. *The Spiritual History of the Dead Sea Sect*. Translated by Carol Glucker. Tel-Aviv: MOD Books, 1989.

Freedman, N. D. "The Flowering of Apocalyptic," in *Apocalypticism*. Ed. Robert W. Funk. JTC 6. New York: Herder and Herder, 1969.

Fujita, Neil S. A Crack in the Jar: What Ancient Jewish Documents Tell us about the New Testament. New York: Paulist Press, 1986.

Gärtner, Bertil. *The Temple and the Community in Qumran and the New Testament* (Cambridge: At the University Press, 1965.

Ginzberg, Louis. *Eine Unbekannte Jüdische Sekte* (1922). Translated in English as *An Unknown Jewish Sect*. New York: The Jewish Theological Seminary of America, 1976.

Golb, N. *Who Wrote the Dead Sea Scrolls? The Search for the Secret of Qumran*. New York: Scribner, 1995.

Greenspahn, F.E. "Why Prophecy Ceased," *JBL* 108 (1989): 37-49.

Imhoof-Blumer, F. *Monnaies grecques*. Koninklijke Nederlandse Akademie van Wetenschappen, Afdeeling Letterkunde, Verhandelingen 14. Amsterdam, 1883.

Jassen, A. P. *Mediating the Divine: Prophecy and Revelation in the Dead Sea Scrolls and Second Temple Judaism*. STDJ 68. Leiden: Brill, 2007.

———. "Prophecy after 'the Prophets': The Dead Sea Scrolls and the History of Prophecy in Judaism," *The Dead Sea Scrolls in Context*. Edited by Armin Lange, Emanuel Tov, and Matthias Weigold. 2 vols. Leiden: Brill, 2011.

———. "Prophets and Prophecy in the Qumran Community," *AJSR* 23 (2008): 299-334.

Jaubert, A. "Le Calendrier des Jubilés et de la Secte Qumrân: Ses origines bibliques," *VT* 3 (1955): 250-64.

Kosmala, H. "The Parable of the Unjust Steward in the Light of Qumran," *Annual of the Swedish Theological Institute*. Edited by H. Kosmala, 114-21. Leiden : Brill, 1964.

Kuhn, H.-W. "The Two Messiahs of Aaron and Israel," in *The Scrolls and the New Testament*. Edited by Kristal Stendahl. New York: Harper & Row, 1957.

Leaney, A.R.C. *The Rule of Qumran and Its Meaning*. Philadelphia: Fortress, 1966.

Martínez, García. "4Q246: ¿Tipo del Anticristo o Libertador escatólogico?," *El misterio de la Palabra: Homenaje a L. Alonso Schökel*. Edited by V. Collado -E. Zurro. Madrid, 1983. In English: "The Eschatological Figure of 4Q246," in *Qumran and Apocalyptic: Studies on the Aramaic Texts from Qumran*. STDJ 9. Leiden: E. J. Brill, 1992.

Mason, Steve. "Did the Essenes Write the Dead Sea Scrolls? Don't Rely on Josephus." *BAR* (November/December 2008).

Mckelvey, R. J. *The New Temple: The Church in the New Testament*. Oxford Theological Monographs (London: Oxford University Press, 1969.

Merrill, Eugene H. *Predestination at Qumran: A Theological Study of the Thanksgiving Hymns* Leiden: Brill, 1975.

Mertens, A. *Das Buch Daniel im Lichte der Texte vom Toten Meer*. Würzburg: Echter, 1971.

Murphy-O'Connor, J. "The Essenes and Their History," *RB* 81 (1974): 215-44.

———. "The Essenes in Palestine," *BA* 40 (1977): 94-124.

Nickelsburg, George W.E. *Jewish Literature Between the Bible and the Mishnah* (Philadelphia: Fortress Press, 1981

———. "Reading the Hebrew Scriptures in the First Century: Christian Interpretations in Their Jewish Context," *W & W* 3:3 (Summer 1983): 238-50.

———. and Michael E. Stone, *Faith and Piety in Early Judaism: Texts and Documents*. Philadelphia: Fortress, 1983.

Nötscher, F. "Geist und Geister in den Texten von Qumran," *Mélanges bibliques: rédigés en l'honneur de André Robert*, 305-16. Trauvaux de l'Institut Catholique de Paris 4. Paris, 1956.

Overholt, T. "The End of Prophecy: No Players without a Program," in The Place Is Too Small for Us: The Israelite Prophets in Recent Scholarship. Edited by R.P. Gordon, 527–538. SBTS 5. Winona Lake: Eisenbrauns, 1995.

Price, Randall. *Secrets of the Dead Sea Scrolls*. Eugene, OR: Harvest House Publishers, 1996.

———. "Old Testament Tribulation Terms." Chap. 3 in *When the Trumpet Sounds*. Oregon: Harvest House Publishers, 1995.

Puech, Emile. "Messianism, Resurrection, and Eschatology," *The Community of the Renewed Covenant*. Edited by Eugene Ulrich and James Vanderkam. Christianity and Judaism in Antiquity Series 10. Indiana: University of Notre Dame Press, 1993.

Ringgren, Helmer. *The Faith of Qumran: The Theology of the Dead Sea Scrolls*. Expanded Edition. New York: Crossroad, 1995.

Rowley, H. H. *The Relevance of Apocalyptic: A Study of Jewish and Christian Apocalypses from Daniel to the Revelation*. New York: Association Press, 1963.

Schaff, Philip. *History of the Christian Church*. Grand Rapids: Eerdmans, 1973.

Schiffman, Lawrence H. *The Eschatological Community of the Dead Sea Scrolls: A Study of the Rule of the Congregation*. Society of Biblical Literature Monograph Series 38. Atlanta, GA: Scholars Press, 1989.

———. *The Halakha at Qumran, and Sectarian Law in the Dead Sea Scrolls: Courts, Testimony and the Penal Codes*. Chico, CA: Scholars Press, 1983.

Scott, J. Julius, Jr., *Customs and Controversies: Intertestamental Jewish Backgrounds of the New Testament* (Grand Rapids: Baker Book House, 1995).

———. "On the Value of Intertestamental Jewish Literature for New Testament Theology," *JETS* 23:4 (December 1980).

Shanks, Hershel. "Searching for Essenes at Ein Gedi, Not Qumran," *BAR* 28:4 (July/August 2002).

Simon, U. *Heaven in the Christian Tradition*. London: Rockliff, 1958.

Sommer, B.D. "Did Prophecy Cease? Reevaluating a Reevaluation," *JBL* 115 (1995): 31-47.

Talmon, Shemaryahu. *The World of Qumran from Within*. Jerusalem: The Magnes Press, 1989.

———. "The Calendar Reckoning of the Sect from the Judean Desert," *Scripta Hierosolymitana* IV. Jerusalem: Magnes Press, 1965.

VanderKam, James C. *The Dead Sea Scrolls Today*. Grand Rapids: Eerdmans, 1994.

———. "2 Maccabees 6, 7a and Calendrical change in Jerusalem," *Journal for the Study of Judaism* 12 (1981).

———. "The Origin, Character, and Early History of the 364-Day Calendar: A Reassessment of Jaubert's Hypothesis," *CBQ* 41 (1979): 390-411.

van der Woude, A. S. "Wicked Priest or Wicked Priests? Reflections on the identification of the Wicked Priest in the Habakkuk Commentary," *JJS* 33 (1982): 349-59.

Vlach, Michael. "The Hermeneutics of Non-Dispensationalism." Paper for the 32nd Annual Pre-Trib Study Group Conference, Sheraton Hotel, Irving, TX, December 4-6, 2023, posted at MichaelJVlach.com.

Wacholder, Ben Zion. *The Dawn of Qumran: The Sectarian Torah and the Teacher of Righteousness*. Monographs of the Hebrew Union College 8. Cincinnati: Hebrew Union College, 1983.

Wenschkewitz, H. *Die Spiritualisierung der Kultusbegriffe Tempel, Priester, und Opfer im Neuen Testament, Angelos*. Beiheft 4. Leipzig: Pfeiffer, 1932.

Wernberg-Møller, P. "A Reconsideration of the Two Spirits in the Rule of the Community (1QSerek 3:13-4:26)," *RQ* 11 (1961).

CHAPTER EIGHT

THE TIMING OF THE EZEKIEL INVASION

by Dr. Ron Rhodes

Some 2,600 years ago, the ancient prophet Ezekiel foretold a remarkable event—the regathering of the Jews from "all the countries" back to their homeland, Israel (Ezek 36:24; 37). This prophecy was followed by a more ominous prediction of a full-scale invasion of Israel by a colossal northern force led by Russia, along with a coalition of Muslim nations, including Iran, Sudan, Turkey, Libya, and other Muslim nations (38:1-6). This invasion is popularly known as the "Ezekiel invasion."

The sinister goal of the invaders will be the complete annihilation of the Jewish people and the plundering of Israel's wealth (Ezek 38:12). Overwhelmed by the sheer magnitude of this assault, Israel will have no chance of defending itself. However, God will intervene and supernaturally destroy the invaders (verses 18-23). All of this is predicted to take place "in the latter years" (verse 8) and "in the latter days" (verse 16), referring to the end times.

More than a few Bible students have observed a striking phenomenon unfolding in our day: *The very nations predicted to unite in this end-time military coalition are now coming together.* What makes this even more remarkable is that this alliance is beginning to take shape *following* the restoration of Israel in 1948. Jews worldwide have returned to their homeland, as prophesied, and today Israel boasts the largest Jewish population on the planet. These developments are fueling speculation that we may be witnessing the groundwork being laid for the long-dreaded invasion of Israel that was foretold by the prophet Ezekiel.

There is ongoing discussion among Christian scholars and pastors about the timing of this invasion. Several scenarios have been suggested. Before we examine these scenarios, let us first consider some basic facts:

1. A precondition for the invasion of Israel by the northern military coalition is that the Jews must first be restored to the Holy Land. Ezekiel proclaimed that this invasion would occur only after the miraculous regathering of the scattered Jews from the farthest corners of the earth. These sons and daughters of Israel, hailing from countless nations around the world, were prophesied to return to "your own land" (Ezek 36:24; 37). Ezekiel 38:8 refers specifically to the Holy Land "whose inhabitants have been gathered from many nations to the mountains of Israel." Israel, of course, became a nation again in 1948. Since that year, we have witnessed the continued regathering of Jews from many nations, all converging upon Israel. With countless Jewish people now back in the land after a long and worldwide dispersion across many nations, a vital piece of the puzzle is now in place, setting the stage for the future invasion of Israel by the northern military coalition.

2. Since the prophecy in Ezekiel 36–37 is being literally fulfilled—with the regathering and relocation of Jews from "many nations" around the world back to the Holy Land—we can expect that chapters 38–39, which

refer to the invasion of Israel, will likewise be literally fulfilled in the future.

3. This invasion will occur in the end times. We know this because in Ezekiel 38:8, God said to Gog, the leader of the northern military coalition: "After many days you will be summoned; *in the latter years* you will come into the land that is restored from the sword, whose inhabitants have been gathered from many nations to the mountains of Israel..." In Ezekiel 38:16, God likewise said to Gog: "You will come up against My people Israel like a cloud to cover the land. *It shall come about in the last days* that I will bring you against My land..." Thomas Ice reminds us that the Old Testament usage of terms like "latter years" and "last days" refer to "a time when Israel is in her time of tribulation."[311] J. Dwight Pentecost agrees that these terms have "specific reference to the latter years and days of God's dealing with the nation Israel...in the seventieth week of Daniel's prophecy."[312]

4. There has never been an invasion in which (1) a massive alliance of nations in the territories of modern Russia, Iran, Turkey, Sudan, and Libya attacked Israel, and (2) God utterly destroyed the alliance with a massive earthquake, fire and brimstone, infighting among the troops, and the outbreak of disease, which (3) resulted in so many casualties that it took seven months to bury all the dead bodies in a large valley. If the invasion hasn't happened *yet*, then it will happen in the future.

---

[311] Thomas Ice, "Are We Living in the Last Days?" Available online at www.pre-trib.org.
[312] J. Dwight Pentecost, *Things to Come* (Grand Rapids: Zondervan, 1965), 346.

5. We can observe that the alignment of the nations mentioned in Ezekiel 38–39 may not have made logical sense at the time of Ezekiel's writing. After all, these nations are not all geographically contiguous, and Islam did not yet exist. (Islam did not emerge until the seventh century AD, long after Ezekiel's time.) Today, the alliance makes perfect sense because the coalition consists primarily of Islamic nations. This alone provides a compelling reason for their unification in launching an attack on Israel.

6. The invasion cannot occur until Israel is living *in security* and is *at rest*. The Jews living in Israel will be "living securely, all of them" (Ezek 38:8). The invasion will target Jews in Israel "who are at rest, that live securely, all of them living without walls and having no bars or gates" (verse 11). Prophecy scholars have two primary views regarding what might lead to this sense of security in Israel: (1) Some believe that Israel is already in a state of relative security because of its peace treaties with major Arab nations, its well-equipped army, its first-rate air force, its effective missile-defense system, its strong economy, and its close relationship with the United States. (2) Others believe that in the face of the continued Muslim threat to Israel, a true sense of security will come only when the leader of a revived Roman Empire—the Antichrist—signs a covenant with Israel. This event will officially begin the tribulation period (Dan 9:27). In this view, Israel's security will be backed by the military might of the revived Roman Empire. Both views are viable.[313]

---

313 See Ron Rhodes, *Northern Storm Rising: Russia, Iran, and the Emerging End-Times Military Coalition Against Israel* (Eugene: Harvest House Publishers, 2008).

We can all agree that this invasion will occur at some point in the future. *But when?* Will it be before the tribulation period? In the middle of the tribulation period? Toward the end of the tribulation? Perhaps after the tribulation but before the millennial kingdom? Or does it occur *during* the millennial kingdom—at its start or at its end?

This is undoubtedly one of the most debated and controversial questions surrounding Ezekiel 38–39. In what follows, I will briefly summarize the various positions. Space limitations require that I be very selective in describing their respective strengths and weaknesses. As you peruse these various scenarios, you will notice that some of them offer similar supporting evidence, but it is described with a slightly different twist.

Scenario 1: Before the Tribulation and Before the Rapture

Tim LaHaye and Jerry Jenkins, in their popular *Left Behind* series, suggest that the invasion of Israel by the northern military coalition will take place before both the tribulation period and the rapture. This view is shared by popular novelist Joel Rosenberg, author of *The Ezekiel Option*.[314]

LaHaye was cautious not to be dogmatic:

"I risk the criticism of colleagues when I suggest that Christ may rapture His church *after* the destruction of Russia—particularly because there is no conclusive biblical teaching for this view. I may be influenced by my yearning to see the mighty soul harvest... But I caution the reader not to be dogmatic. We know Russia will be destroyed, but we cannot determine exactly when in the scenario it will happen."[315]

---
314   Joel Rosenberg, *Epicenter* (Carol Stream: Tyndale House, 2006), 229.
315   Tim LaHaye, *The Coming Peace in the Middle East* (Grand Rapids, MI: Zondervan, 1984), 150.

Rosenberg likewise concedes that the exact timing of the invasion remains uncertain.

The following are the reasons typically suggested for this viewpoint:

1. This viewpoint harmonizes well with the seven-year tribulation period. Specifically, the seven-year period required to burn the enemy's weapons after God's destruction of the invaders (Ezek 39:9) is precisely the same as the seven-year tribulation period. We know that the tribulation period lasts seven years because it is the seventieth week of Daniel (Dan 9:27)— "one week" of years. This period commences when the Antichrist makes a covenant with Israel, intended to last the entire seven-year period.

2. This view may explain why Israel is able to rebuild its temple. After all, if the Muslims were still in power at the beginning of the tribulation period, it would be difficult for Israel to rebuild the temple on the Temple Mount in Jerusalem in the face of Muslim hostility. However, if the Muslim armies are decimated by divine intervention before the tribulation period even begins, this significant obstacle to Israel's Temple restoration will be removed.

3. Some proponents of this view say it must be correct because the other views seem infeasible. They suggest it makes no sense to place the invasion at the end of the tribulation period, the beginning of the millennial kingdom, or the end of the millennial kingdom. "It

---

Thomas Ice, however, reports that "Tim LaHaye has told me personally that even though they represented a pre-rapture position on Ezekiel 38 and 39 in their novel, he tends to place it after the rapture but before the tribulation." See Thomas Ice, "Ezekiel 38 and 39," Part 1, *Pre-Trib Perspectives*, posted at the Pre-Trib Research Center website.

must, therefore, be located before the tribulation because there is no other place for it to occur since the three other suggested dates are impossible."[316]

4. This scenario seems consistent with God's boundless grace and mercy. As God destroys the colossal northern alliance, He will demonstrate His unparalleled power, greatness, and glory before an attentive world (Ezek 39:6-7, 13, 21-22). As a result, there will be numerous conversions among both the Jews and the Gentiles. If this invasion were to occur before the rapture, the countless people who accept Christ because of God's mighty testimony of Himself would be spared the nightmarish tribulation period by being taken out of the world.[317]

Despite the arguments in favor of this position, there are also problems worth mentioning:

1. The idea of the invasion occurring before the rapture seems to contradict Ezekiel's indication that the invasion will occur in the "latter years" or "latter days" (Ezek 38:8, 16). Many pretribulationists have long taught that when these phrases are used about Israel, they refer to the future tribulation period. Given this, the Ezekiel invasion could hardly occur before the rapture since the rapture precedes the tribulation period. However, pretribulationist scholar Arnold Fruchtenbaum contends that this is too strict a view of these terms: "These terms simply apply to the whole period of the end times when prophecy is again being

---

[316] David Cooper, cited in J. Dwight Pentecost, *Things to Come* (Grand Rapids, MI: Zondervan, 1964), 345.
[317] Rosenberg, *Epicenter*, 251.

fulfilled, and so it can very easily apply to the closing days of the Church Age as well."[318]

2. The scenario of the invasion occurring before the rapture may contradict Ezekiel's prophecy that the invasion will occur when Israel is living in security and at rest (Ezek 38:11). As noted previously, some prophecy scholars are convinced that Israel will not experience this strong sense of security and rest until the leader of the revived Roman Empire (the Antichrist) signs a covenant that guarantees Israel's protection (Dan 9:27). John F. Walvoord is representative: "The scene is one of peace which has its best explanation with the seven-year covenant enacted by the ruler of the ten-nation confederacy."[319] Until then, Israel will remain as it is now—always on "high alert" for the possibility of attack by Muslim nations.

3. The New Testament teaches that the rapture is imminent. This means that there is nothing that must be prophetically fulfilled before the rapture occurs. Therefore, it cannot be said that this invasion must take place before the rapture. In fairness, however, those who believe the invasion may occur before the rapture "carefully avoid saying that it *must* occur before the rapture."[320] They still hold to the doctrine of imminence.

4. A slightly more complex argument relates to 2 Thessalonians 2:8, which tells us that the Antichrist is presently being restrained: "He who now restrains" will continue to restrain "until he is out of the way." Many

---

[318] Arnold Fruchtenbaum, *The Footsteps of the Messiah* (San Antonio: Ariel Publishers, 2004), 121.
[319] John F. Walvoord, *Every Prophecy of the Bible* (Colorado Springs: David C. Cook, 2011), 190.
[320] Mark Hitchcock, "The Battle of Gog and Magog," posted at the Pre-Trib Center website, www.pre-trib.org.

pretribulationists interpret this restrainer to be the Holy Spirit, who will be "taken out of the way" at the rapture. In this view, the church is the temple of the Holy Spirit (1 Cor 3:16). When the church is removed from the earth at the rapture, the Holy Spirit—who indwells the church—will also be removed. This poses a problem for the view that the invasion into Israel occurs before both the tribulation *and* the rapture: (1) Israel cannot be invaded until it is living in security. (2) Israel will not have security until the Antichrist signs a covenant with Israel—an event that begins the tribulation period. (3) However, the Antichrist cannot emerge until after the rapture since that is when the restrainer—the Holy Spirit—will be removed. Therefore (4) Israel will not be in security until after the rapture. Hence (5) The invasion of the northern military coalition cannot occur until after this time.

5. I noted previously that proponents of this view say that the seven years needed to burn enemy weapons (Ezek 39:9) correspond nicely with the seven-year tribulation period. The problem is that the Jews will be forced to flee Jerusalem halfway through the tribulation. When the Antichrist desecrates the Jewish temple at the midpoint of the tribulation, Jesus urges the Jewish residents to evacuate the city without any delay and without any personal belongings (Matt 24:17-21). We might paraphrase His words: "Run for your lives or you're dead!" One must ask: How can the Jews complete the task of burning weapons for seven years while having to immediately evacuate Jerusalem—*without packing*—midway through the tribulation period?

Scenario 2: After the Rapture but Before the Tribulation

Some believe the northern military coalition will invade Israel after the rapture but before the tribulation period. Thomas Ice is an advocate of this position: "It will be during the interval of days, weeks, months, or years between the rapture and the start of the seven-year tribulation."[321] Several reasons are offered to support this perspective:

1. After the rapture, the world could plunge into complete disorder. Given the significant Christian population in the United States, the rapture's impact on this country could be severe. This situation could cause Russia and its Muslim allies to seize the moment, seeing it as an ideal time to launch an attack on Israel, which, up till this time, the United States has protected.

2. Once God destroys Russia and the Muslim invaders before the tribulation period, this could open the door for the rise of the antichrist as the leader of the revived Roman Empire—a European superstate. Thomas Ice writes: "If the tribulation is closely preceded by a failed regional invasion of Israel (by Russia and her Muslim allies), then this would remove much of the Russian and Muslim influence currently in the world today."[322] The absence of the Russian and Muslim forces after their defeat significantly eases the Antichrist's path to achieving world domination.

---

[321] Thomas Ice, "Last Days," in *The Harvest Handbook of Bible Prophecy*, eds. Ed Hindson, Mark Hitchcock, Tim LaHaye (Eugene: Harvest House, 2020), 218.

[322] Thomas Ice, "Ezekiel 38 & 39 (Part 1)," Bible Prophecy Blog: News and Commentary from a Biblical Perspective, Jan. 6, 2011, https://www.bibleprophecyblog.com/2011/01/ezekiel-38-39-part-1.html

3. Since the Muslim invaders will be decimated before the tribulation period begins, this might make it easier for the antichrist to sign and enforce a covenant with Israel (Dan 9:27)—a peace pact guaranteeing Israel's security. The Muslim threat would be greatly reduced.

4. This scenario may explain why Israel will be able to rebuild the Jewish temple on the Temple Mount in Jerusalem. With Muslim forces decimated, Muslim opposition to the building of the temple will be markedly reduced.

5. The elimination of the Muslim forces before the tribulation period begins may open the door for the easy emergence of a one-world false religion during the first half of the tribulation period. Christians will have already been raptured before the tribulation. Now the Muslims are out of the way. The resulting religious vacuum will make it much easier for a one-world false religion to emerge and flourish.

6. If the invasion of Israel occurs after the rapture—and if the rapture occurs at least three-and-a-half years before the tribulation period begins—this would allow for the seven-year burning of enemy weapons to be completed by the midpoint of the tribulation period. This is important because, at the midpoint, the Jews will be forced to evacuate Jerusalem without delay and without packing (Matt 24:17-21).

Such points seem persuasive. But critics raise two objections:

1. Some remind us that the invasion will occur in the "latter days" or "latter years" (Ezek 38:8, 16), taken by many pretribulationists to mean the tribulation period.

However, as noted previously, others believe the terms "latter days" and "latter years" refer more broadly to the end times, including the years before the tribulation period.

2. Others remind us that Ezekiel prophesies that the invasion must occur when Israel is living in security and at rest (Ezek 38:11)—something that will reportedly not be the case until the Antichrist, the leader of the revived Roman Empire, signs a peace treaty guaranteeing Israel's protection (Dan 9:27). However, other interpreters believe Israel's security and peace come from its peace treaties with major Arab nations, its military strength, its first-rate air force, its strong economy, and its close relationship to the United States. This subject is widely debated.

Scenario 3: The First Half of the Tribulation — Perhaps Even the Midpoint

Another scenario, advocated by John F. Walvoord, J. Dwight Pentecost, Charles Ryrie, Herman Hoyt, and Mark Hitchcock, places the invasion of Israel by the northern military coalition in the first half of the tribulation period—likely at its beginning, but some interpreters place it closer to the midpoint. In favor of this scenario are the following points:

1. This view is consistent with the requirement that Israel be secure and at rest before the invasion can occur. This state of security will result from Israel signing a peace treaty with the leader of the revived Roman Empire, the Antichrist. Under this agreement, Israel will rest secure under the protection of this world leader.

During this period of tranquility and security, Russia and a group of Muslim nations will suddenly launch an invasion, perhaps as a direct challenge to the antichrist.

2. Proponents of this view contend that when God intervenes to destroy the northern coalition during the first half of the tribulation, it will create a power vacuum that will facilitate the rapid rise of the Antichrist on a global level in the second half of the tribulation period. The absence of the Russian and Muslim forces after their defeat significantly eases the Antichrist's path to achieving world domination, as indicated in Revelation 13. John F. Walvoord says that "when the invading armies are defeated, the ruler of the ten nations will elevate himself and proclaim himself ruler of the entire world."[323] (You will notice that a similar argument favors the scenarios that place the invasion before the tribulation period.)

3. The elimination of the Muslim forces in the first half of the tribulation will open the door for the easy emergence of a false one-world religion. With Christians having already been raptured before the tribulation and Muslim forces now destroyed, the resulting religious vacuum makes it much easier for a one-world false religion to emerge and flourish. (Again, you will notice that a similar argument favors the scenarios that place the invasion before the tribulation period.)

Like the other interpretations, this view is not without problems:

1. If the invasion takes place right at the beginning of the seven-year tribulation period, how will the Jews be

---

[323] John Walvoord, *End Times* (Nashville: Word, 1998), 124.

able to complete the task of burning weapons for seven years while having to evacuate Jerusalem—*without delay* and *without packing*—midway through the tribulation period?

2. If the invasion takes place closer to the midpoint of the tribulation period, several problems emerge. Consider the seven-year burning of weapons as an example. If there is a midtribulational invasion, and God destroys the invaders, the enemy weapons will be burned throughout the second half of the tribulation period and then three-and-a-half years into the millennial kingdom. This is problematic.

3. The view that the invasion takes place closer to the midpoint of the tribulation period raises a conflict between major prophecies. On the one hand, Jesus instructs the Jews in Jerusalem to run for their lives at the midpoint of the tribulation period when the Antichrist desecrates the Jewish temple (Matt 24:15-21). On the other hand, if the northern military coalition launches an invasion into Israel at the midpoint of the tribulation period, and God destroys them, then the Jews will have to spend the next seven months cleansing the land by burying the dead bodies of the invaders (Ezek 39:11-16).[324] You cannot cleanse the land of Jerusalem for seven months at the same time as fleeing Jerusalem.

4. Still further, Jeremiah 30:7 describes the second half of the tribulation period as "a time of distress for Jacob" (or Israel). The Hebrew word for *distress* communicates "unequaled trouble." This will be a time of unparal-

---

[324] Harold Hoehner, "The Progression of Events in Ezekiel 38-39," in Charles Dyer and Roy Zuck, eds., *Integrity of Heart, Skillfulness of Hands* (Grand Rapids, MI: Baker, 1994), 85-86.

leled trouble for the Jewish people. They will be relentlessly persecuted by the antichrist and his forces. This will make the ongoing task of burning enemy weapons difficult at best.

All things considered, an invasion of Israel by the northern military coalition at the outset of the tribulation period is much more plausible than an invasion closer to the midpoint of the tribulation.

Scenario 4: The End of the Tribulation—At Armageddon

Another suggested scenario is that the invasion of Israel by the northern military coalition coincides with Armageddon at the end of the tribulation period. Armageddon, a term meaning "Mount of Megiddo," refers to a location approximately 60 miles north of Jerusalem. This location has historical significance as the site of Barak's conflict with the Canaanites (Judges 4) and Gideon's encounter with the Midianites (Judges 7). It will also be the site of humankind's final cataclysmic battles just before the second coming of Christ (Rev 16:16).

Several arguments are offered in support of equating Armageddon with the Ezekiel invasion:

1. Armageddon unfolds during the tribulation period (Rev 16:16). Likewise, the northern military coalition's invasion of Israel occurs "in the latter years" (Ezek 38:8) and "in the latter days" (verse 16), terms that many pretribulationists believe point to the tribulation. Hence, the events must be the same.

2. In both the Ezekiel prophecy (Ezek 39:4, 17-20) and the account of Armageddon (Rev 19:17-18), there are references to birds and predatory animals feasting on

the bodies of the fallen invaders. Hence, the events must be the same.

3. Zechariah 12:10 predicts that many Jews will turn to the Lord at the end of the tribulation in the final stages of Armageddon. Similarly, Ezekiel 39:22 affirms that "the house of Israel shall know that I am the LORD their God, from that day forward," and Ezekiel 39:29 quotes God as saying, "I will not hide my face anymore from them, when I pour out my Spirit upon the house of Israel." Such redemptive similarities must mean that the events are the same.

Despite such similarities, there are also notable dissimilarities:

1. Armageddon involves virtually all the nations of the earth (Joel 3:2; Zeph 3:8; Zech 12:3; 14:4). The northern military coalition is geographically limited, comprising Russia, Iran, Sudan, Turkey, Libya, and some other Muslim nations (Ezek 38:1-6). Hence, Armageddon and the Ezekiel invasion cannot be the same.

2. Armageddon's destruction is unleashed at the "Mount of Megiddo," approximately 60 miles north of Jerusalem. The Ezekiel invasion unfolds on the mountains of Israel. These are different events.

3. Armageddon's casualties result from the personal appearance of Jesus Christ at the second coming (Rev 19:15). Four catastrophic factors cause the casualties of the northern military coalition in the Ezekiel invasion: (1) a great earthquake, (2) infighting among the troops, (3) the outbreak of disease, and (4) fire and brimstone falling upon the troops (Ezek 38:20-22). These are different events.

4. At the end of the tribulation, during Armageddon, the Jews will not be living in security and peace because they will be heavily persecuted and targeted for attack by the antichrist's forces (Jer 30:7; Rev 12:13; Matt 24:16-20). Since living in security is a prerequisite for the Ezekiel invasion (Ezek 38:8), these must be different events.

5. At the outset of the Ezekiel invasion, certain nations protest the invasion (Ezek 38:13). No such protest is expressed at Armageddon since all the nations of the world are involved (Rev 16:14).

6. Armageddon occurs at the end of the tribulation period. If Ezekiel's invasion is equated with Armageddon, this implies that the burial of the invader's bodies (for seven months) and the burning of their weapons (for seven years) will extend well into the millennial kingdom. This does not seem feasible, and hence these must be different events.

7. Armageddon is led by the Beast, the Antichrist (Rev 19:19). The Ezekiel invasion is led by Gog (Ezek 38:7). Gog is not the antichrist.

8. The Ezekiel invasion targets Israel alone (Ezek 38:8-13). The armies gathered at Armageddon will ultimately align themselves against Jesus Christ at the second coming (Rev 19:19).

To sum up, one might find some similarities between the Ezekiel invasion and Armageddon. However, the differences between the two far outweigh any similarities. This view does not seem tenable.

Scenario 5: A Gap Between the End of the Tribulation and the Beginning of the Millennium

A minority of interpreters place the Ezekiel invasion in a gap between the end of the tribulation period and the inauguration of the millennial kingdom. Proponents of this view contend that if there is a gap between the rapture and the beginning of the tribulation period, it is reasonable to propose a comparable gap between the end of the tribulation and the beginning of the millennium. This gap would allow sufficient time for the burial of the dead over seven months.

This view recognizes that the invasion cannot occur until Israel is secure and at rest (Ezek 38:8). There could be no greater sense of security than that which will follow the second coming of Christ.

The primary challenge with this perspective is not the notion of a gap per se, but the requirement for a gap long enough to accommodate all the detailed events in Ezekiel 38–39. Most scholars recognize the need for at least a minimal gap to accommodate the small number of prophetic events that take place following the second coming, such as the judgment of the nations in Matthew 25:31–46. However, to fully explain the events in Ezekiel 38–39, this interim period would have to be at least seven years long to include the burning of enemy weapons. This means the gap would have to be as long as the tribulation period itself.

One might argue for a shorter interlude, suggesting that the burial of bodies for seven months and the burning of weapons for seven years could continue into the millennial kingdom. However, such an approach seems unsatisfactory.

Besides, Daniel 12:12 seems to indicate that the period between the end of the tribulation and the beginning of the millennial kingdom is limited to 75 days. Here's how we arrive at this number: Daniel 12:12, in a context which deals with the end of the tribulation period, states: "Blessed is he who waits and arrives at the 1,335 days." We already know that the second half of the tribulation period is 1260 days (or three-and-a-half years). So, here's some simple math: 1335 minus 1260 equals 75. Since the millennial kingdom has not yet begun, this must mean that there is a period of 75 days between the end of the tribulation period and the beginning of the millennial kingdom. Such a short gap would be insufficient to accommodate the burial of bodies and burning of weapons.

Scenario 6: The Beginning of the Millennium

Some interpreters, such as Arno Gaebelein, suggest that the northern military coalition's invasion of Israel will occur at the beginning of the millennial kingdom. These interpreters base this on the notion that Israel will experience profound peace and tranquility during the millennial reign of Christ. This is consistent with the aforementioned precondition of security and rest prior to the invasion (Ezek 38:8).

There are significant challenges to this perspective:

1. Isaiah 2:4 predicts perpetual and unbroken peace during Christ's millennial reign: "They shall beat their swords into plowshares, and their spears into pruning hooks; nation shall not lift up sword against nation, neither shall they learn war anymore." This would seem to rule out the possibility of a northern military alliance invading Israel during the millennium. The only millennial conflict we read about in prophetic Scripture relates to Satan's final revolt at the end of the millennial kingdom (Rev 20:7-9).

2. Considering the events following Christ's return, the prospect of an invasion of Israel at the beginning of the millennium seems highly unlikely. The judgment of the nations will result in the execution of unbelievers: "These will go away into eternal punishment" (Matt 25:46). None of the wicked—none of Israel's adversaries—will enter the millennial kingdom (see Jer 25:32-33; Rev 19:15-18). Put another way, *only believers* will enter Christ's millennial kingdom, and these followers of Christ will not be attacking Israel.

3. Ezekiel 39:12 suggests that the land will remain contaminated for seven months following the invasion until all the dead bodies are buried. This scenario seems incongruous with the inaugural phase of Christ's millennial kingdom, which is marked by peace, harmony, righteousness, and a vastly enhanced living environment (Isa 11:6-7; 29:18; 30:23-24; 35:1-2; 65:20).

4. It is inconceivable that any nation or group of nations would consider attacking Israel when Christ (God) reigns over the kingdom.

These and other scriptural challenges render this view untenable.

Scenario 7: The End of the Millennium

The idea that the Ezekiel invasion will occur at the end of the millennial kingdom has generated considerable debate among scholars. While some proponents of this view argue that it is consistent with certain aspects of biblical prophecy, some significant challenges and inconsistencies must be addressed. Let's consider the details:

Revelation 20:7-10 states:

> When the thousand years are ended, Satan will be released from his prison and will come out to deceive the nations that are at the four corners of the earth, Gog and Magog, to gather them for battle; their number is like the sand of the sea. And they marched up over the broad plain of the earth and surrounded the camp of the saints and the beloved city, but fire came down from heaven and consumed them, and the devil who had deceived them was thrown into the lake of fire and sulfur where the beast and the false prophet were, and they will be tormented day and night forever and ever.

This passage details the events that will occur at the end of the thousand-year millennial kingdom. Some interpreters find direct parallels with Ezekiel 38:

- Gog and Magog are mentioned in both Revelation 20:8 and Ezekiel 38:2.

- The massive size of the invading army is highlighted in both accounts. Revelation says of the invaders: "Their number is like the sand of the sea" (Rev 20:8). The Ezekiel invaders are described as being "like a cloud covering the land" (Ezek 38:9).

- In both accounts, the defeat of the invading forces is attributed to God.

While such factors may seem persuasive to some, there are significant problems with this viewpoint:

1. There is a notable discrepancy in what precedes each of these invasions. The Ezekiel invasion, described in

Ezekiel 38–39, is situated within a more extensive section of the book dealing with the restoration of Israel after a long and worldwide dispersion (chapters 33–39). In other words, Israel is first restored to the land and then, sometime later, is invaded by a northern military coalition. In contrast, the invasion described in Revelation 20:7–10 occurs after Israel has been in a state of restoration *for a thousand years.*

2. The idea of a seven-month burial period following the Ezekiel invasion does not fit well with an end-of-millennium scenario. Revelation 20:9 says that during the attack, "fire came down from heaven and consumed them." The fact that they are "consumed' means there are no bodies left to bury.

3. Following the great white throne judgment in Revelation 20, the narrative quickly proceeds to the commencement of the eternal state in Revelation 21. This transition presents challenges concerning the seven-year burning of weapons mentioned in connection with the end-of-millennium invasion. More specifically, the burning of these weapons would apparently need to extend into the eternal state. To avoid this problem, some propose that there must be a gap after the millennial kingdom that could last seven years.

4. The Ezekiel invasion involves a coalition of regional nations, including Russia and various Muslim nations (Ezek 38:1-6). Conversely, the end-of-millennium invasion described in Revelation 20:8 comprises an international army recruited from "the nations that are at the four corners of the earth." These are two distinct invading forces.

5. All things considered, it appears that the apostle John may have employed the terms "Gog and Magog" in a metaphorical way, akin to modern metaphors like "Wall Street" denoting the stock market. In this interpretation, "Gog and Magog" would symbolize a coalition of nations attacking Israel without necessarily suggesting a direct link to the Ezekiel invasion. In other words, the invasion of Revelation 20 will be a Gog-Magog-like invasion.

My Assessment

Given all the arguments *for* and *against* each of these views, it would probably be unwise to take a rigid position on the precise timing of the Ezekiel invasion. We must approach this issue with humility, recognizing that while we should study it and come to our own conclusions on the matter, we should also be charitable toward those who have different perspectives.

That said, allow me to offer my assessment of the issue:

- I respectfully disagree with the two millennial scenarios that suggest the invasion occurs either at the beginning or at the end of the millennium. Both views seem difficult to harmonize with other key prophecies of the millennial kingdom and the eternal state.

- I also respectfully disagree with the idea that the invasion occurs during a gap between the end of the tribulation and the beginning of the millennial kingdom. The gap would have to be at least seven years, but Scripture seems to limit it to seventy-five days (Dan 12:12).

- Furthermore, I do not accept the scenarios that place the invasion near the middle or the end of the tribulation period. These views seem difficult to harmonize with other prophecies of the tribulation period and the beginning of the millennial kingdom.

- The two positions I find most plausible are:

  1. The Ezekiel invasion occurs at the beginning of the tribulation period. The burning of the weapons for seven years seems to coincide with the seven-year tribulation period. This view satisfies the precondition for the invasion—Israel must be at rest and be living in security. The covenant that the Antichrist signs with Israel will facilitate this. However, the big problem with this view remains: What happens to the burning of the weapons when the Jews must suddenly take flight from Jerusalem at the midpoint of the tribulation following the antichrist's desecration of the Jewish temple (Matt 24:15-18)? A possible solution may relate to where the weapons are stored and burned during the first part of the tribulation period. Since these burning weapons are likely to produce enormous amounts of smoke, perhaps they will not be burned in or near Jerusalem but at a place in the wilderness where such smoke wouldn't be so bothersome. If this is the case, it may be that when the Jews flee Jerusalem, some group from among these Jews will make a quick detour to the weapons site and transport them to their place of refuge, wherever that may be. I concede that this is speculative, but it is possible.

2. A second plausible view is that the invasion could occur sometime after the rapture but before the tribulation period. If the rapture occurs, and if the Ezekiel invasion then takes place three-and-a-half years before the tribulation period, this would provide enough time for the Jews to finish burning all the enemy weapons by the midpoint of the tribulation period. This would consequently make their escape from Jerusalem much easier. A potential weakness of this view may relate to the aforementioned prerequisite for the invasion: Israel must be living in peace and security. However, it is quite conceivable that Israel's security will be based not on the antichrist's covenant but on factors already in place before the tribulation period. As previously noted, these would include Israel's peace treaties with major Arab nations, its well-equipped army, its formidable air force, its effective missile defense system, its robust economy, and its strong alliance with the United States.

Ed Hindson's View

Since this is a book written in honor of Ed Hindson, it is appropriate to close this chapter with a summary of his position on when Russia and various Muslim nations attack Israel. In the book *Target Israel*, which Hindson coauthored with Tim LaHaye, we read: "One common question asked by people who want to understand Bible prophecy is, 'When will the destruction of Russia occur—before the rapture, or after?' We do not think the Bible makes this crystal clear." They ultimately conclude that "Russia's destruction is a Tribulation event, so it won't occur until after the 'blessed hope,' or the rapture." However, they then concede: "The events of Ezekiel 38 will likely take place after the rapture, although nothing in Scripture prohibits them from occurring before the rapture. That's why we say the Bible isn't crystal clear on this."[325]

The debate goes on!

---

[325] Tim LaHaye and Ed Hindson, *Target Israel* (Eugene: Harvest House Publishers, Apple Books Edition 2015), 179.

BIBLIOGRAPHY

Fruchtenbaum, Arnold. *The Footsteps of the Messiah*. San Antonio: Ariel Publishers, 2004.

Hitchcock, Mark. "The Battle of Gog and Magog." https://www.pre-trib.org/dr-robert-thomas/message/the-battle-of-gog-and-magog/read.

Hoehner, Harold "The Progression of Events in Ezekiel 38–39," in Charles Dyer and Roy Zuck, eds., *Integrity of Heart, Skillfulness of Hands*. Grand Rapids: Baker, 1994.

Ice, Thomas. "Are We Living in the Last Days?" https://www.pre-trib.org/dr-robert-thomas/message/are-we-living-in-the-last-days/read.

———. "Ezekiel 38 and 39," *Pre-Trib Perspectives*, https://www.pre-trib.org.

———. "Last Days." *The Harvest Handbook of Bible Prophecy*, eds. Ed Hindson, Mark Hitchcock, Tim LaHaye. Eugene: Harvest House, 2020.

LaHaye, Tim. *The Coming Peace in the Middle East*. Grand Rapids: Zondervan, 1984.

LaHaye, Tim and Ed Hindson, *Target Israel*. Eugene: Harvest House Publishers, 2015. Apple Books edition.

Pentecost, J. Dwight. *Things to Come*. Grand Rapids: Zondervan, 1964.

———. "Where Do the Events of Ezekiel 38–39 Fit into the Prophetic Picture?" *Bibliotheca Sacra*. Dallas Theological Seminary, 1955–1995. Logos Bible Software.

Rhodes, Ron. *Northern Storm Rising: Russia, Iran, and the Emerging End-Times Military Coalition Against Israel*. Eugene: Harvest House Publishers, 2008.

Rosenberg, Joel. *Epicenter*. Carol Stream: Tyndale House, 2006.

Walvoord, John F. *The Prophecy Knowledge Handbook*. Wheaton: Victor Books, 1990. Logos Bible Software.

———. *End Times*. Nashville: Word, 1998.

———. *Every Prophecy of the Bible*. Colorado Springs: David C. Cook.

CHAPTER NINE

THE CAPITAL OF THE COMING KING IN PSALM 2:6

by Tim M. Sigler, PhD

It was such a pleasure for me and my wife Bernice to welcome Dr. Hindson and his wife Donna to the campus of Shepherds Theological Seminary to teach his famous Isaiah course in May 2021. The following year, he gave us the royal tour of the John W. Rawlings School of Divinity at Liberty University on January 10, 2022, driving us around the campus in his sporty BMW and sharing the Dean Emeritus parking privileges to speed up the process. Our shared love for the Hebrew Scriptures, the land and people of Israel, biblical archaeology, ANE backgrounds, Bible prophecy, dispensationalism, and many other things always fostered a joyous conversation. The Blessed Hope of the Rapture promises a reunion with our Messiah when we see Him face to face and are gathered with those fellow believers who have gone on before us. Dr. Hindson knew that one day the King is coming, and he loved to learn all he could about that future day.

Looking forward to the joys that await us was a major focus of Dr. Hindson's contributions both to the church and the academy. In one of his last publications, *Future Glory: Living in the Hope of the Rapture, Heaven, and Eternity*, he writes of the twelvefold description of the coming King from Revelation 19:11-16 and draws upon the imagery and symbolism from various other passages to observe the following details:

> 1) His Conquest: He rides the white horse (Rev 6:2); 2) His Character: He is called Faithful and True (Rev 3:14); 3) His Commission: He judges and makes war (2 Thess 1:7-8); 4) His Clarity: His eyes are like a flame of fire (Rev 1:14); 5) His Coronation: He wears many crowns (Rev 4:10); 6) His Code: His secret name (Jud 13:18; Isa 9:6); 7) His Clothing: Robe dipped in blood (Isa 63:1-6); 8) His Confirmation: Called the Word of God (Jn 1:1); 9) His Communication: Sword is in His mouth (Rev 19:15, 21); 10) His Command: Rules with a rod of iron (Ps 2:9); 11) His Conquest: Treads the winepress of the wrath of God (Rev 14:14-29); and 12) His Celebration: King of kings and Lord of lords (Rev 17:14).[326]

To this list may be added a further detail concerning the coming King described throughout Scripture—namely, His City or Capital: the renewed Jerusalem of the millennial kingdom where Messiah will rule on the throne of His father, David. The passage which best brings together the themes of royal imagery, divine appointment, authority over rebellious nations, and a capital city where this kingly rule will be established on this earth during the millennial kingdom and from which Messiah's rule will go forth is Psalm 2, and specifically verse 6.

---

[326] Ed Hindson, *Future Glory: Living in the Hope of the Rapture, Heaven, and Eternity* (Eugene, OR: Harvest, 2021), 115-20.

"But as for Me, I have installed My King
Upon Zion, My holy mountain." (NASB 1995)

This essay will examine Psalm 2:6 in its literary context and tie its themes to the broader issues of Zion theology and eschatology within the Psalter and the canon as a whole. We will explore its eschatological significance and why it must be fulfilled literally, physically, and militarily on this earth during the millennium and not merely spiritually or in the eternal state. This study will not attempt to lay again the foundation that direct (not indirect) messianic prophecies culminate in the person and work of Jesus of Nazareth as that has been done by many others. It will instead assume that the Son of Psalm 2 is the Son of God, as did Paul in his preaching in the book of Acts: "And we preach to you the good news of the promise made to the fathers, that God has fulfilled this *promise* to our children in that He raised up Jesus, as it is also written in the second Psalm, "You are My Son; today I have begotten You" (Acts 13:32–33).

Psalms 1 and 2 and the Macrostructure of the Psalter

Psalms 1 and 2 introduce the entire collection of 150 psalms or praises (Heb. *tehilim*) by describing the type of person who will sing them, memorize them, ponder their lyrics, obey their commands, pray them back to God, tell them to others, and apply their truths to the deepest struggles of their lives. Psalms 1 and 2 are rightly seen as the double-door entry or gateway to the Psalter.[327]

Psalm 1 shows that there are two ways to live and that there is a choice to be made. Psalm 2 shows there are consequences to that choice. Psalm 1 has been called a wisdom psalm due to its

---

[327] Robert L. Cole, *Psalms 1–2: Gateway to the Psalter.* Hebrew Bible Monographs 37 (Sheffield: Sheffield Phoenix Press, 2013).

parallel vocabulary with Proverbs and a Torah psalm due to its reference to God's law. Psalm 2 has been called a royal, coronation, and messianic psalm due to its special vocabulary that connects it thematically with the Davidic covenant. But as Robert Cole suggests, when we see this "intended coherent reading of the pair" together and link them as the double-door entry to all the praises, we observe that "Psalms 1 and 2 were intended as prophecy in the ultimate sense."[328] These psalms together tell us the fate of those who praise and those who refuse to praise. Notably, neither of these psalms has superscriptions, while 116 of the 150 do. Located where they are, it is possible to appreciate them as a lengthy superscription over the entire collection—a prophetic introduction. This double-door entry teaches us how to read the rest of the collection: we are to read them theologically, cosmically/nationally, personally, messianically, and eschatologically.

As Hill and Walton observe, "The analysis of Psalms 1 and 2 and the seam Psalms has led to the conclusion that the five books of the Psalter are intended to trace the history of Israel, particularly with regard to the Davidic covenant, which is the covenant of kingship."[329] They further helpfully emphasize the prophetic significance of Psalms 1 and 2 both in terms of personal eschatology and the future of the nation.

> David is a prime example of the righteous man vindicated. He was vindicated in his conflict with Saul, in his conflict with Absalom, and ultimately on a national and eschatological scale in the development of the Davidic covenant. This shows us a "wisdom" aspect to the editor's message (the righteous will be vindicated) as it addresses the indi-

---

328 Cole, 3-4. I am not convinced of all of Cole's claims, especially about identifying the blessed man of chapter 1 with the Son/King/Messiah of chapter 2, but he provides otherwise very helpful analysis.

329 Andrew E. Hill and John H. Walton, *A Survey of the Old Testament* (2nd ed.; Grand Rapids: Zondervan, 2000), 347-48.

vidual and an "eschatological" aspect (God's commitment to Davidic kingship) addressing the nation.[330]

While they may not go far enough in recognizing Psalms 1 and 2 as direct messianic prophecies, their emphasis on the Davidic covenant assists readers in seeing how the entirety of the Psalter is structured around God's promises to David which are ultimately fulfilled in David's greater Son, revealed in the New Covenant Scriptures in the person and work of Messiah Jesus. Their chart illustrating the structure and message of the Psalter as a cantata about the Davidic covenant is most helpful.[331]

A Cantata About the Davidic Covenant

Introduction Psalms 1–2	Psalm 1 Ultimate vindication of the righteous Psalm 2 God's choice and defense of Israelite king		
Book	Seam	Theme	Content
Book 1 Psalms 1–41	41	David's conflict with Saul	Many individual laments; most psalms mention enemies
Book 2 Psalms 42–72	72	David's kingship	Key psalms: 45, 48, 41; 54–64; mostly laments and "enemy" psalms
Book 3 Psalms 73–89	89	Eighth-century Assyrian crisis	Asaph and Sons of Korah collections; key psalm: 78

---

330 Hill and Walton, 348.
331 Hill and Walton, 348.

Book 4 Psalms 90–106	106	Introspection about the destruction of temple and exile	Praise collection: 95–100; key psalms: 90, 103–105
Book 5 Psalms 107–150	145	Praise/reflection on return from Exile and beginning of new era	Hallelujah collection: 111–117; Songs of Ascent: 120–134; Davidic reprise: 138–145; key psalms: 107, 110, 119
Conclusion 146–150		Climactic praise to God Ps 150 The Great Hallelujah	

A canonical reading of the Psalter that focuses on the intentional ordering of individual psalms into a collective whole with an overarching message or theme is a departure from the long-standing approach of Hermann Gunkel's form criticism which analyzed and grouped psalms by literary genre or style (e.g., wisdom psalms, royal psalms, hymns, psalms of individual or collective thanksgiving or lament, etc.). This movement away from form criticism was occasioned by the canonical approach of Yale scholar Brevard Childs who accepted many of the assumptions of higher criticism but also challenged the status quo by questioning how any of those scientific and atomistic analyses of various passages had any lasting effect on the community that actually read those texts. He emphasized that the final form of the biblical text is what affected the ancient communities of faith and thus dismissed the importance of trying to get behind the biblical text through the critical methods (source, form, redaction, etc.). One of Childs's students was Gerald Wilson whose dissertation, *The Editing of the Hebrew Psalter*, "initiated a fresh approach for reading the Psalms as a book, intentionally arranged. According to

Wilson's conclusions, the book of Psalms should not be read as a compendium of unrelated poems, prayers, and hymns; rather,... readers should be sensitive to the literary context created by thematic groupings of psalms."³³²

Michael Snearly's dissertation draws upon the work of Childs and Wilson to press further the issue of an intentional narrative emphasis in the Psalter. He summarizes his approach as follows: "I inquire into the narrative trajectory of the Psalms up to Book V (Psalms 107-150) by giving special attention to the key seam psalms of the Psalter (Psalms 1-2 and 89)." Yet, he disagrees with Wilson and the consensus of scholars who see in the Psalms an initial hope in "a royal/Davidic figure who will inaugurate Yahweh's purposes," but ultimately his rejection. "The last two books of the Psalter, then, affirm that Yahweh alone is king (see Psalms 93-100) and the messianic hope is democratized among the people, that is, the promises made to David are fulfilled in the people."³³³ According to this reading, the Davidic covenant is considered invalid and no longer about David or his line.

> But You have cast off and rejected,
> You have been full of wrath against Your anointed.
> You have spurned the covenant of Your servant;
> You have profaned his crown in the dust. (Ps 89:38-39)

Yet, contra Wilson, Snearly argues:

> ...that Book V reaffirms the importance of the Davidic figure in the Psalter. This is built from a proper interpretation of Psalm 89 and the key-word relations between Psalms 1-2, 89, and Book V. The key words הרות ("Torah" in Psalm 1), צוין ("Zion" in Psalm 2), מלך ("king" in Psalm

---

332 Michael K. Snearly, "The Return of the King: Book V as a Witness to Messianic Hope in the Psalter," in *The Psalms: Language for All Seasons of the Soul*, ed. Andrew J. Schmutzer and David M. Howard, Jr. (Chicago: Moody, 2013), 209-10.
333 Snearly, 211.

2), חסד ("covenant loyalty" in Psalm 89), and עולם ("eternal" in Psalm 89) are integral to the macrostructure of Book V: yes, Yahweh remembers his servant and his covenant loyalty is eternal.

The storyline of the Psalter begins with Psalms 1–2, which jointly introduce the royal theme that permeates Books I–III. Instead of reading a caesura in the promises of the Davidic covenant in Psalm 89, the psalm should be understood as a lament over the present, shameful state of the Davidic dynasty. Yet hope remains that Yahweh's covenant loyalty will reverse this deplorable condition. Book IV, then, highlights the sovereign reign of Yahweh, which should not be read as a rejection of the human, Davidic line, but rather as consistent with the program introduced at the beginning of the Psalter (see Psalm 2 where Yahweh and his king reign together—Yahweh appoints the king, and the king represents Yahweh's rule).[334]

Similarly, Satterthwaite argues for a renewed hope for and from Zion in Book V.:

> Psalms 132-134 conclude the Songs of Ascents on a fundamentally optimistic note. Psalm 132 stands out by reason of its length and marks a climactic point in the collection: Jerusalem and David become, so to speak, the "goal" of the collection, the note on which it ends. Psalm 132 is an appeal to the initial event which constituted Zion as YHWH's "resting place" (vv. 8, 14), the first procession of the ark up to Zion. and a plea to remember the human agent who gave the lead in that event, David (v. 1). The first half of Psalm 132 asks that the hopes which surrounded that initial event may be fulfilled, bringing joy for those com-

---

334 Snearly, 212.

mitted to YHWH (v. 9) and restoration for David's descendant (v. 10). The second half of Psalm 132 is structurally parallel to the first (very closely so) and gives the answer to this plea, YHWH's oath (in the first person) concerning David and his descendants, and his promises concerning Zion. Among all the voices heard in the Songs of Ascents, here YHWH's voice is for the first time heard. The effect is that many of the petitions which have been made up to this point now find their definitive answer in a reaffirmation of YHWH's choice of Zion and of David's royal line: "this is my resting place forever...here I will make a horn grow for David..." (vv. 14, 17).[335]

Finally, in appreciating the literary context of Psalms 1–2, it should be observed that these two introductory psalms form an inclusio or bracket around the entire Psalter when compared with the collection's closing in Psalm 149 before the great Hallelujah of 150. The introductory themes that resurface include Zion's king (2:6; 149:2) versus rebellious kings (2:2; 149:8), Messiah's rod of iron (2:9) versus their fetters of iron (149:8), and the counsel for the wicked to worship and rejoice with trembling (2:11) versus the consistent culminating praises (149:1, 3, 6, 9). The macrostructure of the Psalter points to Zion's king throughout.

Psalm 2:6 in its Immediate Context

Psalm 2 shows the futility of conspiracy against the Lord in four segments of three verses each: the rebellion of earthly kings (2:1–3); the wrath of the heavenly King (2:4–6); the rod of Zion's King (2:7–9); and the refuge for repentant kings (2:10–12). It has been observed that various speakers are represented in each segment:

---

[335] Philip Satterthwaite, "Zion in the Songs of Ascents," in *Zion, City of Our God*, ed. Richard S. Hess and Gordon J. Wenham (Grand Rapids: Eerdmans, 1999), 126.

the psalmist opens with his incredulous question about international rebellion against the Lord and His Anointed (2:1-3); the LORD Himself laughs and speaks (2:4-6); the divine Son is the speaker in what can be understood as an inner-trinitarian dialogue (2:7-9); and the final unit concludes with the psalmist speaking on behalf of God in warning the rebellious kings and offering them wise counsel and blessing if they repent (2:10-12).

Numerous word plays, parallels, and repetitions are at work between Psalms 1 and 2 and within each. The term *hagah* is translated as "devise" or "plot" in a negative context of imagining a vain thing (2:1) but can be translated positively as "meditate" when the imagination is focused on God's instruction (1:2). The kings *yatzav* "set themselves" (2:2) against the Lord and His Anointed, but the King *yashav* "sits" (2:4) on His throne! The concluding section is reminiscent of the two ways to live, wise or foolish, outlined in Proverbs but also emphasized in these two Psalms (Pss 1:1, 6; 2:12). The "Son" (Heb. *ben*) in 2:7 is the same "Son" (Aram. *bar*) in 2:12 as these words are commonly used interchangeably within Jewish literature. Note the inclusio with the word "blessed" at the beginning of Psalm 1 and the close of Psalm 2. The term *derek* was used first in 1:1 about the "way" or "path" of sinners, then contrasted at the end of 1:6 concerning the "way of the righteous" versus the "way of the wicked." It is repeated again after this two-chapter introduction in the warning to avoid the Son's wrath lest you "perish in the way" (2:12). One can heed the instruction (Heb. *torah*) of the Lord and be wise to His warnings, submit to His rule, worship His Son, with the result of being "blessed." Or, one can refuse His warnings, His wisdom, His worship, and experience His wrath. Psalm 1 opens with "blessed" and closes with "perish" as these two outcomes are starkly contrasted. Psalm 1 points to the ultimate Blessed One, to the Son of Psalm 2.

In this context of warnings to rebellious kings, the divine response of 2:6 is pronounced. Ross explains, "The speech begins with a strong contrast: 'But as for Me.' God is in effect saying, 'they may do such and so, but as for me, I will do this...."[336] The confidence with which this divine appointment is accomplished is evidenced by using the perfect tense (like the English past tense) to demonstrate the certainty with which this future act is announced. "This use is especially frequent in prophetic address (hence it is also called the 'prophetic perfect' or 'perfective of confidence')."[337] Waltke and O'Connor note the emphatic use of the independent first-person pronoun with the finite verb in the phrase "I have installed my king." They note a psychological focus in this grammatical construction and cite the observations of Takamitsu Muraoka, who observes a "strong emotional heightening" and "focused attention or deep self-consciousness."[338] They note that in relation to the phrase "I have installed my king," the emphatic use of the independent first-person pronoun with the finite verb involves the first person "in flashes of self-assertion."[339] In the divine plan, the appointment of Zion's king is as good as done and is as certain as if it were already complete. Nevertheless, its accomplishment is clearly in the prophetic future.

"I have installed my king" could be understood as "consecrating," "coronating," "crowning," "enthroning," "installing," "appointing," or even "anointing."[340] Ross comments further on this

---

336 Allen P. Ross, *A Commentary on the Psalms 1–89*, vol. 1, Kregel Exegetical Library (Grand Rapids: Kregel Academic, 2011–2013), 206.

337 Bruce Waltke and M. O'Connor, *An Introduction to Biblical Hebrew Syntax* (Winona Lake: Eisenbrauns, 1990), 490.

338 Waltke and O'Connor, 296; citing T. Muraoka, *Emphatic Words*, 58.

339 Waltke and O'Connor, 58.

340 On *nasakti*, Avrohom Chaim Feurer summarizes rabbinic commentaries by the medieval grammarian David Kimhi (Radak) and nineteenth-century Meir Leibush ben Yehiel Michel Wisser (Malbim) as follows: "HASHEM will chastise the nations: 'How dare you attempt to remove David after I have chosen and anointed him?' (Radak), Furthermore, rather than undermining David's authority, your rebellion will reinforce his power, for now I, HASHEM, am forced to openly display my choice of David by destroying my adversaries (Malbim)." In *Tehillim: A New Translation with a Commentary Anthologized from Talmudic, Midrashic and Rabbinic Sources*; Artscroll Series (Brooklyn, NY: Mesorah, 2013), 68. On the semantic connections between *nasak* and *mashakh*, see C. Dohmen, "נסך," in *TDOT* (Grand Rapids: Eerdmans, 1998), 9:457; Richard E. Averbeck, "נסך," in *NIDOTTE* (Grand Rapids: Zondervan, 1997), 3:113-17. C. John Collins, "משח," in *NIDOTTE*, 2:1123-27; J.A. Soggin, "משח," *TLOT* 2:676-77; Klaus Seybold, "משח," *TDOT* 9:43-54; Jeffrey H. Tigay, "Divine Creation of the King in Psalms 2:6," in *Hayim and Miriam Tadmor Volume*. Eretz-Israel: Archaeological, Historical and Geographical Studies 27 (2003): 246-51;

perfect tense verb "set, install" (וְתִכַּסָּנ). "Since this is the coronation psalm, the tense might best be classified as an instantaneous perfect, meaning 'Here and now I set my king.' This fits well with the king's designation 'today' (v. 7)."[341] Waltke and O'Connor observe that "The epistolary perfective may be seen as a special case of the instantaneous perfective. Another overlapping subtype is the performative, in which not only are speaking and acting simultaneous, they are identical."[342] If this is the correct understanding of the perfect tense verb, the "here and now" sense would have to relate to a future time when the Father will pronounce what He is doing at that moment in time. Thus, this writer prefers to understand the verb as a prophetic perfect.

The announcement that the LORD has set His king in Zion, the Davidic capital, cannot be appreciated apart from the context of the Davidic covenant and kingly line. Ross observes,

> The announcement also states that the coronation is on Mount Zion, meaning the palace on the mountain (a metonymy of subject). Zion was a unique mountain, "set apart" for the worship and service of the LORD, which is why it is designated "holy." This designation made it even more explicit that God was behind this Israelite king.[343]

Monson notes, "With the transferral of the ark to Jerusalem. Yahweh officially chose Mount Zion as his dwelling (Ps. 132:13-14). The place became a conduit of spiritual and political power. David's successful campaigns demonstrated anew that the God of Israel was also Lord of the entire world."[344] As Avrohom Chaim Feurer notes, "Zion was not conquered by Israel until after Da-

---

Gerald H Wilson, *Psalms I*, NIVAC, 111 n.17.
341 Ross, *Psalms*, 206.
342 Waltke and O'Connor, 489.
343 Ross, *Psalms*, 207.
344 John M. Monson, "The Temple of Solomon: Heart of Jerusalem," in *Zion, City of Our God*, ed. Richard S. Hess and Gordon J. Wenham (Grand Rapids: Eerdmans, 1999), 6.

vid rose to the throne, therefore Zion and Jerusalem are always referred to as 'David's City.'"[345] Among numerous connections between Psalms 2 and 110, Rydelnik observes that "the King is to reign from Zion. In Ps 110:2, the Lord stretches forth the King's scepter 'from Zion.' Accordingly, Ps 2:6 presents the King as enthroned on 'Zion,' God's 'holy mountain.'"[346] The centrality of Zion in the plan to redeem Israel and the nations is clear from numerous texts. "For out of Jerusalem will go forth a remnant, and out of Mount Zion survivors. The zeal of the LORD will perform this" (2 Kgs 19:31). Strong notes, "Zion theology, serving as the royal theology of the Davidic dynasty, asserted that the Lord is the divine Great King, who controls all forces of chaos, thereby providing for the protection and fertility of the nation."[347]

The term "Zion" has often been the catchword of hope for the Jewish people surrounded by powerful enemy nations. As Robert Alter comments on 2:6,

> The geo-theological paradox of these words runs through many of the psalms. Zion is a modest mountain on the crest of which sits a modest fortified town, the capital of a rather small kingdom, surrounded by vast empires. Yet, the poet boldly imagines it as God's chosen city, divinely endorsed to be queen of nations and the splendor of humankind.[348]

There are various other names for Jerusalem (the city of peace) in Scripture: Jebus (Jud 19:10), the city of our God (Ps 48:1); the city of the great King (Ps 48:2; Matt 5:35); the city of the LORD of

---

345 Avrohom Chaim Feurer, *Tehillim*, 68.
346 Michael Rydelnik, *The Messianic Hope: Is the Hebrew Bible Really Messianic?* NAC Studies in Bible & Theology (Nashville, TN: B & H Academic, 2010), 180-81.
347 John T. Strong, "Zion, Theology of" *NIDOTTE*, ed. Willem VanGemeren (Grand Rapids: Zondervan, 1997), 4:1314-21.
348 Robert Alter, *The Book of Psalms: A Translation with Commentary* (New York: W. W. Norton, 2007), 6.

hosts (Ps 48:8); Salem (Gen 14:18; Ps 76:2); the city of righteousness (Isa 1:26); the faithful city (Isa 1:26); Ariel, i.e., Lion of God (Isa 29:1); City of Holiness (Isa 48:42; 51:1; Dan 9:24; Neh 11:1; 11:18); the city of David (2 Sam 5:7–10); the holy city (Isa 52:1); city of the LORD (Isa 60:14); "My Delight Is in Her" (Isa 62:4); the throne of the LORD (Jer. 3:17); the LORD is our righteousness (Jer 33:16); the perfection of beauty (Lam 2:15); the joy of all the earth (Lam 2:15); the LORD Is There [YHWH Shammah] (Ezek 48:35); the holy mountain (Zech 8:3). But the most common synonym for Jerusalem by far, used thirty-nine times in the Psalter, and employed in numerous examples of synonymous parallelism is Zion (Pss 51:18; 76:2; 102:21; 128:5; 135:21; 147:12).

Being set in Zion, the Son has a responsibility to judge. He will "break them with a rod of iron" (2:9), a repeated theme in the Apocalypse (Rev 2:27; 12:5; 19:15). Despite the emphasis on the doom of all who rebel, Psalm 2 concludes with an invitation to all who will repent (2:10–12).

For repentant rebels, there is a refuge in God's Son, Messiah, and King. There is no refuge *from* the Son, but only *in* the Son!

Timing of the Fulfillment of Psalm 2:6

When will this prophetic psalm be fulfilled? Is this to be a spiritual kingdom in the heavenly realm or an earthly kingdom established by a literal military victory? What do the words in the passage indicate about the author's intent, and how should readers understand their significance? References to "nations" (2:1, 8), "peoples" (noting the plural to designate people groups in 2:1), "rulers" (2:2), "kings" (2:2, 10), and "judges" (2:10) provide the lexical indication that this victory is political. The use of terms like "inheritance" or "heritage" (2:8), and "earth" (2:2, 8, 10) indicate an earthly—in this world—context. The words "bonds" and "cords" or "fetters" (2:3), "break" and "dash" (2:9) emphasize a military conquest. The terms "wrath" (2:5, 12), "terrify" and "fury" (2:5), "decree" (2:7), "perish" and "refuge" (2:12) speak of judgment.

The various lexical data converge to require a political, earthly, militaristic judgment in which the Son will "break them with a rod of iron" (2:9) providing the inner-biblical basis for the repeated phrase used to describe the events of the Second Coming when "he will rule them with a rod of iron, as when earthen pots are broken in pieces, even as I myself have received authority from my Father" (Rev 2:27); or when He will "rule all the nations with a rod of iron" (Rev 12:5); or when "from his mouth comes a sharp sword with which to strike down the nations, and He will rule them with a rod of iron. He will tread the winepress of the fury of the wrath of God the Almighty" (Rev 19:15). The nations will unite against God and His Anointed King/Son/Messiah and against His capital city of Jerusalem (Zech 12; 14:1–3). But this unity will only set them up like a populous profane piñata prepared for the messianic collision and confrontation with His rod of iron. Refuge for the inhabitants of Jerusalem will come in the context of Armageddon and Israel being hidden in Bozrah in the same place where the Second Coming will occur and from where He will come to trample "down the peoples in [His] anger" (Isa 63:1–6).

George Gunn notes, "Some who would like to interpret Christ's present session in heaven as the fulfillment of this verse would make "Zion" equal to heaven. However if Christ is "poured out" ("installed") from heaven to Zion, it would seem better to understand Zion as the earthly Zion, and the fulfillment to be millennial."[349] For instance, Robert Cole sees the Zion of 2:6 in connection with "the heavenly holy mountain of Zion" in a "celestial location."[350] Willem VanGemeren has led the way in argu-

---

349 George A. Gunn, "Psalm 2 and the Reign of the Messiah," *BSac* 169 (October-December 2012): 431.

350 Cole, 108; idem. "Psalm 1–2: The Divine Son of God," *The Moody Handbook of Messianic Prophecy*, ed. Michael Rydelnik and Edwin Blum (Chicago: Moody, 2019), 477-90.

ing that the mention of "Israel" indicates "a hermeneutical crux in the interpretation of prophecy" with special permission to see in such promises eschatological blessings for the church.[351]

Like much Christian exposition and theological commentary, early medieval Jewish liturgy began to emphasize the heavenly rule of the Davidic Messiah and downplay the significance of an earthly transformation and rule that was still the expectation of apocalyptic and early rabbinic literature.[352] Christian interpreters who spiritualize Israel's promises of a literal military victory under the divine Messianic Son/King/Judge can find common ground with the medieval Jewish philosopher Maimonides, who "made room for the Messianic idea among his thirteen principles of the Jewish faith," but "accepted it only together with anti-apocalyptic restrictions."[353] Maimonides counsels as follows:

> Do not think that the Messiah needs to perform signs and miracles, to bring about a new state of things in the world, revive the dead, and the like. It is not so.... Rather it is the case that in these matters that the statutes of our Torah are valid forever and eternally. Nothing can be added or taken away from them. And if there arise a king from the House of David who meditates on the Torah and practices its commandments like his ancestor David in accordance with the Written and Oral Law, prevails upon all Israel to walk in the ways of the Torah and to repair its breeches [i.e., to eliminate the bad state of affairs resulting from the incomplete observance of the law], and

---

[351] Willem A. VanGemeren, "Israel as a Hermeneutical Crux in the Interpretation of Prophecy [II]," *WTJ* 47 (1984), 271-97, esp. p. 272.

[352] Ulrike Hirschfelder, "The Liturgy of the Messiah: The Apocalypse of David in *Hekhalot* Literature," *JSQ* 12 (2005): 148-193.

[353] Gershom Scholem, *The Messianic Idea in Judaism* (New York: Schocken, 1971), 27. See Brettler and Levine for a modern Orthodox explanation about why there was a departure from the majority rabbinic interpretation of the messianic, son, king view (Marc Zvi Brettler and Amy-Jill Levine, "Psalm 2: Is the Messiah the Son of God?" TheTorah.com, https://thetorah.com/article/psalm-2-is-the-messiah-the-son-of-god).

fights the battles of the Lord, then one may properly assume that he is the Messiah. If he is then successful in rebuilding the sanctuary on its site and in gathering the dispersed of Israel, then he has in fact [as a result of his success] proven himself to be the Messiah. He will then arrange the whole world to serve only God, as it is said: "For then shall I create a pure language for the peoples that they may all call upon the name of God and serve him with one accord" (Zeph 3:9).

Let no one think that in the days of the Messiah anything of the natural course of the world will cease or that any innovation will be introduced into creation. Rather, the world will continue in its accustomed course. The words of Isaiah: "The wolf shall dwell with the lamb and the panther shall lie down with the kid" (Isa 11:6) are a parable and an allegory which must be understood to mean that Israel will Dwell securely even among the wicked of the heathen nations who are compared to a wolf and a panther. For they will all accept the true faith and will no longer rob or destroy. Likewise, all similar scriptural passages dealing with the Messiah must be regarded as figurative. Only in the Days of the Messiah will everyone know what the metaphors mean and to what they refer. The sages said: "The only difference between this world and the Days of the Messiah is the subjection of Israel to the nations.[354]

The approach of Maimonides has much in common with many Christian interpreters today who devalue the plain reading of Scripture, disparage a literal-historical-grammatical approach to biblical interpretation, and decline to take Israel's promises at

---
354 Scholem, 28-29.

face value. He is clear about his disinterest in the careful exegesis of prophetic texts:

> From the simple meaning of the words of the prophets it appears that at the beginning of the Days of the Messiah the war between Gog and Magog will take place... [With regard to these Messianic wars and the coming of the prophet Elijah before the End, Maimonides then continues:] concerning all these things and others like them, no one knows how they will come about until they actually happen, since the words of the prophets on these matters are not clear. Even the sages have no tradition regarding them but allow themselves to be guided by the texts. Hence there are differences of opinion on the subject. In any case, the order and details of these events are not religious dogmas. Therefore a person should never occupy himself a great deal with the legendary accounts nor spend much time on the Midrashim dealing with these and similar matters. He should not regard them as of prime importance, since devoting himself to them leads neither to the fear nor of the love of God...[355]

Despite the popularity of such exegetical practice among both Jewish and Christian interpreters, Robert Thomas is correct to observe, "Without some special qualification, Scripture never uses Mount Zion to denote a celestial abode of God or His people."[356] Describing the victorious followers of the Lamb in Revelation 14:1-5, he argues, "Since the focus of this scene is immediately after the storm of persecution has passed, this must be the millennial kingdom of 20:4-6 not the eternal kingdom of

---

355 Scholem, 29.
356 Robert L. Thomas, *Revelation 8–22 Exegetical Commentary*; Wycliffe Exegetical Commentary (Chicago, IL: Moody, 1995), 190.

21:1-22:5."[357] He continues,

> The dominant biblical connotation of the name fits here too. Jewish tradition expected a rallying of the faithful remnant at Mount Zion (Ps 48:1-2; Isa 11:9-12; 24:23; Joel 2:32) after the difficulties of the latter days (Moffatt, Charles, Johnson). Of the possible meanings whether this hilly area of southeast Jerusalem, the temple mount, the whole city of Jerusalem, or the whole land of Judah and the Israelite nation, any one would amount to a literal understanding of the earthly Zion. Since John has Psalm 2 in mind in this larger context (cf. 11:18; 12:5), a reference to earthly Zion is probable. This locality also corresponds to the prophecy of Zech 14:4-5. So this advance projection pictures the Warrior-King of 19:11-16 as having already returned to earth bringing with Him that select number who have suffered martyrdom at the hand of the beast (13:15).[358]

He further helpfully argues for the literal understanding of Zion references as follows: "The uses of Psalm 2 in Acts 4:25ff and in the Apocalypse furnish a prime indication that a NT nonliteral application of an OT prophecy, in conjunction with Christ's first advent or the church, does not necessarily exhaust or nullify the divine intention of its ultimate and future fulfillment in a literal way."[359]

Returning to the psalmist's incredulity, it is still a wonder today. "Why do the nations rage, and the peoples devise a vain thing?" (Ps 2:1). If God declared that Israel is His inheritance (and He has), then why does the world at large believe that the city of Jerusalem and the surrounding Promised Land belong to

---

357 Thomas, 190.
358 Thomas, 190-191.
359 Thomas, 555 n.38.

someone other than His chosen people? Paul Wilkinson assists in explaining this conundrum.

> In the final reckoning, Israel's story is not about the nation of Israel but about the God of Israel! Since May 14, 1948, the nations of the earth have been confronted every day with the reality of Israel's existence as a sovereign state, but instead of blessing Israel, they have cursed her. The clamor of contempt toward God's earthly inheritance is rising to a crescendo, but He hears and records every note and sound. Many Palestinian Arabs mistakenly and malevolently claim God's inheritance as their own while powerful nations like Russia look on, poised to plunder a piece of Israel's pie and 'seize great spoil' (Ezek. 38:10-13). Many nations are indifferent and much of the church is ignorant, but God is indignant![360]

Among several dispensational interpreters who will now be surveyed, Paul Enns helpfully argues for the fulfillment of the prophecy of Psalm 2:6 with the establishment of Jerusalem as the capital of Messiah's reign during the millennial kingdom.

> Numerous Old Testament passages refer to Christ's future millennial reign on earth. Psalm 2 describes the installation of Christ as king in Jerusalem, ruling over the nations of the world (Ps. 2:6-9). Psalm 24:7-10 depicts the victorious, returning king triumphantly entering Jerusalem to rule. Isaiah 9:6-7 describes Christ as the Son in His governmental rule. Isaiah 11:1-16 indicates Christ's reign will be a reign of justice (vv. 1-5), a peaceful reign (vv. 6-9), and a rule over restored Israel and the nations of the world (vv.10-16). Isaiah 24:23 prophesies Christ's reign will be in Jerusalem. Isaiah 35:1-10 emphasizes the blessings of

---

360 Paul Wilkinson, *Israel: The Inheritance of God* (San Antonio, TX: Ariel, 2021), 250-51.

the restored land and nation in Messiah's kingdom. Daniel 7:13-14 emphasizes Christ's rule will be over all people and nations. Zechariah 14:9-21 prophesies the destruction of Israel's enemies and Christ's rule over the nations of the world.[361]

Andy Woods also describes the importance of the capital of the divine King during the Millennium.

> During the millennial kingdom, the nation of Israel will not merely occupy a place of equal co-existence among the Gentile nations. Rather, in fulfillment of her divine destiny, she will be elevated to a place of preeminence over them (Deuteronomy 28:13; Isaiah 13:2; 49:22-23; Zechariah 8:22-23). Therefore, it should come as no surprise that the prophetic Scriptures reveal that the millennial kingdom's capital city will be Jerusalem (Isaiah 2:3; Zechariah 14:17). Revelation 20:9, describing a rebellion that will take place at the end of the millennium, says, "They marched across the breadth of the earth and surrounded the camp of God's people, *the city he loves*" (NIV). This beloved city is a clear reference to Jerusalem (Psalm 78:68; 87:2). When Satan is released from the abyss at the end of the millennium, this city will become the target of his attack since it is the headquarters, or nerve center, of the millennial kingdom.[362]

Commenting on the millennial Jerusalem, Arnold Fruchtenbaum notes, "While Ezekiel gives only a short description of the millennial Jerusalem, other Scriptures mention additional characteristics of the city. The authors of the Psalms in particular

---

361 Paul Enns, *The Moody Handbook of Theology* (Chicago, IL: Moody, 1997, c1989), 220. See also John F. Walvoord, *The Prophecy Knowledge Handbook* (Wheaton, IL: SP Publications, 1990), 81.
362 Andy Woods, "Millennium," in *The Harvest Handbook of Bible Prophecy*, ed. Ed Hindson, Mark Hitchcock, and Tim LaHaye (Eugene, OR: Harvest House Publishers, 2020), 260.

took delight in describing and characterizing the millennial Jerusalem."363

On the final verse of Ezekiel's prophecy (48:35), Charles Dyer observes,

> The most remarkable aspect of the new city of Jerusalem will be the presence of the Lord. God's glory had departed from the city as a prelude to its judgment (cf. chaps. 10–11), and His return will signal Jerusalem's blessing. This fact so impressed Ezekiel that he wrote that the city will be given a new name: THE LORD IS THERE. As the Prophet Ezekiel had stated repeatedly, God will return to dwell with His people. No longer worshiping lifeless idols and engaged in detestable practices, Israel will enjoy the Lord's holy presence in the Millennium.364

Much more could be observed from numerous prophetic texts concerning the millennial Jerusalem: its geography (physical features, topography, demography, agriculture, and human activities), its geopolitics (king, Davidic covenant, Israelite monarchy, and historical battles), its geometry (distance, shape, size, and relative position of figures), and glory (divine presence, beauty, holiness, and source of blessing to the world).

This magnificent millennial city will be the precursor to the New Jerusalem, which will descend after Messiah's final victory over Satan, who will surround "the camp of the saints and the beloved city" (Rev 20:9). The adversary will be cast into the lake of fire in preparation for the great white throne judgment (20:11–15) and the descent of the heavenly city (21:1–4) as John saw "the holy city, new Jerusalem, coming down out of heaven from God"

---

363 Arnold G. Fruchtenbaum, *Footsteps of the Messiah: A Study of the Sequence of Prophetic Events* (Revised; San Antonio, TX: Ariel Ministries, 2021), 465.
364 Charles H. Dyer, "Ezekiel," in *The Bible Knowledge Commentary: An Exposition of the Scriptures*, ed. J. F. Walvoord and R. B. Zuck, vol. 1 (Wheaton, IL: Victor Books, 1985), 1317.

(21:2, 10). Even into eternity, God's choice of Jerusalem will be remembered and celebrated. On the New Jerusalem, Dr. Hindson cited Bernard Ramm as follows in describing what awaits all those who love our coming King:

> The curtain of revelation drops with a final vision of glorification. The glorified shall reign for ever and ever. It is a *reign*! That is, it is a condition of complete glorification...a perfect sharing in the wonder of God. And it is *eternal*. It will last forever and ever...knowing an existence free from all pain, death, and mourning, and knowing an existence only of happiness, bliss, joy and glory without end.[365]

---

[365] Hindson, *Future Glory*, 154, citing Bernard Ramm, *Them He Glorified* (Grand Rapids: Eerdmans, 1963), 136.

BIBLIOGRAPHY

Alter, Robert. *The Book of Psalms: A Translation with Commentary*. New York: W. W. Norton, 2007.

Averbeck, Richard E. "נסך," in NIDOTTE. 3:113-17.

Brettler, Marc Zvi and Amy-Jill Levine, "Psalm 2: Is the Messiah the Son of God?" TheTorah.com, https://thetorah.com/article/psalm-2-is-the-messiah-the-son-of-god.

Cole, Robert L. *Psalms 1–2: Gateway to the Psalter*. Hebrew Bible Monographs 37. Sheffield: Sheffield Phoenix Press, 2013.

——. "Psalm 1–2: The Divine Son of God," *The Moody Handbook of Messianic Prophecy*, edited by Michael Rydelnik and Edwin Blum, 477-90. Chicago: Moody, 2019.

Collins, C. John. "חשמ," in NIDOTTE, 2:1123-27.

Dohmen, C. "נסך," in TDOT. 9:457.

Dyer, Charles H. "Ezekiel," in *The Bible Knowledge Commentary: An Exposition of the Scriptures*, edited by J. F. Walvoord and R. B. Zuck, Vol. 1. Wheaton, IL: Victor Books, 1985.

Enns, Paul. *The Moody Handbook of Theology*. Chicago, IL: Moody, 1997, c1989.

Feurer, Avrohom Chaim. *Tehillim: A New Translation with a Commentary Anthologized from Talmudic, Midrashic and Rabbinic Sources*. Artscroll Series. Brooklyn, NY: Mesorah, 2013.

Fruchtenbaum, Arnold G. *Footsteps of the Messiah: A Study of the Sequence of Prophetic Events*. Revised. San Antonio, TX: Ariel Ministries, 2021.

Gunn, George A. "Psalm 2 and the Reign of the Messiah," *BSac* 169 (October-December 2012).

Hill, Andrew E. and John H. Walton, *A Survey of the Old Testament*. 2nd ed. Grand Rapids: Zondervan, 2000.

Hindson, Ed. *Future Glory: Living in the Hope of the Rapture, Heaven, and Eternity*. Eugene, OR: Harvest House Publishers, 2021.

Hirschfelder, Ulrike. "The Liturgy of the Messiah: The Apocalypse of David in Hekhalot Literature," *JSQ* 12 (2005): 148-93.

Monson, John M. "The Temple of Solomon: Heart of Jerusalem," in *Zion, City of Our God*, edited by Richard S. Hess and Gordon J. Wenham. Grand Rapids: Eerdmans, 1999.

Ross, Allen P. *A Commentary on the Psalms 1–89*, Vol. 1. Kregel Exegetical Library. Grand Rapids: Kregel Academic, 2011-2013.

Rydelnik, Michael. *The Messianic Hope: Is the Hebrew Bible Really Messianic?* NAC Studies in Bible & Theology. Nashville, TN: B & H Academic, 2010.

Satterthwaite, Philip. "Zion in the Songs of Ascents," in *Zion, City of Our God*, edited by Richard S. Hess and Gordon J. Wenham. Grand Rapids: Eerdmans, 1999.

Scholem, Gershom. *The Messianic Idea in Judaism*. New York: Schocken, 1971.

Seybold, Klaus. "חשמ," TDOT 9:43-54.

Snearly, Michael K. "The Return of the King: Book V as a Witness to Messianic Hope in the Psalter," in *The Psalms: Language for All Seasons of the Soul*, edited by Andrew J. Schmutzer and David M. Howard, Jr. Chicago: Moody, 2013.

Soggin, J.A. "חשמ," TLOT 2:676-77.

Strong, John T. "Zion, Theology of." NIDOTTE, 4:1314-21.

Thomas, Robert L. *Revelation 8–22 Exegetical Commentary*. Wycliffe Exegetical Commentary. Chicago: Moody, 1995.

Tigay, Jeffrey H. "Divine Creation of the King in Psalms 2:6," in *Hayim and Miriam Tadmor Volume*. Eretz-Israel: Archaeological, Historical and Geographical Studies 27 (2003): 246-51.

VanGemeren, Willem A. "Israel as a Hermeneutical Crux in the Interpretation of Prophecy [II]," *WTJ* 47 (1984): 271-97.

Waltke, Bruce and M. O'Connor. *An Introduction to Biblical Hebrew Syntax*. Winona Lake: Eisenbrauns, 1990.

Walvoord, John F. *The Prophecy Knowledge Handbook*. Wheaton, IL: SP Publications, 1990.

Wilson, Gerald. "Psalms I", NIVAC, 111 n.17.

Wilkinson, Paul. *Israel: The Inheritance of God*. San Antonio, TX: Ariel, 2021.

Woods, Andy. "Millennium," in *The Harvest Handbook of Bible Prophecy*, edited by Ed Hindson, Mark Hitchcock, and Tim LaHaye. Eugene, OR: Harvest House Publishers, 2020.

CHAPTER TEN

THE KINGDOM OF GOD AND THE KINGDOM OF MAN IN THE BOOK OF DANIEL

by Dr. Daniel Sloan

The book of Daniel is one of the great books of the Old Testament. It is unique because it combines narrative, prophetic, and apocalyptic elements throughout the book.[366] Daniel was also a unique prophet because he did not serve as a traditional prophet. He did not preach messages of repentance and give sermons to the people. Instead, he served as an administrator in two different

---

[366] The book of Daniel was very dear to the heart of Ed Hindson. He taught the Daniel-Revelation class at Liberty University for decades.

empires while also serving in a prophetic role, mainly through dream interpretation.[367]

One of the major themes found in the book of Daniel is that of the distinction between the kingdom of man and the Kingdom of God. The kingdom of man, represented by both the Jewish and Gentile nations of the world, is a kingdom with a future end in history. On the other hand, the future Kingdom of God, as presented in the book of Daniel, is an everlasting kingdom that will one day replace the kingdom of man. This chapter will look at the trajectory of these two contrasting kingdoms throughout the Book of Daniel, culminating with the Son of Man passage in Daniel 7.

Daniel 1:1-2

In the third year of the reign of Jehoiakim king of Judah, Nebuchadnezzar king of Babylon came to Jerusalem and besieged it. And the Lord gave Jehoiakim king of Judah into his hand, with some of the articles of the house of God, which he carried into the land of Shinar to the house of his god; and he brought the articles into the treasure house of his god. (NKJV)

The first two verses of the book of Daniel established the limitations on the kingdom of man from a Jewish perspective. In 605 BC, Nebuchadnezzar attacked the city of Jerusalem for the first of three invasions. It was in this invasion that Daniel and his friends were taken away to Babylon as political prisoners, along with some of the treasures from Solomon's Temple. A Jewish reader might immediately question this event. Why would Yahweh allow a pagan king to successfully invade Yahweh's own people?

---

[367] This is most likely the reason that Daniel was not placed in the prophet section in the Hebrew canon. He was not a true "prophet" in the traditional sense. However, Jesus called him a prophet in Matt 24:15.

The book of Daniel does not directly answer this question. The closest Daniel ever came to answering this question in the book was found in his prayer in chapter 9, when he addressed the sinfulness of the nation. However, the key phrase in these early verses was the phrase "the Lord gave." Judah was given to Nebuchadnezzar as a gift from Yahweh because of their sin, not because of Nebuchadnezzar's greatness. Sprinkle writes, "Whereas the Babylonians would likely attribute the plundering of the temple of Yahweh to the superiority of their god Marduk, Daniel attributes these events to the sovereign will of Yahweh."[368] Many of the prophets, such as Isaiah and Jeremiah, had warned of this coming judgment for the nation if the nation refused to repent and turn back to Yahweh and His ways. "Delivered" is the Hebrew word *nātan*, "gave." God in his sovereignty had permitted Nebuchadnezzar to come against Judah to judge Jehoiakim and the sinful nation.[369]

The importance of these verses cannot be overstated and offer two important keys to remember for the rest of the book. First, it was Yahweh that allowed for nations to conquer other nations, even His own people. Longman rightfully asserts, "Nebuchadnezzar's might, though considerable, was not the reason why Jerusalem fell under his influence; it was the result of the will and action of God himself."[370] Second, it also began a line of human kingdoms that would fail throughout the book. Starting with God's people as the primary example of this failure of human kingdoms made it very clear that any nation could suffer the same fate as Judah as long as Yahweh permitted it.[371]

---

[368] Joe M. Sprinkle, *Daniel*, ed. T. Desmond Alexander, Thomas R. Schreiner, and Andreas J. Köstenberger, Evangelical Biblical Theology Commentary (Bellingham, WA: Lexham Press, 2020), 49-50.

[369] Stephen R. Miller, *Daniel*, The New American Commentary, vol. 18 (Nashville: Broadman & Holman Publishers, 1994), 58.

[370] Tremper Longman III, *Daniel*, The NIV Application Commentary (Grand Rapids: Zondervan, 1999), 2463.

[371] Judah was in a unique situation where Yahweh had promised their restoration in the future.

Daniel 2:44–45

And in the days of these kings the God of heaven will set up a kingdom which shall never be destroyed; and the kingdom shall not be left to other people; it shall break in pieces and consume all these kingdoms, and it shall stand forever. Inasmuch as you saw that the stone was cut out of the mountain without hands, and that it broke in pieces the iron, the bronze, the clay, the silver, and the gold—the great God has made known to the king what will come to pass after this. The dream is certain, and its interpretation is sure." (NKJV)

In Daniel 1 it was established that the Jewish nation would not be able to survive their sinfulness and Yahweh had allowed them to fall into the hands of Nebuchadnezzar. The question that may have arisen in many Jewish minds at that time would be what would happen to this Gentile king and his nation? Would they survive where Judah had not?[372] This question was clearly answered in Daniel 2. Daniel argued that no human kingdom, no matter how strong and mighty, would be able to compare to the Kingdom of God.

At the start of chapter 2, Nebuchadnezzar had a terrible dream about a statue made of various kinds of metals. Nebuchadnezzar called for his wise men and religious advisors to give him an interpretation of his dream, but he also did not tell them the dream. Some argue that he himself forgot the dream, but that was probably not the case. Instead, it was much more likely that Nebuchadnezzar did not trust the wise men's ability to interpret it if he told them the dream. Dream books were common in the ancient world and therefore, if Nebuchadnezzar told them the dream, they could simply use those resources to make up any in-

---

Most other Gentile nations do not have that same kind of promise throughout history.
372 The book of Habakkuk offers a very similar argument.

terpretation that they wanted without actually proving that they had any power from the gods.

The wise men countered Nebuchadnezzar and instead argued that it was impossible to interpret the dream without hearing the dream because the gods did not work in this way in giving direct revelation to humanity. His wise men and religious advisors could not interpret his dream; only Daniel, through the power of Yahweh, was able to interpret the dream. Specifically, Daniel described a dream that incorporated four future empires, the head of gold, the arms of silver, the thigh of bronze, and the legs/feet of iron and clay. There is clearly a pattern found in these materials. The materials start with the most valuable, gold, then silver, bronze, and finally iron. However, the strength of the materials is in reverse since gold is very weak, then silver, bronze, and ending with iron, clearly the strongest of the four materials. This seems to argue that the empires that the materials represent will grow stronger throughout history. Some argue that only the head of gold can be understood definitively since that is the only nation that Daniel specifically named in the passage. For example, Andrew Hill writes, "Beyond the immediate historical situation of the Babylonian Empire, the revelation of the dream and its interpretation in ch. 2 is not intended as a precise schematic of world history."[373]

Other scholars argue that the nations can be established because of our modern knowledge of history, either as Babylon, Media-Persia, Greece, and Rome (the conservative view) or Babylon, Media, Persia, and Greece (the Maccabean hypothesis).[374] Regardless of which view one holds on this issue, the same key is present; the kingdom of man is constantly in flux.[375] Nations destroy and

---

[373] Andrew Hill, *Daniel*, The Expositor's Bible Commentary (Grand Rapids: Zondervan, 2008), loc. 2989-90.

[374] Some, like Ed Hindson and I, also see a hint at the kingdom of the Antichrist in this passage as well, although Daniel 7 is much clearer on this issue.

[375] I find the Maccabean thesis quite inadequate. The Medes never had an empire that controlled

conquer other nations and thus the balance of power in history is always in constant movement. Babylon one day would fall, which happened in 539 BC to Cyrus the Great. Persia would then fall to Alexander the Great, and then the Greek Empire would fall to the Roman Empire. Even mighty Rome, the greatest of the ancient empires, eventually fell. Thus, Daniel established that the kingdoms of the world were only temporary powers.

This failure of the kingdom of man became even more pronounced when compared to the last kingdom (the Kingdom of God as represented in the vision as the large stone). The large stone that Daniel saw had two purposes. First, it destroyed the statue in its entirety, blowing it away like chaff. The worldly kingdoms cannot compare to the Kingdom of God and are simply inferior to its composition. James Hamilton, Jr. sums it up nicely when he writes, "God's kingdom destroys all human kingdoms and fills the earth, pointing to the way that his kingdom will enjoy dominion over the entire world as his glory fills the earth."[376]

When this occurs is up for debate depending on one's eschatological position. Amillennialists see this occurring with the first coming of Christ and His defeat of Satan at the cross. Premillennialists argue against this position because human government still exists after Christ's crucifixion and ascension. Indeed, Christianity and human government have mixed throughout much of church history, especially through the power of the Catholic Church. Postmillennialists see this kingdom as being fulfilled through the Church. Premillennialists argue against this position as well, arguing that the kingdom cannot be enacted unless King Jesus Himself is present. One cannot have the

---

the region comparable to Babylon, Persia, Greece, and Rome. They were only able to find power by combining with the Persians under Cyrus. They simply do not fit in the listing alongside these other superpowers. Also, the Medes and the Persians were combined as one nation in the book of Daniel itself in 6:8.

376 James M. Hamilton, Jr., *With the Clouds of Heaven: The Book of Daniel in Biblical Theology*, ed. D. A. Carson, vol. 32, New Studies in Biblical Theology (Downers Grove, IL: InterVarsity Press, 2015), 89.

Kingdom of God without God present to lead the Kingdom. Instead, Premillennialists look forward to Christ's Second Coming when He will destroy all forms of human government and instead set up His kingdom during His millennial reign on earth (Rev. 20:1-6).[377]

A second point made in this passage was the timing elements of the Kingdom of God compared to the kingdom of man. The kingdom of man had a clear end when the stone destroyed the statue. However, the Kingdom of God was designated as a kingdom "which shall never be destroyed…shall not be left to other people…shall stand forever." These three points show the distinction between the two kingdoms. First, The Kingdom of God would never be destroyed, unlike the kingdoms represented by the statue, which would destroy each other and then finally be destroyed by the Kingdom of God. Throughout the history of the world, the kingdoms of man have fallen time and time again. Egypt, Babylon, Persia, Greece, and Rome were all at one time in history the strongest nations in the world, and yet eventually they would be destroyed.

Second, the Kingdom of God would not be left to another people. The pattern of the kingdoms of the world, especially in the Ancient Near East, was that when one kingdom was destroyed and replaced by the next great kingdom, that kingdom was assimilated into the new kingdom. When the Persians conquered Babylon, Babylon's empire became a part of the Persian empire. When Alexander the Great conquered Persia, Persia became a part of the Greek empire. Greece eventually became a part of the Roman Empire. However, the Kingdom of God was not like these nations. Instead, it was the final form of government in history

---

[377] One of the main arguments from this passage for an earthly Messianic Kingdom is that the four kingdoms of the statue were all earthly and physical. Therefore, it only makes sense if the kingdom replacing them is also earthly and physical as well. Also, the kingdom is said to "fill the earth", which seems strange if it is not an earthly kingdom. Miller, 101. J. Paul Tanner, *Daniel*, Evangelical Exegetical Commentary (Bellingham, WA: Lexham Press, 2020), 208.

and would never be conquered and therefore never become a part of the next empire in line.

Third, the most striking element of the Kingdom of God is its longevity as Daniel wrote that "it shall stand forever." Why would Daniel have needed to add this element when he had already stated that the kingdom would not be conquered? Sprinkle makes a connection between the idea of the eternality of the Kingdom with the eternality of the Davidic line established in the Davidic Covenant in 2 Samuel 7.[378] Twice in that passage, in verses 13 and 16, the Davidic line is stated to continue forever. Thus, Daniel appears to be making a clear connection between the Kingdom of God and the Davidic line in this passage. While he did not specifically name the Messiah in this passage, it laid the groundwork for Daniel 7 in which more details would be given about this kingdom and its King.

Finally, the passage ended with the statement "The dream is certain, and its interpretation is sure." Miller writes,

> Christ's kingdom will certainly come. In the latter part of v. 45, Daniel concludes his interpretation of the dream revelation by telling Nebuchadnezzar that "the great God has shown the king what will take place in the future" and emphasizes the certainty of the fulfillment of the revelation (the dream is true and certain to occur) and the interpretation is trustworthy...The prophecies of Daniel concerning past events (the four empires) have been accurately fulfilled, and his inspired messages concerning events yet future will just as assuredly occur.[379]

Believers do not have to worry about whether Satan will in some way be able to interrupt or even stop the plans and prophecies of God. The Kingdom of God will come because God Him-

---

378 Sprinkle, 85.
379 Miller, 102.

self, through Daniel's prophecy, has already declared it as such and nothing in the universe has the power to change the plan of God.

Daniel 4:1–3, 34

> Nebuchadnezzar the king, to all peoples, nations, and languages that dwell in all the earth: Peace be multiplied to you. I thought it good to declare the signs and wonders that the Most High God has worked for me. How great are His signs, and how mighty His wonders! His kingdom is an everlasting kingdom, and His dominion is from generation to generation... And at the end of the time I, Nebuchadnezzar, lifted my eyes to heaven, and my understanding returned to me; and I blessed the Most High and praised and honored Him who lives forever: For His dominion is an everlasting dominion, and His kingdom is from generation to generation.

There is perhaps no greater transition in all the Bible than the transition between Daniel 3 and Daniel 4:1-3. Daniel 3 told the story of the prideful King Nebuchadnezzar who built a statue and tried to burn anyone who would not worship the statue. While Nebuchadnezzar admitted that Yahweh was powerful in chapters 2 and 3, he still had not concluded that he was worthy of worship. However, Daniel 4 opened with a personal message from King Nebuchadnezzar himself declaring the greatness of Yahweh and not himself. It is almost unbelievable to think that this king in chapter 4 could even be the same person from the previous chapters. The story of Nebuchadnezzar's insanity in the chapter explains the transition of him from a self-lover to a follower of Yahweh.[380]

---

[380] Critical scholars' approach ch. 4 in one of two ways. Many argue that it is simply a complete fabrication and therefore is simply a legend. They argue that there is no historical record of Nebuchadnezzar ever suffering from this type of sickness. However, the records for the second

When the first three verses of the chapter are read, one must question what could possibly have made Nebuchadnezzar change so dramatically so quickly. The answer is then given. Nebuchadnezzar had another dream, like the one in chapter 2, in which a great tree was cut down. Nebuchadnezzar attempted to get the wise men to interpret the dream, but ultimately Daniel alone could give him the interpretation, which entailed that Nebuchadnezzar would suffer from insanity for seven years because of his immense pride, believing himself to be some type of cow or ox. He would sleep in the field, look completely disheveled, and then eventually turn to acknowledge Yahweh as the ruler of the earth. It was only after that point that Nebuchadnezzar's sanity would be healed and his kingdom would be restored to him.

Therefore, the problem in the passage was that Nebuchadnezzar saw his kingdom as equal to or greater than the Kingdom of God. It was seen in chapter 3 when he created a gold statue, likely connected to the head of gold from the statue in chapter 2, that he demanded to be worshipped. It also was seen in 4:30 when he stated, "Is not this great Babylon, that I have built for a royal dwelling by my mighty power and for the honor of my majesty?" Nebuchadnezzar's pride made him think that he was greater than anything in the universe, especially the God of the people he had recently conquered.[381] He was surely mistaken in this belief and

---

half of Nebuchadnezzar's reign are spotty at best and even if they were found, it is unlikely that the official records would have recorded such an embarrassing tale about the king. Others argue that the author of the book mistook Nabonidus for Nebuchadnezzar. This is because a historical document, called the Prayer of Nabonidus, has been found that states that Nabonidus was sick for seven years and was healed. Carol Newsom, *Daniel* (Louisville, KY: Westminster John Knox Press, 2014), 128. However, when one looks at the details of this prayer, they do not line up with the details of the passage in Daniel, especially with the idea of the king believing that he was an animal and living out in the field.

381 In the ANE mindset, gods were associated with their territory. The Babylonian gods only controlled the land that Babylon controlled, etc. This is one of the main reasons that nations were constantly trying to expand their territory. It was not just for natural resources or political power alone, but also to show that your gods were more powerful than the gods of the other nations. This is also why conquered nations would have their temples robbed and their idols taken to be placed in the temple of the conqueror to show their gods' superiority. With this mindset, Nebuchadnezzar clearly would have believed that because he conquered Judah, then his gods were more powerful than Yahweh. He did not understand that Yahweh had simply allowed him to do

suffered the consequences with his insanity.

Verses 1–3 then were written by Nebuchadnezzar after this event to describe his new relationship with Yahweh. While the text was not definitive if Nebuchadnezzar was "saved," it at least showed that he had a healthy respect for the Hebrew God. In verse 1, he attached his name to the statements. If he was not saved at this point, this would be the only example of Scripture written by a pagan. He then identified his audience, the people across the earth. This form, Longman argues, reads like an ancient official royal proclamation. He writes, "The outburst is more than spontaneous; it has the form of an official proclamation directed throughout the world. As a matter of fact, Nebuchadnezzar's kingdom stretched from what is today Egypt to western Iran and from modern Syria into Saudi Arabia, encompassing many different cultures and language groups."[382] While his kingdom was not the entire world, it hyperbolically consisted of much of the known world at that time and thus very much served as a major proclamation throughout the entire region.

Next, Nebuchadnezzar declared the "signs and wonders" that the Most High God had given to him in his life. While he was most likely addressing the issue of his insanity found in the chapter, one must remember that was not the first time that Nebuchadnezzar had seen the power and uniqueness of Judah's God. In chapter 2, it was Yahweh that had allowed him to understand his dream about the statue. In chapter 3, it was Yahweh that had spared Shadrach, Meshach, and Abed-Nego from his rage in the fiery furnace. Indeed, for perhaps decades Nebuchadnezzar had seen the miraculous works of Yahweh's power in his life. The prediction and fulfillment of his insanity was simply the final step in his acceptance of Yahweh's power.

---

this or that Yahweh controlled the entire earth, not simply Judah's territory.
382 Longman, 2547.

One cannot help but compare the Pharaoh of the Exodus with Nebuchadnezzar, as both were confronted by Yahweh with signs and wonders. Pharaoh saw the miracles of Yahweh time and time again through the plagues that Moses put on his nation. However, even after finally allowing Israel to leave, he again rebelled against Yahweh by sending his army after Israel. Nebuchadnezzar similarly was confronted by Yahweh with numerous miracles and after much resistance, finally changed and surrendered to the power and glory of Yahweh.

Nebuchadnezzar shifted his focus from the miracles that he had seen to the Kingdom of God that he now recognized. He described the Kingdom of God as an everlasting kingdom that never ends. One might wonder where he received this information since he was a pagan king. He had heard this type of information from Daniel years before in chapter 2 when Daniel described the stone that destroyed the statue in the vision. However, it is also likely that Daniel himself had continued to talk to Nebuchadnezzar about his God, either before or after his insanity. Daniel had served with the king for many years at this point and was one of the king's most trusted advisors. Tanner argues, "It is entirely possible that Daniel had ministered to him somewhere in the process (near the end of his illness? shortly after his restoration?) with the words from Ps 145, and that by the grace of God Nebuchadnezzar came to faith and fully trusted in God and this revelation about God's kingdom."[383] Wherever he had received the information from, he was admitting that God's Kingdom was greater than his kingdom, showing the new level of humility that he now had after his insanity episode.

---

[383] Tanner, 269-70.

Daniel 5:26–31

This *is* the interpretation of *each* word. MENE: God has numbered your kingdom and finished it; TEKEL: You have been weighed in the balances and found wanting; PERES: Your kingdom has been divided, and given to the Medes and Persians." That very night Belshazzar, king of the Chaldeans, was slain. And Darius the Mede received the kingdom, *being* about sixty-two years old.

After Daniel 4, the book moves forward drastically, skipping over the end of Nebuchadnezzar's reign and toward at least twenty-three years to 539 BC during the co-regency of Nabonidus and his son Belshazzar, Nebuchadnezzar's grandson.[384] Nabonidus was the ruling king of Babylon but created a co-regency with his son Belshazzar that allowed him to be away from Babylon and put Belshazzar in charge.[385] During this time, Cyrus the Great came to power in Persia, combined with the Medes, and was on the outskirts of Babylon. Thus, the city was in the charge of an unproven leader who was not even the ruling king and was about to be attacked by a brilliant military and political leader in Cyrus.

At the beginning of the chapter, Belshazzar showed no signs of worry about the impending invasion. In fact, he was throwing a party in the palace, possibly for the Babylonian New Year. Babylon was a fortress during this time and would have been almost impossible to directly assault, which was probably why the Babylonians did not take the threat from Cyrus very seriously. At the party, Belshazzar called for the items taken from the Jewish Temple decades before to be used in a completely desecrating manner, while he also worshiped the pagan idols that were associated with Babylonian religion.

---

384 Tanner, 317.
385 Nabonidus spent several years away from Babylon in both Harran and Arabia.

It was at this point that a miraculous event began to occur in the throne room; a hand began to write a message on the wall of the palace. This terrified everyone present, causing Belshazzar to make a promise to the wise men that if anyone could interpret the message, they would be promoted to third in the kingdom. However, the wise men, as usual throughout the book, failed in their task. This commotion caused the queen, possibly Nebuchadnezzar's wife and Belshazzar's grandmother, to enter and tell Belshazzar to summon Daniel.[386] When Daniel arrived, in his eighties probably at this point, he was unknown to Belshazzar, showing that he was probably retired or driven to obscurity in the palace.

Daniel reminded Belshazzar about Nebuchadnezzar's miraculous encounters and how Nebuchadnezzar had eventually turned to acknowledge Yahweh, something that Belshazzar was unwilling to do. Belshazzar chose to follow the pattern of Pharaoh by ignoring the message and warning of Yahweh through a miracle but instead followed his own grandfather Nebuchadnezzar who had humbled himself before Yahweh. Daniel finally gave Belshazzar the answer to the writing on the wall, but it was probably not the answer that Belshazzar was hoping to receive. The interpretation of the three words, *mene*, *tekel*, and *peres*, usually translated as numbered, weighed, and divided, was a sign of the immediate judgment that was about to fall upon Belshazzar. The idea of God weighing actions and motivations was common in both Hebrew thought (Proverbs) and Egyptian thought, weighing of souls on a balance scale before Osiris, god of the underworld.[387] Goldingay sums it up well when he writes, "Belshazzar's sin has exceeded Nebuchadnezzar's, and so will his fall, not merely to banishment

---

386 Some argue that this was Belshazzar's wife, but that is unlikely as the chapter had already mentioned that Belshazzar's wives were present at the party. It also would not make sense that Belshazzar would have no knowledge of Daniel and yet one of his wives would not only know Daniel but also know the type of information that she had about Daniel's interaction with Nebuchadnezzar decades ago.

387 Hill, loc. 4173-75.

in humiliation, but to death and the end of his dynasty, without finding repentance."[388]

Interestingly, the chapter ended with two key elements. First, Daniel told Belshazzar that his kingdom, the Babylonian empire, had been given to the Medes and Persians by Yahweh. This was a fulfillment of the prophecy that Daniel had interpreted in chapter 2 when he had told Nebuchadnezzar that his empire would be conquered and replaced by another kingdom, the arms of silver. Unlike the Kingdom of God which would never be conquered and left to another people, the kingdom of Babylon would be conquered and folded into the Medio-Persian Empire. Second, the idea that it was Yahweh that gave the Babylonians into the hands of the Persians was reminiscent of chapter 1 when Yahweh allowed Judah to be given into the hands of the Babylonians. Thus, both Jew and Gentile kingdoms would be given to their enemies if they were not deemed acceptable before a holy God. While the Kingdom of God was unending and forever, the kingdom of man was setting the pattern of constant turnover and destruction.

This prediction was historically fulfilled through Cyrus the Great. The Babylonians were correct in believing that Cyrus could not directly conquer the city. However, Cyrus was able to get around the walls of the city through ingenuity. His army diverted the river and went under the wall through the newly formed gap in the wall. On the Cyrus Cylinder, Cyrus boasts that he took the city of Babylon without a battle, aided by the Babylonian deity, Marduk:

> Marduk, the great lord, a protector of his people/worshipers, beheld with pleasure his (i.e., Cyrus') good deeds and his upright mind (lit.: heart) (and therefore) ordered him to march against his city Babylon.... He made him set out on the road to Babylon...going at his side like a real friend. His

---

[388] John Goldingay, *Daniel*, Word Biblical Commentary (Grand Rapids: Zondervan, 2019), 116.

widespread troops—their number, like that of the water of a river, could not be established—strolled along, their weapons packed away. Without any battle, he made him enter his town Babylon..., sparing Babylon...any calamity.[389]

Daniel had predicted decades before that the Babylonian empire would fall, and he lived to see that very event be fulfilled.

Daniel 6:25-27

Then King Darius wrote: To all peoples, nations, and languages that dwell in all the earth: Peace be multiplied to you. I make a decree that in every dominion of my kingdom men must tremble and fear before the God of Daniel. For He is the living God, and steadfast forever; His kingdom is the one which shall not be destroyed, and His dominion shall endure to the end. He delivers and rescues, and He works signs and wonders in heaven and on earth, Who has delivered Daniel from the power of the lions.

Daniel 6 is the most famous chapter in the book of Daniel and one of the most famous stories in the entire Bible. It is also a chapter that is very similar to both chapters 3 and 4, almost combining the events in those two stories into a new story in a different context. In chapter 3, Nebuchadnezzar tried to force the three Hebrews to abandon their faith under pain of death through the fiery furnace. In chapter 4, Nebuchadnezzar was driven insane to the point that he finally admitted that his nation was nothing compared to the Kingdom of God. In chapter 6, Daniel faced both a call to abandon his faith under pain of death as well as influencing another pagan ruler to declare the greatness of the Kingdom of God.

---

389 Cited in Tanner, 355.

The chapter began with the new Persian government under King Darius taking over from the Babylonian empire. Daniel was given a place within this new administration and proved himself so well that Darius planned to promote him over the Persian administrators. This caused the Persian administrators to create a plan to trap Daniel, tricking Darius into signing a law that outlawed prayer for thirty days. They told Darius that the administrators had agreed that this was a good idea. It is clear that they had not consulted Daniel about this manner. Daniel heard about the regulations but refused to abide by them and was therefore arrested by the other administrators. Even though Darius liked him and wanted to protect him, he had no choice but to throw him in the lion's den.[390] When Darius arrived the next morning, Daniel was not dead but alive, saved by the power and intervention of Yahweh. It was after this occurrence that Darius made a proclamation to declare the greatness of the Hebrew God.

When one first reads the beginning of Darius's proclamation, one cannot help but see the connections between Darius's proclamation with Nebuchadnezzar's proclamation given decades earlier in Daniel 4. Sprinkle writes,

> This proclamation of Darius to various peoples echoes the earlier proclamations of Nebuchadnezzar (3:28–4:3). Both Nebuchadnezzar and Darius addressed every people, nation, and language (4:1; 6:25). Nebuchadnezzar's decree provokes fear by threatening to destroy the family of anyone who speaks against the God of Shadrach, Meshach, and Abednego (3:29), while Darius destroyed the families of Daniel's enemies (6:24) and exhorts people to fear and

---

[390] The Medes and Persians had a rather unique law in which once a law was given, it could not be revoked under any circumstance. In the story of Esther, Xerxes had the very same issue of not being able to change a law and had to pass a separate law instead as a workaround to the initial law. Darius either did not think to do this or the law was written in a way that a workaround was impossible.

tremble before the God of Daniel (6:26a).[391]

While the proclamation was certainly written in the ANE style of their day, it also would make sense that Daniel also had something to do with its composition similarities since he was the common denominator with both proclamations. Why would Darius make that proclamation to his people based solely on Daniel's deliverance? One reason could have been that Darius, like Nebuchadnezzar, had been influenced by both Daniel's faith and Yahweh's miraculous deliverance and had been pushed toward Judaism. Another option was that Darius simply saw the power of Daniel's God and did not want to alienate that powerful deity.

The proclamation next stated that Yahweh was the "living God" and that He was "steadfast forever." This showed that Darius recognized the mighty act of deliverance that Yahweh had done for Daniel. Longman writes, "Darius proclaims the God of Daniel 'the living God.' This indicates that he not only exists but is active in the world. Certainly, the prophet's rescue shows that in a dramatic fashion. God and his kingdom will never end, and he rescues his people in astounding ways."[392] While this declaration was vague enough to make it impossible to determine Darius's specific religious observations, it did show that Darius understood that Yahweh was a force in the universe that he did not want to tangle with in any meaningful way.[393]

Darius then stated, "His kingdom is the one which shall not be destroyed, and His dominion shall endure to the end." This declaration clearly showed that Darius had been greatly influenced by Daniel. Nebuchadnezzar made a similar statement in his proclamation, but he had received a similar statement in Dan-

---

[391] Sprinkle, 163.
[392] Longman, 2601.
[393] While this may seem like Darius has converted to Judaism, one must remember that Darius was a polytheist. He easily could declare the power of Daniel's God without becoming a monotheistic Jew.

iel's interpretation of his dream. Darius had never had a dream that allowed him to receive this type of interpretation. Therefore, the only possible explanation for him to have received this information about the Kingdom of God would have been through Daniel's teaching. Daniel's influence therefore spread to two different rulers of two massive empires, both acknowledging, at least in words, that the Kingdom of God was a force that was beyond anything the worldly empires could compete against.

Daniel 7:13–14, 27

> "I was watching in the night visions, and behold, *One* like the Son of Man, coming with the clouds of heaven! He came to the Ancient of Days, and they brought Him near before Him. Then to Him was given dominion and glory and a kingdom, that all peoples, nations, and languages should serve Him. His dominion *is* an everlasting dominion, which shall not pass away, and His kingdom *the one* Which shall not be destroyed… Then the kingdom and dominion, and the greatness of the kingdoms under the whole heaven, shall be given to the people, the saints of the Most High. His kingdom *is* an everlasting kingdom, and all dominions shall serve and obey Him."

The narrative section of Daniel, chapters 1-6, sets the stage for chapter 7, which is not only the key chapter in the book of Daniel but one of the key chapters in the entire Old Testament. The first six chapters show that the kingdom of man, represented by the human kingdoms of the world, was woefully impotent when compared to the Kingdom of God, which was an everlasting kingdom. Daniel 7 not only continued this argument but also expanded the argument by showing that even the greatest form of the kingdom of man, the future kingdom of the Antichrist, was nothing compared to the Kingdom of God, which Daniel argued was ruled by a Messianic figure.

The chapter begins by noting that the dream given to Daniel occurred during the first year of Belshazzar's reign, placing it between the events of chapters 4 and 5. Unlike the visions in the first half of the book, this vision is given directly to Daniel. The vision begins with four beasts: a lion, a bear, a leopard, and a monster. Scholars generally connect these beasts with the four empires associated with the statue in chapter 2. Thus, if one has the statue representing Babylon, Medio-Persia, Greece, and Rome, then the beasts also represent those nations as well. However, more details are given in the passage, especially about the fourth beast.

This fourth beast represents the Roman Empire. However, it also has what appears to be some future elements attached to it, the ten horns and then the little horn. The little horn has generally been recognized by conservative scholars as the future Antichrist, and the ten horns are represented as part of his kingdom. Verses 24-25 offered further explanation of these elements, showing that the horns arose from the fourth kingdom and then the little horn also came from that fourth kingdom. These ten kings empower the little horn and then the little horn, empowered by these kings, will both attack Yahweh and persecute his saints.[394] Thus, the final form of the kingdom of man will be led by this Antichrist figure and control much of the world.

However, verses 9-13 explain how this empire would end. The Ancient of Days, God the Father, was seen seated on the heavenly throne. He then put judgment on the beast (little horn or Antichrist) and the beast was slain. Tanner writes,

> Such a wicked one as the antichrist will not succeed, however. Verse 11 reveals that he will be killed and his body given to the burning fire. The reference to his body substantiates

---

[394] Rev 12-18 expands upon these elements.

that he is a real human. He may be indwelt or empowered by a demon(s), but he is not a demon or spirit-being. This verse must be correlated with Rev 19:17-21. In the latter passage, the "beast" (= little horn of Daniel) leads a number of the kings of the earth in war against the Lord Jesus at the second coming. The beast has no chance of success but is quickly seized and thrown alive into the lake of fire.[395]

One minor issue found in the passage when comparing the passage with Revelation 19 is the source of the Antichrist's defeat. Daniel attributed this to the Ancient of Days while John attributed this to Jesus at the Second Coming. However, this can be correlated by simply arguing that God the Father is the One that sends Jesus down for the Second Coming. The passage ends with a statement that the other beasts had their "dominion taken away." Thus, the defeat of this final Kingdom of Man culminates in the ending of all human government.

What then would be able to replace human government? Daniel is given this answer in verses 13-14. Daniel next sees "One like the Son of Man, coming with the clouds of heaven." The identity of this figure is hotly debated. Some argue that this figure is simply a collective term for Israel. However, John Collins argues "The traditional interpretation of the 'one like a human being' in the first millennium overwhelmingly favor the understanding of this figure as an individual, not as a collective symbol."[396] If the figure is an individual, then who is this individual? Some, such as Collins, argue that this figure was Michael the Archangel.[397] He argues this because of Daniel 12:1.

However, both ancient Jewish and Christian scholars throughout church history have identified this figure as the Messiah. This

---

395 Tanner, 425.
396 John J. Collins, *Daniel*, Hermeniaeia (Philadelphia, PA: Fortress, 1994), 308.
397 Collins, 310.

was the view of Rabbi Aqiba in the Talmud, who identified the one like a son of man as the Messiah, "one [throne] for Him [the Ancient of Days], and one for David."[398] In the Gospels, Jesus consistently refers to Himself as the "Son of Man."[399] Perhaps the most important example was found in Matthew 26:64 when Jesus addressed the high priest. Also, the idea of the Son of Man "coming with the clouds of heaven" was a connection to deity, both in the Old Testament and in other ANE texts.[400]

This Messianic figure then is brought forth before the Ancient of Days and is given the rulership of the Kingdom of God. This Kingdom of God is the same Kingdom of God that had been identified throughout the first half of the book, first seen in chapter 2 and then again in chapters 4 and 6. Miller writes, "Since the 'son of man' was 'given' a kingdom and authority to rule, this scene evidently describes the coronation of the 'son of man' by the Ancient of Days. According to the text, therefore, this individual will be crowned as the sovereign ruler of the world. His reign will never end."[401] Thus, the future Messiah would rule the Kingdom of God. Steinmann sees a strong connection between this verse and Psalm 2 and Psalm 110, which both connect the Messiah as the divine king.[402]

While the idea of the Kingdom of God being eternal had already been established in Daniel, verse 14 adds a new element to the kingdom. The kingdom would consist of "all peoples, nations, and languages." This kingdom is not only eternal, but it is one that is universal, unlike the kingdoms of man that would be limited in scope and would eventually be destroyed. That this Son of Man will rule this eternal kingdom shows that He is not simply

---

398 Sprinkle, 180.
399 Matt 8:20, 9:6, 10:23, 11:19, etc.
400 For example, Ps 68:4.
401 Miller, 207.
402 Andrew Steinmann, *Daniel*, Concordia Commentary (St. Louis, MO: Concordia Publishing, 2008), 359.

a mortal man and contrasts with the temporary dominions of the four kingdoms and especially the fourth beast, which comes to an abrupt and complete end (v. 11).[403]

Verse 27 expands on the idea of the Kingdom of God once again. Daniel writes that the kingdom and dominion would be given "to the people, the saints of the Most High." At first, this passage looks confusing because earlier in verses 13-14 the kingdom had been given to the Son of Man. Now, it is given to the saints of the Most High. Does this mean that the Son of Man and the saints of the Most High are the same? Those who argue for the collective interpretation of the Son of Man use this verse as evidence for their argument. However, there is another explanation that can still hold a singular view of the Son of Man while accounting for verse 27.

The saints of the Most High are given the kingdom, but that does not automatically mean that they will rule the kingdom in the same way that the Son of Man will rule the kingdom. Tanner sums this up well, stating,

> This kingdom will be given to "one like a son of man" (just as Dan 7:13-14 promised), but in another sense it is "given to the people who are the saints of the Most High." That is, the kingdom is first and foremost entrusted to the Lord Jesus Christ. He is the king *par excellence*, the king over everything, or as Heb 1:2 puts it, he is "heir of all things." Then those who belong to him are allowed to enter the kingdom and participate in various capacities of its administration... In this kingdom there may be sub-rulers (having authority), but all will be in absolute submission and obedience to the Lord Jesus Christ.[404]

---

403 Sprinkle, 182-83.
404 Tanner, 463-64.

Therefore, the believers that make up the Kingdom of God will have places of authority within the kingdom, all under the ultimate Kingship of the Messiah.[405] Thus, Daniel 7 establishes that a future final form of the kingdom of man, under the direction of the Antichrist, would arise but will be defeated and replaced by the Kingdom of God under the rulership of the Messianic King.

Conclusion

The kingdom of man and the Kingdom of God play a major role in the theology of the book of Daniel. The kingdom of man, represented by the superpowers of Daniel's day, Babylon and Persia, as well as Greece and Rome, show throughout the book that while the kingdom of man throughout history was very powerful and sometimes even used by Yahweh Himself in judgment, they are doomed to be replaced in the future. In their place, the Kingdom of God, under the command of the Messianic King, will one day reign. That Kingdom will be undefeatable and will reign for eternity.

How does this concept impact believers today? It does so in two important ways. First, believers should never put their utmost trust in the kingdom of man. It is easy to think that if we just fix the government and make it have more Christian values and laws, then that will solve everything. While we should try to influence the government to follow stronger Christian values, that cannot be our end goal because the kingdom of man is doomed to fail and be replaced one day.

Second, believers can take heart that while the forces of Satan and the sinfulness of the world can be a challenge to us today, these forces will not win in the end. People generally look to the end of Revelation for this belief, which is certainly true, but Dan-

---

405 Matt 19:28, Luke 22:30, Rev 20:4.

iel established the ultimate victory of King Jesus and the Kingdom of God centuries before John was able to write Revelation. God has spoken and the kingdom of man will one day be finished. The Kingdom of God is on the way and we believers will one day take part in this glorious kingdom. The King is Coming!

BIBLIOGRAPHY

Collins, John J. *Daniel. Hermenieia.* Philadelphia, PA: Fortress, 1994.

Goldingay, John. *Daniel. Word Biblical Commentary.* Grand Rapids: Zondervan, 2019.

Hamilton, James M., Jr. *God's Glory in Salvation through Judgment: A Biblical Theology.* Wheaton, IL: Crossway, 2010.

Hill, Andrew. *Daniel. The Expositor's Bible Commentary.* Grand Rapids: Zondervan, 2008, Kindle edition.

Longman III, Tremper. *Daniel. The NIV Application Commentary.* Grand Rapids: Zondervan, 1999.

Miller, Stephen R. *Daniel.* Vol. 18. *The New American Commentary.* Nashville: Broadman & Holman, 1994.

Newsom, Carol. *Daniel.* Louisville, KY: Westminster John Knox Press, 2014.

Sprinkle, Joe M. *Daniel. Evangelical Biblical Theology Commentary*, edited by T. Desmond Alexander, Thomas R. Schreiner, and Andreas J. Köstenberger. Bellingham, WA: Lexham, 2020.

Steinmann, Andrew. *Daniel. Concordia Commentary.* St. Louis, MO: Concordia Publishing, 2008.

Tanner, J. Paul. *Daniel. Evangelical Exegetical Commentary.* Bellingham, WA: Lexham, 2020.

EPILOGUE

Whether in the Old Testament's many prophecies of a coming King or the New Testament's spiritual realization of the King and prediction of the physical manifestation of his kingdom in the new heavens and new earth, God's people in all epochs of time have been able to say with great accuracy and expectation "the King is Coming." It is this hopeful anticipation of Jesus—both his person and his work—that served as a uniquely central preoccupation of Dr. Ed Hindson and all who sat under his teaching throughout his long and storied career. Each chapter contained in this volume celebrates this theme in a unique way (either directly or indirectly), and while the present collection of investigations does not begin to exhaust the prophetic elements related to Christ and his ministry, the contributors hope that each essay galvanizes further research and investigation of the Scriptures and how they point to the realization of Jesus' work (anticipated, executed, and realized).

While the contributions contained in this book are wide-ranging in scope and focus, the theme that all share is a high regard for God's Word and the Word that incarnated himself in the first century and will one day return in glory for his people. Some of the articles in this collection have turned over stones that Hindson and others have previously left unbothered. Others have re-examined familiar stones from a different lens. All in their own way adopt the same alacrity that Hindson so passionately applied and instilled in those who had the benefit of reading his works, hearing his lectures, or listening to his sermons in the arena of both messianic and prophetic studies.

How now shall readers respond to the contents of this passionate compendium? First, the reverence for Scripture and its principal protagonist on display in these pages should inspire readers to adopt similar values in their personal studies/devotions. One cannot rightly interpret or apply the special revelation of God nor fully/responsibly understand the central focus of that revelation without a high view of Scripture (2 Tim 3:16-17) and its Christo-centric design (Col 3:15-17). Therefore, what has been modeled hermeneutically in these chapters ought to be implemented in subsequent investigations that they may have inspired.

Second, this work intends to spark joyful enthusiasm among those who read it concerning both messianic prophecy and eschatology with the hopes that the excitement surrounding Jesus' rule (now essential and one day existential) might echo in the next generation of God's people. After all, as Revelation 1:3 reminds us, "Blessed is he who reads and those who hear the words of the prophecy, and heed the things which are written in it; for the time is near." God's people need not be distracted by those things that would keep them from looking up and looking ahead to the One who is coming for them—that same One who came to provide hope through redemption. Pervasive fear and anxiety, even among the saved, are remedied when one rightly turns his/her eyes upon Jesus and trusts that the things of this world will, by comparison, grow strangely dim in the light of his glory and grace.

Finally, if as the title and theme of this work suggest, "the King is Coming," one might expect that a sense of urgency may inform the witness of God's people on the world's stage. As a more complete understanding of Christ and his work has been reached after reading this book (as is hoped), it stands to reason that those who receive such knowledge become disseminators of what has been gleaned. Many do not yet know the King or that his coming is near. It is up to the King's subjects who know and expect his glorious return, in the wake of such glory, to shine as bright lights in an ever-darkening world. The words of Paul ring true now just as they did in his day:

> How then will they call on Him in whom they have not believed? How will they believe in Him whom they have not heard? And how will they hear without a preacher? How will they preach unless they are sent? Just as it is written, "How beautiful are the feet of those who bring good news of good things!" (Rom 10:14-15)

Scripture has revealed the King and the imminence of his glorious return. So many investigations/discussions point, in their own way, to this inescapable truth and beckon God's people everywhere to be on a mission in a world of inferior despots and fallen regimes. This is what motivated Hindson and that which continues to propel those he influenced forward for Christ as they await his rule. "He who testifies to these things says, 'Yes, I am coming quickly.' Amen, Come Lord Jesus" (Rev 22:20).

— Jeffrey R. Dickson, PhD

ALSO AVAILABLE FROM LAMPION HOUSE PUBLISHING

LOOK FOR THESE AND OTHER GREAT TITLES AT:
LAMPIONHOUSEPUBLISHING.COM

LAMPION
House Publishing